Embedded Multitasking

Embedded Multitasking

Keith Curtis

AMSTERDAM • BOSTON • HEIDELBERG • LONDON
NEW YORK • OXFORD • PARIS • SAN DIEGO
SAN FRANCISCO • SINGAPORE • SYDNEY • TOKYO
Newnes is an imprint of Elsevier

Newnes

Newnes is an imprint of Elsevier
30 Corporate Drive, Suite 400, Burlington, MA 01803, USA
Linacre House, Jordan Hill, Oxford OX2 8DP, UK

 Recognizing the importance of preserving what has been written, Elsevier prints its books on
acid-free paper whenever possible.

Library of Congress Cataloging-in-Publication Data

Curtis, Keith, 1961-
  Embedded multitasking / Keith Curtis.
    p. cm.
  Includes index.
  ISBN 0-7506-7918-2 (pbk. : alk. paper) 1. Embedded computer systems. 2.
Computer firmware--Design. 3. Embedded computer systems--Programming. I.
Title.
  TK7895.E42C87 2006
  004'.35--dc22

                          2005029822

British Library Cataloguing-in-Publication Data
A catalogue record for this book is available from the British Library.

ISBN-13: 978-0-7506-7918-3
ISBN-10: 0-7506-7918-2

For information on all Newnes publications
visit our website at www.books.elsevier.com.

Dedication

Paraphrasing an old saying:

"Give a man a tool, he becomes a repair man."

"Teach him how to make his own tools, he becomes an engineer!"

This book is dedicated to all the embedded engineers out there adding intelligence to the everyday things in our lives.

And to my wife Shirley, who has put up with this, and all my other projects, through a combination of patience and understanding.

Contents

About the Author

I am fortunate in that I grew up the son of an engineer. My father was, and is, an electrical engineer, so is it not surprising that I also became an electrical engineer, earning my BSEE from Montana State University in 1986.

Being a somewhat rebellious youth, I didn't go into RF like my father. Instead I embraced digital logic and microprocessors. My workbench at home was littered with surplus TTL parts, and the odd EEPROM and LED display; it was this early fascination with microprocessors that first led me down the path to embedded programming.

In fact, my interest in embedded programming led to my first full-time summer job, working for a company that used the 6502 microprocessor to build numerical controls for lathes and mills. I have held a number of jobs since that first summer: a year in avionics, eight years in gaming, six years in RF, and now five years in semiconductors. But through it all, I have always retained my interest in microprocessor-based design.

It was my interest in microprocessors, in fact, that led me to apply the design of hardware state machines to the process of software development. During my time at MSU, I attended a class taught by an engineer on sabbatical from Hewlett-Packard. The class subject was the design of embedded controls using linked state machines instead of microprocessors. While I didn't immediately make a connection between hardware and software state machines, I did keep the textbook; after a stint as a consultant, and as time passed, I came to apply many of the techniques from hardware design to software design. The result has been the content of this book, a method for multitasking using linked software state machines.

I hope you find the process useful, and I encourage you to evolve it as needed to fit your specific design style. Good luck, and remember, be verbose in your documentation, lest you be added to the product support groups' speed dial.

What's on the CD-ROM?

When I began this book, I decided that I wanted to keep it as generic as possible. My examples don't favor a specific microcontroller family, and with the exception of including examples in C, I tried not to favor a specific language or compiler. With this in mind, I was somewhat hesitant to include a CD-ROM given that the purpose of the book is to teach a new design methodology, not create a specific embedded design example. However, there are templates and tools that help in the design process, so after consulting with my editor, I came to the decision that a CD-ROM that included these tools would be useful, while remaining true to the original intention of keeping the text generic.

The CD-ROM contains three main directories: examples, templates, and tools. The Examples directory contains all of the algorithm listings and code snippets from the book. They are included for anyone who would like to use them as a seed to start their own personal code library. The Templates directory contains template files for creating all three types of state machines: the various communications protocols in C, the example priority handlers, and the various timing systems. The final directory, Tools, contains two spreadsheets, one for calculating a system tick, and another for building an execution time database used in the Time Remaining priority handler. The Tools directory also contains an example document that outlines a naming convention.

To keep the files as universal as possible, all of the documents, algorithms, code snippets, and templates are in a DOS text file format. The spreadsheets, however, had to be put in a format that could be loaded into a spreadsheet, so I chose Excel®, as it is the spreadsheet that I know best. However, I also included the equations for the important cells so the tool can be translated into another spreadsheet package if the reader should desire to do so.

The reader is encouraged to use and modify the files, and I hope that it helps the reader develop a good coding technique. Just remember that the intent is to learn a new program development technique.

Note: Copying and distributing the files is restricted, as outlined in the license agreement at the back of this book. In addition, the files are provided "AS IS." Compatibility with a specific compiler, applicability to a specific purpose, or a completely error-free condition is neither warranted nor guaranteed. The sole purpose of the files is to aid in the understanding of the design methodology presented.

"Excel is a registered trademark of Microsoft Corporation in the United States and/or other countries."

1

What's In This Book, and Why Should I Read It?

When I told my friends that I was writing a book, several of them told me that I had to have a very good opening. "A good opening," they said, "fires the reader's imagination and draws them into the book." The theory being, I suppose, if the reader is drawn in, then they will have to buy the book.

Well, being an engineer, I very seldom say things that fire the imagination. In fact, at parties, most people's eyes tend to glaze over right after I tell them I am an engineer. So, I have decided instead to appeal to the universal sense of enlightened self-interest. In short, I will begin this book by demonstrating why good programming is in the best interest of every software designer. Now, it may not get you a cubicle with a window, or even an office with a door. But I can promise that producing products that are not profitable is the surest way to become unemployed. So, while there may not be a direct cash benefit to producing profitable products, the alternative is definitely worse.

However, before we get into the explanation of profitability and engineering, we need to take a few moments and discuss some basic business concepts—specifically, how the price of a product is divided up between the various costs and profit.

If we consider a generic product, the sale price of the product is divided into two parts: the cost of producing the product and the profit on the sale. The cost of producing the product includes recurring and nonrecurring production costs, general and administrative overhead costs, cost of sales, and support costs. The profit is the difference between what the company spent to produce the product and what it was paid for the product. Essentially, profit is the company's return on the investment it made in producing the product.

So, let's take a little closer look at the costs, starting with the recurring and nonrecurring production costs.

A recurring production cost is any expense that is incurred each time a product is made. It includes the cost of the materials used to produce the product and the labor expense of having workers assemble the product. It can also include the cost of packaging, printing a user's manual, license fees, even the material cost of the shrink wrap to seal up the package.

Nonrecurring production costs, on the other hand, are expenses that are incurred to enable a production run, and typically cover expenses such as investments in equipment, product testing such as Conformity European (CE®)/Underwriter's Laboratory (UL®)/Canadian Standards Association (CSA®)[1], and materials that enable production, but are not part of the product produced. For example, the cost of the plastic used to injection mold the case for a product is a recurring cost because it is incurred each time a unit is produced. However, the cost of testing for UL acceptance, assembly benches, tools, even the mold used to produce each unit are nonrecurring costs because they are incurred just once during the production cycle.

Nonrecurring costs are also often referred to as fixed production costs, because they do not increase and decrease with the number of units produced. They can also be thought of as an investment in the production process. For instance, the cost of having a special tool produced would be considered an investment because it reduced the recurring cost through shortening the assembly time. Nonrecurring costs are also typically amortized, or divided up, over some portion of the product's lifetime. If a mold is to be used over the production of a million units, then .00001% of the cost of the mold is then added to the cost of each of the first one million units produced. Of course, the one million and first unit produced does not incur this cost, and as a result, the profit on that unit, and every one produced after it, is correspondingly higher, assuming the price and other costs remain constant.

---

[1]   CSA is a registered trademark of the Canadian Standards Association. UL is a registered trademark of Underwriters Laboratories. CE is a registered trademark of The Council of the European Communities.

The next cost is also typically considered a fixed cost, that being the administrative and overhead cost. This cost, typically listed as the G&A (General and Accounting), is the expense of operating a business. It includes administrative cost, including the salaries of the company executives, the secretaries, the accountants, and even the janitors. It also includes costs for services, such as electricity, water, and phones. Basically, any expense that is incurred to pay for a general support function of the company will be lumped into this category. And, like a nonrecurring production cost, it is also divided up and tacked onto the production cost of the products. However, unlike a nonrecurring production cost, it never goes away.

A similar cost to that of G&A is the cost of sales. It includes expenses for things like advertising, shipping, product promotions, customer contests, even commissions paid to salesmen. These costs are those associated with putting the product in front of the customers, either through advertising, or through placing the product on the shelf in a local store. Any cost incurred that is directly tied to the act of selling the product typically falls under this category. This is one of the few general costs that is typically allocated based on the number of units sold. So, if the cost of sales is high for a group of units, then the profits for that group of units will be correspondingly lower. As a result, management will generally pay close attention to the cost of goods sold.

The final costs are those tied to support of the product after the sale. These typically include expenses like a 24-hour support phone line, repair technicians, failure analysis, repair costs, and upgrades/bug fixes. Like G&A, support cost is also spread across the production run as a fixed expense.

Note: Because the support cost is typically treated like an overhead expense, it is often hidden from management supervision. This leads some management to the mistaken assumption that a product is reliable and well-liked by the customer when in fact there is a quality problem and customer satisfaction is dropping.

A closer look at profits reveals that it is also divided up into multiple sections. Some of the profits are spent as dividends paid out to the investors. This increases the desirability of the stock in the company and can serve to attract additional investors who, in turn, add money to the company by buying stock. Some of the profit is held as a cash reserve, to cover future equipment purchases and expansion. And, most importantly to engineering, some of the profits are used to fund new product development.

See, I told you there was a reason why engineers should have a personal interest in making sure the products they design are profitable. The larger the profit on a product, the more money will be available to fund new equipment, hire more engineers, and pay for new projects. Now, this is not to say that all of the profits will be channeled into engineering. However, it does say that if the products are not profitable, then any new product development must be paid for using borrowed money. That means that the product will not only have to repay the money, plus interest, but will also have to do that before it generates any new monies to pay for future projects.

Engineering and Profits

So, if a profitable product produces the necessary surplus of cash required to fund new projects, and if engineers are responsible for the design of the profitable products, then it falls to us as software and hardware engineers to generate designs that will produce the best product for the least cost.

OK, how do we do that? We could just increase the cost of the product. Some companies have tried this, although most who have are now owned by their competitors, so for now we will ignore that option. The better place to start is by understanding where the costs of a product come from, and then analyze what we can do as designers to minimize those costs. To do that, we have to understand the product life cycle.

A typical product has multiple phases in its lifetime. For the purpose of discussion here, we will limit this to five general phases:

1. *Product definition*: In this phase, the initial concept for the product is generated and market research is conducted.

2. *Design*: Engineering is charged with developing the product that will meet the market requirements, including performance, price and profit.

3. *Initial production*: The design then moves to production, where a production facility is configured to produce the design. Product support will also analyze the design at this point to determine its support requirements.

4. *Sustained production*: At this point in the product's life cycle, the production facility has reached its optimal production volume, and support is managing the day-to-day customer support requirements of the product.

5. *End of life*: At this point, the product has reached the end of its profitability. The production facility will ramp down production, and support will plan for any remaining customer support needs.

Let's start our analysis, with a quick description of each of the phases of a product's life. We can then examine the different phases to determine where changes in a design strategy can be employed to help reduce cost.

The birth of a product is in the *product definition* phase of its life. The marketing group within a company is generally tasked with ongoing market research, looking for new product ideas. When they find a potential product idea, they then do further research to determine how big the market is for the proposed product. What is the share of the market which the company can reasonably expect to capture? What features will the product need to be successful in the market? And what price point is needed to capture the anticipated market share?

Estimating the total size of a potential market is somewhat of an art, and I am certainly not qualified to either explain or critique the process. For our purposes here, just take it for granted that the marketing group is well versed in the subject and that their evaluation will result in a reasonably accurate estimate of the total number of products that the proposed market will demand and the expected market share that the company can expect to capture. They will also estimate the minimal number of features required by potential users and the optimal price point that will allow capture of the market share. These numbers will then be analyzed to determine the potential profitability that the company can expect for the product.

If it looks as if the product will bring in a reasonable profit to justify the investment in a development phase, then the product idea will be summarized in a *requirements document* and passed on to the design phase. If the profitability of the product does not justify the development cost, the product idea will either be shelved for future consideration, re-evaluated by marketing with a different set of features, or just dropped.

In the *design phase*, engineering will then generate a design based on the requirements document. Once the design of the product is complete, engineering then oversees any certification testing required, such as FCC, CE, CSA, or UL. Any changes to the design required to correct any design deficiencies will then be made, and the product will be resubmitted until it passes.

The final step in the design process is to generate any collateral material required for the sale of the product. This material typically includes testing procedures and fixtures, user's manuals, documentation for both the production and support groups, and any packaging or shipping containers.

Once the design phase is complete, *initial production* begins. In this phase, the production group works with engineering to determine the most cost-effective method to produce the design. The production group will also create any quality assurance documentation needed, as well as production jigs required by the design. The production and test staff will also receive training in the product production process.

The support group will also begin its analysis of the design with engineering, evaluating potential sources of faults and failures. They should also become fluent in the operation of the design to facilitate fault analysis and repair. The result of this analysis and training will be troubleshooting procedures and the purchase of the appropriate test equipment and stocks of repair parts. Further, the repair technicians and the help desk operators will be trained to handle problems, perform fault analysis, and do cost-effective repairs.

Following the initial production phase of the product's life, the product will enter *sustained production*. At this point, the production facility has ramped up to the normal production rate for the product. The production personnel are operating with only minimal support from engineering, and the production yields are at or above expected levels.

The support group at this time is analyzing failures, processing repairs, answering customer questions, and making any corrections to the design to fix bugs found either in production or in the field. The support group should also be performing an ongoing analysis of the type and number of failures to identify any potential problems with the design. If any are found, they are tasked with making the appropriate changes to the design to eliminate or minimize the potential fault.

In addition, the marketing group may also suggest changes and enhancements to the operation of the product, in an effort to extend the product lifetime. Engineering will be tasked to work with support to roll-in the proposed changes and work out a conversion process for product already in the field.

Once the design has reached the end of its production, the product enters the *end-of-life* phase of its product life. This could be due to either the obsolescence of key components, low profitability due to less-expensive competition, or the disappearance of its target market. For whatever reason, the company has decided that continued production is not profitable, and it has decided to terminate production.

For the production group, this means the disassembly of any custom production facilities and the retraining of production personnel for work on other active product lines. Production and test jigs will be put into storage or sold as scrap, and all relevant documentation will be archived.

For the support group, the challenge at end of a product's life is to provide the expected level of customer support needed to support users that are still using the product. This means the support group will have the task of buying appropriate quantities of repair parts while they are still available, or finding suitable substitutes for the repair parts if they are not available or run out before support is terminated.

During the course of a product's life several costs are impacted directly by the design. As we have already established, reducing these costs is in the interest of the engineers working for the company. So our job at this point is to determine what the costs are, how the method of design affects the costs, and what can be done to minimize the cost.

Let's start with costs affecting the product definition phase of the new product. In this phase, the purpose is to define a new product and determine if it is profitable. To do this, engineering must be able to give reasonable estimates of what the product will cost over the course of its life. These costs come from all phases of the life cycle, including design, initial and sustained production, and even end of life.

Typically, the production and end-of-life numbers are estimated based on labor costs from similar recent products and a material cost based on a preliminary design and bill of material (BOM) from engineering. The design phase cost estimate will also rely on the preliminary design and BOM from engineering; however, it will also need an estimate of the time required to write and test the software associated with the project.

If the estimate for the design time is low, then a marginally profitable project may be approved and the company will end up investing its money in a product that will contribute little or no profit. If the estimate for the design time is high, then potentially profitable products may be passed over. So, it is important that engineering be able to produce an accurate estimate of what the software development will cost.

So, in the product definition phase it is important to be able to do an accurate preliminary design of the software system and this design must be sufficiently detailed so that accurate estimates for finishing the design are possible. This means that engineering's opportunity to increase profit, is based on a design system that allows an accurate preliminary design of the system, with sufficient detail to allow accurate time estimates for the remainder of the design work.

In the design phase of the life cycle, engineering is charged with the development and test of the product. They have the preliminary software design and the estimates for the remaining work. The preliminary design for the hardware is also finished, with its estimates for completion and testing. If engineering continues along this established design flow, then the product should complete at or near the preliminary estimates.

However, there are almost always unforeseen problems in any design effort. To prevent these problems from spinning a design out of control, the design process must be sufficiently flexible to be able to modify the design in process, without starting over. So, another opportunity for cutting costs is to use a design system that is also reasonably flexible, allowing changes in one section of the design to be isolated from most, if not all, other sections.

Another opportunity for cost reduction is the replacement of hardware peripherals with software-based peripherals. This is the so-called hardware/software tradeoff, and it is a trade of processing power for the cost of a hardware peripheral. While this appears to be a bottomless well of cost savings, there are several drawbacks to any tradeoff:

1. Using software-based peripherals requires additional program memory to hold the additional code.

2. Software-based peripherals require more processor time to execute.

3. The additional execution overhead may require a higher clock speed or faster processor.

4. Using software-based peripherals increases the complexity of the software design and testing.

So, any decision to replace a hardware peripheral can only be made with accurate estimates of processing load and program memory requirements. This means that the tradeoffs can only be made later in the design, after the processing load and memory requirements are established, or that the design methodology is capable of making accurate predictions early in the design.

One of the most valuable means of saving development costs is code reuse. This involves having a library of previously developed and tested software routines for common functions—for example, the math library bundled with a compiler. Rather than force users to develop their own math functions, the compiler designer has generated a library of previously developed and tested functions, saving the user a considerable amount of time and research. There is every reason to believe that engineering can also benefit from this practice by reusing previously developed code in their new designs. Note: this does incur some overhead in engineering due to the building and documentation of the library. However, if the design methodology used by engineering is modular and encourages documentation, this process can be relatively simple and inexpensive.

One of the early tasks of software development is to supply test code to the hardware group for the purpose of testing the prototype hardware. While most groups simply write a quick block of code to exercise the various inputs and outputs, a more extensive system can significantly shorten the testing performed by the hardware group. The typical objection to this practice is that the code will be thrown away after the design, so why put too much work into it? However, if a modular design approach is taken, then the routines used to exercise the hardware during testing can be reused, not only in the final software system, but also in production as part of the hardware testing performed in production. So, once again, a modular design methodology can help in the reduction of design costs.

Next, what about testing the software? Testing a complete software system is certainly more complex and takes longer than incremental testing during the design. Incremental testing also simplifies the debugging process because the potential list of suspects is significantly reduced. Further, if the incremental testing can be automated, then the depth of testing possible is also increased, producing significantly better code quickly.

Once the individual blocks of the software design are tested, then they can be combined together block by block in an incremental fashion. This again limits the number of suspects when there are problems, and the test data from the individual blocks can also be useful in finding problems.

For this to work, the design must be modular with clearly defined specifications on the functions of each module, as well as the interface between the modules. There must also be a method for building a software test jig that allows the inputs from other blocks to be simulated during automated testing.

The final requirement of the design phase is the generation of the design collateral. This includes testing procedures and fixtures, user's manuals, documentation for both the production and support groups, and any packaging or shipping containers. All too often, no thought is given to this requirement until after the design is complete. As a result, the material is typically generated though a form of criminal investigation, reverse engineering the details from the final design, interviewing the designers, and trying to piece together the details of the system's operation. All of this takes time and costs money. So, what can a well-designed and documented product do to reduce cost at this phase?

In testing, good documentation will provide a clear explanation of how the product is supposed to work. This gives the test group a clear set of criteria for their testing procedures. It also defines which sections of the design are active during each operation, so the test procedure can skip over redundant test conditions, shortening the test time. The same information will also show the most efficient method for exercising all the functions in the shortest time possible.

A modular design also means that sections of the product software may be reused as test software for production. This shortens the job of generating the test software. It allows testers on the production line to exercise the various sections of the hardware design "on demand," reducing the time and equipment required for testing. And custom test software can be used to partially debug any problems, reducing repair time.

Writing the various user manuals for the design also benefits from a top-down design with good documentation. A top-down design starts with a good overall description, and then flows down through each level of the design. This is the same format used by most manuals, so the writers will have a complete outline to work from, with all the information they need present in the documentation. If the documentation is sufficiently complete, there should only be minimal involvement from the actual design team during the writing. This should free the design team to start work on the next product definition or design.

For support, good documentation and a clear design flow are critical for their work. They will need it to understand the operation of the product, both when it is operating correctly and when it fails. This will help them not only design their own debugging documentation, but also train their people in the potential problems that customers will face. It will also allow them to find flaws quickly and produce fixes in a timely manner.

Finally, a good design can even ease the burden of generating packaging. With predictable behavior and fewer bug fixes, there will be little need to add markings on the packaging for production revision. And the packaging is less likely to be opened repeatedly by production to include the latest bug fix, so the packaging can be made less expensive, without the requirement that it be a re-openable design.

In the design phase, the cost reduction opportunities are primarily in two areas: shortening the design and test process, and creating an easily understood and well-documented design. The design and testing portion of the opportunity require a good top-down design approach and a modular format. This produces software that can be incrementally tested, reused in later designs and production test software, and more easily understood by the writers and support teams. Good documentation is also beneficial to the writers and the support teams in that it provides a clear picture of what the design is intended to do, as well as how it will respond to various failures.

In the initial and sustained production phases of the product life, most of the benefits outlined in the design phase come to fruition. The documentation provided on the design allows the production and support teams to become fluent in the design quickly in the initial production phase. The modular nature of the design allows the generation of test software as well. And the combination of the documentation and the modular nature of the design assist in the generation of troubleshooting guides and procedures for the support group.

Additional cost-saving opportunities arise when the design transitions to sustained production. Any recurring material cost savings from a tradeoff of software for hardware begin in the sustained phase of the production, as do production labor cost savings from automated testing provided by custom test software. And, on the support side, good documentation and a modular format allow the support team to identify the source of any software bugs early, and assist in their quick removal from the design.

Together, the initial and sustained production phases of the product life cycle are the source of the majority of the cost savings for the product. This is largely due to the volume of the production run. Any material cost savings in the unit cost will translate directly into a significant cost savings over the production of the product.

However, the volume can also increase costs for the support team. If a problem is found in the design, a high production volume can produce a significant volume of flawed units to be repaired. The best way to minimize this cost, without dropping production, is to identify problems early and fix them quickly. This requires both a good support team fluent in the design, and a clean modular design that allows the incorporation of changes with a minimum of testing.

For maximum cost savings in production, both initial and sustained, the design must use a modular, well-documented design method that supports easy modification and the ability to tradeoff software for hardware. The ability to automate testing is also valuable in that it shortens the time required to qualify new bug fixes.

A final note on the sustained phase of the product's life cycle: This is the time when the product is typically selling well, and marketing and management is looking for ways to stretch out the production. Usually, this means the introduction of similar products, some products with a subset of feature from the original design and a reduced price tag, or products with a specialized set of features designed to meet a specific market niche. These products may not have a sufficient profit margin to justify their own development, but if they can be spun off the existing product with a minimum of design effort, they can extend the profitability of the original design.

The best way to start this type of product development is to begin with the original product's definition as a baseline. Marketing and engineering can then evaluate the various tradeoffs required to produce the spin-off product. This means that, once again, the design method used by engineering must be able to accurately predict what the new features and functions will cost in design and production. It also means that the documentation of the original produce development and the design notes from the original design must be accurate and complete so the projected costs for the new product are accurate.

Given that the design time available for this type of spin-off is typically minimal, the design process of modifying the original design must be fast and efficient. For that to work, engineering cannot afford to restart the development from scratch. They can only generate new software when needed to handle the new or modified features and functions. This means that the original design must be a top-down, modular, well-documented design that will allow engineering to reuse the majority of the software design generated for the original product.

An added advantage to this form of spin-off design is that much of the collateral design and documentation generated for the original design will translate into collateral for the spin-off design. This means that manuals, test procedures, test fixtures, and the troubleshooting documentation generated by the support group will need only minimal modification to work for the new designs, provided that the groups generating this collateral know what has changed from the original design and how it will affect the collateral generated originally. This means that, just like the original design, the spin-off design must be a top-down design with good documentation and a modular format.

The final phase of the product life is the end-of-life support of the product. This can be one of the most difficult to estimate because so much of the hardware used in the design may have been obsolete by the manufacturer. In fact, making end-of-life buys on components can be one of the most significant costs associated with end-of-life support.

It follows that replacing obsolete material with either a suitable substitute, or software, is one of the cost savings options. For the most part, this will entail searching for similar products that can either be adapted or used directly for the obsolete hardware. However, there will be instances in which the missing hardware may be replaced with software. When this happens, it is important that the software design be modular to allow the replacement of the software driver associated with the hardware. It is also important to have good documentation on the original design, so that the impact of replacing the hardware with a software function can be gauged accurately. Customers will be happy if their system can be fixed, but they are typically very annoyed if the fix significantly changes the operation of the system. Knowing what to expect with a fix is important, before the customer is told that the fix is possible.

So, over the life of the product, there are several opportunities to reduce costs. In fact, some of the changes have the potential to significantly reduce costs. And, as we discussed previously, reductions in costs increase the profitability of a product and make more capital available for use by engineering in the next design. Therefore, following the principle of enlightened self-interest, it is in every engineer's best interest to design products using a design method with the following features:

1. A top down design method
2. Modularity
3. Good documentation

And, one final requirement that has not been specifically named so far:

4. Multitasking

While multitasking has not been specifically mentioned so far, it is one of the main points of this book, so it must have some advantage beyond a flashy title. And it does—the ability to run several functions at the same time, the ability to replace a hardware peripheral with software and still retain the real-time nature of the peripheral, and the ability to temporarily add automated testing routines to simulate virtual input and output hardware.

OK, that makes sense, but why not just use an RTOS? It is certainly simpler than designing the software to be multitasking. Yes, an RTOS is simpler, the code can be written as linear segments and with the multiple tasks, it does promote modular design.

However, there are some drawbacks to using an RTOS: it has a minimum footprint in the design, it will likely have a fee associated with its use, and it will have an impact on the performance and hardware requirements of the system.

So, let's start with the minimal footprint. A typical RTOS has a minimum memory requirement for both data and program memory. Program memory is needed for the routines used by the RTOS, and for the *kernel*. The kernel is the core software for the RTOS that handles the swapping in and out of the tasks, communications between the tasks, timing, and establishing priorities in the system. Data memory is also needed to support the communications between tasks and storage of each task's context information. Together, these requirements establish the minimum memory sizes required, just for the RTOS.

An RTOS also typically has a fee associated with its use. The fee may be recurring, meaning that some nominal fee will be charged for each product that uses it, or a nonrecurring fee will be charged when the RTOS is initially purchased. In either case, some cost will be incurred for the use of the software.

Next, there is the impact on the performance and hardware requirements of the system. We have already established the costs associated with the RTOS memory requirements. Additionally, there will be an impact on the processing load for the system, in the form of lost execution cycles required to execute the kernel and its associated routines. There may also be requirements on the hardware itself, such as interrupt capability and access to the system stack. Finally, there may also be limitations on which high-level language compilers are compatible with the RTOS.

So, while an RTOS does simplify the design, there are design tradeoffs; additional memory requirements, recurring or nonrecurring fees, specific hardware requirements, and a requirement for specific development software. Therefore, additional cost savings can be accomplished through the use of a design methodology that produces software that is multitasking without the use of an RTOS.

That pretty much defines the requirements for our proposed design method. Each one is firmly rooted in one or more methods for reducing cost, so the profitability of the product is increased, and more capital is available for future design. Basically, use a design method that achieves the stated goals and the result should be a happier, healthier company which can afford to spend more money on engineering and new designs.

Now I know that this may not sway some engineers. There will be some that feel that it is their right to design as they see fit and no one can tell them how to do their job. Well, as an author, I would be remiss if I did not make an effort to try and bring these designers back into the fold. So, I will try to point out some of the immediate drawbacks.

First of all, poor documentation typically guarantees that the wayward engineer will be spending weeks to months at the end of every project with a technical writer camped out at the door of their cubical. Remember the collateral material requirement for a user's manual and test procedures? And, if the technical writer has too much trouble with the documentation, management may decide to simply let the engineer write the documents. Not an appealing prospect when everyone else in engineering is gearing up on a new project.

Next, there are the long hours at the end of the project. If the design method can't accurately predict the time needed to do the design, management may simply decide to go with the low estimate, leaving the engineer to guess what their milestones should be to get the job done. And yes, this is a recipe for disaster, resulting is lost weekends and late nights. These occur on their own, the design method used by the engineer should not increase their frequency.

With all these problems, specifically problems that come to management's attention due to late deliveries, there is also the very real probability that management may not entrust the hot new project to an engineer that has to struggle to meet dates. Typically these engineers are the ones lamenting, "I have seniority, why didn't *I* get that project?" And the answer is, "Because we needed it on time."

Finally, for all those engineers that feel "it was hard to design the software, so it should be hard to understand it," let me point out that there is an innate flaw in being the only person that understands the software. It means the original engineer will also be the only person to work on the software. While it does mean that no one will mess up the code, it also means that when a bug is found, that engineer will have to drop any new projects and jump into the old project until the bug is found and fixed. This means that the new project will be later and later, resulting in long nights and weekends to get caught back up to the schedule. It means that the engineer will lose the respect of both their manager and the support people that have to answer the calls on the product. It means that the engineer runs the risk of a lateral move in occupation from engineering to support when the product becomes their entire career.

Basically, using a poor design methodology to generate software will pretty much guarantee:

- That everyone else will get the new hot projects.
- That the support people will have your extension on speed dial.
- That you can plan on late nights and working weekends until you retire.
- That other more efficient designers will be promoted over you.
- And that during the next downsizing you can plan on being offered the option of layoff or transfer to support.

One final note, before we move on to the next chapter: throughout this book, you will note that I will use the term "designer" when talking about the person generating the software design. This is deliberate because I consider a designer to be someone that actually plans out, or designs, the development of their software. Because this is a book on the design of software, then anyone reading this book is either a designer already, or working to become one, so the title is appropriate in either case.

Basic Embedded Programming Concepts

The purpose of this chapter is to provide the designer with some basic concepts and terminology that will be used later in the book. It covers not only basic multitasking but also binary numbering systems, data storage, basic communications protocols, mathematics, conditional statements, and state machines. These concepts are covered here not only to refresh the designer's understanding of their operations but also to provide sufficient insight so that designers will be able to "roll their own" functions if needed. While this chapter is not strictly required to understand the balance of the book, it is recommended.

It is understandable why state machines and multitasking need review, but why are all the other subjects included? And why would a designer ever want to "roll my own" routines? That is what a high-level language is for, isn't it? Well, often in embedded design, execution speed, memory size, or both will become an issue. Knowing how a command works allows a designer to create optimized functions that are smaller and/or faster than the stock functions built into the language. It also gives the designer a reference for judging how efficient a particular implementation of a command may be. So, while understanding how a command works may not be required in order to write multitasking code, it is very valuable when writing in an embedded environment.

For example, a routine is required to multiply two values together, a 16-bit integer and an 8-bit integer. A high-level language compiler will automatically type-convert the 8-bit value into a 16-bit value and then perform the multiplication using its standard 16-by-16 multiply. This is the most efficient format from the compiler's point of view, because it only requires an 8 × 8 multiply and 16 × 16 multiply in its library. However, this does creates two inefficiencies; one, it wastes two data memory locations holding values that will always be zero and, two, it wastes execution cycles on 8 additional bits of multiply which will always result in a zero.

The more efficient solution is to create a custom 8 × 16 multiply routine. This saves the 2 data bytes and eliminates the wasted execution time spent multiplying the always-zero MSB of the 8-bit value. Also, because the routine can be optimized now to use an 8-bit multiplicand, the routine will actually use less program memory as it will not have the overhead of handling the MSB of the multiplicand. So, being able to "roll your own" routine allows the designer to correct small inefficiencies in the compiler strategy, particularly where data and speed limitations are concerned.

While "rolling your own" multiply can make sense in the example, it is *not* the message of this chapter that designers should replace all of the built-in functions of a high-level language. However, knowing how the commands in a language work does give designers the knowledge of what is possible for evaluating a suspect function and, more importantly, how to write a more efficient function if it is needed.

Numbering Systems

A logical place to start is a quick refresher on the base-ten number system and the conventions that we use with it. As the name implies, base ten uses ten digits, probably because human beings have ten fingers and ten toes so working in units or groups of ten is comfortable and familiar to us. For convenience in writing, we represent the ten values with the symbols "0123456789."

To represent numbers larger than 9, we resort to a position-based system that is tied to powers of ten. The position just to the left of the decimal point is considered the ones position, or 10 raised to the zeroth power. As the positions of the digits move to the left of the decimal point, the powers of ten increase, giving us the ability to represent ever-larger large numbers, as needed. So, using the following example, the number 234 actually represents 2 groups of a hundred, 3 groups of ten plus 4 more. The left-most value, 2, represents 10^2. The 3 in the middle represents 10^1, and the right-most 4 represents 1 or 10^0.

Example 2.1

```
234
2    *10^2=   200
  3  *10^1=    30
    4 *10^0= +   4
              234
```

By using a digit-position-based system based on powers of 10, we have a simple and compact method for representing numbers.

To represent negative numbers, we use the convention of the minus sign '–'. Placing the minus sign in front of a number changes its meaning from a group of items that we have, to a group of items that are either missing or desired. So when we say the quantity of a component in the stock room is –3, that means that for the current requirements, we are tjree components short of what is needed. The minus sign is simply indicating that three more are required to achieve a zero balance.

To represent numbers between the whole numbers, we also resort to a position-based system that is tied to powers of ten. The only difference is that this time, the powers are negative, and the positions are to the right of the decimal point. The position just to the left of the decimal point is considered 10^0 or 1, as before, and the position just to the right of the decimal point is considered 10^–1 or 1/10. The powers of ten continue to increase negatively as the position of the digits moves to the right of the decimal point. So, the number 2.34, actually presents 2 and 3 tenths, plus 4 hundredths.

Example 2.2

```
2.34
2    *10^0  =   2.
  3  *10^-1 =    .30
    4 *10^-2 = + .04
              2.34
```

For most everyday applications, the simple notation of numbers and a decimal point is perfectly adequate. However, for the significantly larger and smaller numbers used in science and engineering, the use of a fixed decimal point can become cumbersome. For these applications, a shorthand notation referred to as *scientific notation* was developed. In scientific notation, the decimal point is moved just to the right of the left-most digit and the shift is noted by the multiplication of ten raised to the power of the new decimal point location. For example:

⟶

Example 2.3

Standard notation	Scientific notation
2,648.00	2.648x10^3
1,343,000.00	1.343x10^6
0.000001685	1.685x10^-6

As you can see, the use of scientific notation allows the representation of large and small values in a much more compact, and often clearer, format, giving the reader not only a feel for the value, but also an easy grasp of the number's overall magnitude.

Note: When scientific notation is used in a computer setting, the notation 10^ is often replaced with just the capital letter E. This notation is easier to present on a computer screen and often easier to recognize because the value following the ^ is not raised as it would be in printed notation. So, 2.45x10^3 becomes 2.45E3. Be careful not to use a small "e" as that can be confusing with logarithms.

Binary Numbers

For computers, which do not have fingers and toes, the most convenient system is *binary* or base two. The main reason for this choice is the complexity required in generating and recognizing more than two electrically distinct voltage levels. So, for simplicity, and cost savings, base two is the more convenient system to design with. For our convenience in writing binary, we represent these two values in the number system with the symbols "0" and "1". Note: Other representations are also used in boolean logic, but for the description here, 0 and 1 are adequate.

To represent numbers larger than one, we resort to a position-based system tied to powers of two, just as base 10 used powers of ten. The position just to the left of the decimal point is considered 2^0 or 1. The power of two corresponding to each digit increases as the position of the digits move to the left. So, the base two value 101, represents 1 groups of four, 0 groups of two, plus 1. The left-most digit, referred to as the most significant bit or MSB, represents 2^2 (or 4 in base ten). The position of 0 denotes 2^1 (or 2 in base ten). The right-most digit, referred to as the least significant bit or LSB (1), represents 1 or 2^0.

Example 2.4

```
101
1   *2^2=  100 (1*4 in base ten)
 0  *2^1=   00 (0*2 in base ten)
  1 *2^0= +  1 (1*1 in base ten)
          101 (5 in base ten)
```

So, binary numbers behave pretty much the same as they do for base 10 numbers. They only use two distinct digits, but they follow the same system of digit position to indicate the power of the base.

Signed Binary Numbers

To represent negative numbers in binary, two different conventions can be used, *sign and magnitude*, or *two's complement*. Both are valid representations of signed numbers and both have their place in embedded programming. Unfortunately, only two's complement is typically supported in high-level language compilers. Sign and magnitude can also be implemented in a high-level language, but it requires additional programming for any math and comparisons functions required. Choosing which format to use depends on the application and the amount of additional support needed. In either case, a good description of both, with their advantages and disadvantages, is presented here.

The sign and magnitude format uses the same binary representation as the unsigned binary numbers in the previous section. And, just as base-ten numbers used the minus sign to indicate negative numbers, so too do sign and magnitude format binary numbers, with the addition of a single bit variable to hold the sign of the value. The sign bit can be either a separate variable, or inserted into the binary value of the magnitude as the most significant bit. Because most high-level language compilers do not support the notation, there is little in the way of convention to dictate how the sign bit is stored, so it is left up to the designer to decide.

While compilers do not commonly support the format, it is convenient for human beings in that it is a very familiar system. The sign and magnitude format is also a convenient format if the system being controlled by the variable is vector-based—i.e., it utilizes a magnitude and direction format for control.

For example, a motor speed control with an H-bridge output driver would typically use a vector-based format for its control of motor speed and direction. The magnitude controls the speed of the motor, through the duty cycle drive of the transistors in the H-bridge. The sign determines the motor's direction of rotation by selecting which pair of transistors in the H-bridge are driven by the PWM signal. So, a sign and magnitude format is convenient for representing the control of the motor.

The main drawback with a sign and magnitude format is the overhead required to make the mathematics work properly. For example:

1. Addition can become subtraction if one value is negative.
2. The sign of the result will depend on whether the negative or positive value is larger.
3. Subtraction can become addition if the one value is negative.
4. The sign of the result will depend on whether the negative or positive value is larger and whether the positive or negative value is the subtracted value.
5. Comparison will also have to include logic to determine the sign of both values to properly determine the result of the comparison.

As human beings, we deal with the complications of a sign and magnitude format almost without thinking and it is second nature to us. However, microcontrollers do not deal well with exceptions to the rules, so the overhead required to handle all the special cases in math and comparison routines makes the use of sign and magnitude cumbersome for any function involving complex math manipulation. This means that, even though the sign and magnitude format may be familiar to us, and some systems may require it, the better solution is a format more convenient for the math. Fortunately, for those systems and user interfaces that require sign and magnitude, the alternate system is relatively easy to convert to and from.

The second format for representing negative binary numbers is two's complement. Two's complement significantly simplifies the mathematics from a hardware point of view, though the format is less humanly intuitive than sign and magnitude. Positive values are represented in the same format as unsigned binary values, with the exception that they are limited to values, that do not set the MSB of the number. Negative numbers are represented as the binary complement of the corresponding positive value, plus one. Specifically, each bit becomes its opposite, ones become zeros and zeros become ones. Then the value 1 is added to the result. The result is a value which, when added to another value using binary math, generates the same value as a binary subtraction. As an example, take the subtraction of 2 from 4, since this is the same as adding –2 and +4:

First, we need the two's complement of 2 to represent –2

Example 2.5

```
0010    Binary representation of 2
1101    Binary complement of 2 (1s become 0s, and
        0s become 1s)
1110    Binary complement of 2 + 1, or -2 in two's
        complement
```

```
Then adding 4 to -2
 1110    -2
+0100    +4
 0010    2 with the msb clear indicating a positive
         result
```

Representing numbers in two's complement means that no additional support routines are needed to determine the sign and magnitude of the variables in the equation; the numbers are just added together and the sign takes care of itself in the math. This represents a significant simplification of the math and comparison functions and is the main reason why compilers use two's complement over sign and magnitude in representing signed numbers.

Fixed-Point Binary Numbers

To represent numbers between the whole numbers in signed and unsigned binary values we once again resort to a position-based system, this time tied to decreasing negative powers of two for digit positions to the right of the decimal point. The position just to the left of the decimal point is considered 2^0 or 1, with the first digit to the right of the decimal point representing 2^–1. Each succeeding position represents an increasing negative power of two as the positions of the digits move to the right. This is the same format used with base-ten numbers and it works equally well for binary values. For example, the number 1.01 in binary is actually 1, plus 0 halves and 1 quarter.

Example 2.6

```
1.01
1    *2^0  =   1          (1*1  in base ten)
  0  *2^-1 =    .0        (0*½  in base ten)
  1  *2^-2 = +  .01       (1*¼  in base ten)
                1.01      (1¾   in base ten)
```

While any base-ten number can be represented in binary, a problem is encountered when representing base-ten values to the right of the decimal point. Representing a base-ten 10 in binary is a simple 1010; however, converting 0.1 in base ten to binary is somewhat more difficult. In fact, to represent 0.1 in binary (.0000110011) requires 10 bits to get a value accurate to within 1%. This can cause intermittent inaccuracies when dealing with real-world control applications.

For example, assume a system that measures temperature to .1 degrees C. The value from the analog-to-digital converter will be an integer binary value, and an internal calibration routine will then offset and divide the integer to get a binary representation of the temperature. Some decimal values, such as .5C will come out correctly, but others will have some degree of round-off error in the final value. Then, converting values with round-off error back into decimal values for the user interface will further increase the problem, resulting in a display with a variable accuracy.

For all their utility in representing real numbers, fixed-point binary numbers have little support in commercial compilers. This is due to three primary reasons:

1. Determining a position for the decimal point is often application specific, so finding a location that is universally acceptable is problematic.

2. Multiply, and specifically divide, routines can radically shift the location of the decimal point depending upon the values being used.

3. It has difficulty in representing small fractional base-ten values.

One alternative to the fixed-point format that does not require a floating-point format is to simply scale up all the values in a system until they are integers. Using this format, the temperature data from the previous example would be retained in integer increments of .1C, alleviating the problem of trying to represent .1C as a fixed-point value. Both the offset and divider values would have to be adjusted to accommodate the new location of the decimal point, as would any limits or test values. In addition, any routines that format the data for a user interface would have to correctly place the decimal point to properly represent the data. While this may seem like a lot of overhead, it does eliminate the problem with round off error, and once the constants are scaled, only minimal changes are required in the user interface routines.

Floating-Point Binary Numbers

Another alternative is to go with a more flexible system that has an application-determined placement of the decimal point. Just as with base-ten numbers, a fixed decimal point representation of real numbers can be an inefficient use of data memory for very large or very small numbers. So, binary numbers have an equivalent format to scientific notation, referred to as *floating-point*.

In the scientific notation of base-ten numbers, the decimal point was moved to the right of the leftmost digit in the number, and an exponent notation was added to the righthand side. Floating-point numbers use a similar format, moving the decimal point to the right of the MSB in the value, or *mantissa*, and adding a separate *exponent* to the number. The exponent represents the power of two associated with the MSB of the mantissa and can be either positive or negative using a two's complement format. This allows for extremely large and small values to be stored in floating-point numbers.

For storage of the value, typically both the exponent and the mantissa are combined into a single binary number. For signed floating-point values, the same format is used, except the MSB of the value is reserved for the sign, and the decimal point is placed to the right of the MSB of the matissa.

In embedded applications, floating-point numbers are generally reserved for highly variable, very large or small numbers, and "rolling your own" floating-point math routines are usually not required. It is also beyond the scope of this book, so the exact number of bits reserved for the mantissa and exponent and how they are formatted will not be covered here. Any reader desiring more information concerning the implementation of floating-point numbers and mathematics is encouraged to research the appropriate industry standards for additional information. One of the more common floating-point standards is IEEE® 754.

Alternate Numbering Systems

In our discussion of binary numbers, we used a representation of 1s and 0s to specify the values. While this is an accurate binary representation, it becomes cumbersome when we move into larger numbers of bits. So, as you might expect, a couple of short-hand formats have been developed, to alleviate the writer's cramp of writing binary numbers. One format is *octal* and the other is *hexadecimal*. The octal system groups bits together into blocks of 3 and represents the values using the digits 0–7. Hexadecimal notation groups bits together into blocks of 4 bits and represents the values using the digits 0–9, and the letters A–F.

	Decimal	Binary	Octal	Hexadecimal
Table 2.1	0	0000	00	0
	1	0001	01	1
	2	0010	02	2
	3	0011	03	3
	4	0100	04	4
	5	0101	05	5
	6	0110	06	6
	7	0111	07	2
	8	1000	10	8
	9	1001	11	8
	10	1010	12	A
	11	1011	13	B
	12	1100	14	C
	13	1101	15	D
	14	1110	16	E
	15	1111	17	F

Octal was originally popular because all 8 digits of its format could be easily displayed on a 7-segment LED display, and the 3-bit combinations were easy to recognize on the binary front panel switches and displays of the older mainframe computers. However, as time and technology advanced, problems with displaying hexadecimal values were eliminated and the binary switches and LEDs of the mainframe computer front panels were eventually phased out. Finally, due to its easy fit into 8-, 16-, and 32-bit data formats, hexadecimal eventually edged out octal as a standard notation for binary numbers. Today, in almost every text and manual, values are listed in either binary, decimal (base ten), or hexadecimal.

Binary-Coded Decimal

Another binary numeric format is binary-coded decimal or *BCD*. BCD uses a similar format to hexadecimal in that it groups together 4 bits to represent data. The difference is that the top 6 combinations, represented by A–F in hexadecimal, are undefined and unused. Only the first 10 combinations represented by 0–9 are used.

The BCD format was originally developed for use in logic blocks such as decade counters and display decoders in equipment to provide a base-ten display and control format. The subsequent development of small 8-bit microcontrollers carried the format forward in the form of either a BCD addition/subtraction mode in the math instructions of the processor, or as a BCD adjust instruction that corrects BCD data handled by a binary addition/subtraction.

One of the main advantages of BCD is its ability to accurately represent base-ten values, such as decimal dollars and cents. This made BCD a valuable format for software handling financial and inventory information because it can accurately store fractional base-ten decimal values without incurring round-off errors. The one downside to BCD is its inefficiency in storing numbers. Sixteen bits of BCD can only store a value between 0 and 9999, while 16-bit binary can represent up to 65535 values, a number over 60 times larger.

From this discussion, you may think that BCD seems like a waste of data storage, and it can be, but it is also a format that has several specific uses. And even though most high-level languages don't offer BCD as a storage option, some peripherals and most user interfaces need to convert binary numbers to and from BCD as a normal part of their operation. So, BCD is a necessary intermediate format for numbers being converted from binary to decimal for display on a user interface, or communication with other systems. Having an understanding of the format and being able to write routines that convert binary to BCD and back are, therefore, valuable skills for embedded designers.

ASCII

The last format to be discussed is ASCII. ASCII is an acronym for the American Standard Code for Information Interchange. It is a 7-bit code that represents letters, numbers, punctuation, and common control codes.

A hold-over data format from the time of mainframe computers, ASCII was one of two common formats for sending commands and data serially to terminals and printers. The alternate code, an 8-bit code known as EBIDIC, has since disappeared, leaving ASCII as the de-facto standard with numerous file formats and command codes based on it. The following is a chart of all 128 ASCII codes, referenced by hexadecimal:

Table 2.2

Hex	ASCII	Hex	ASCII	Hex	ASCII	Hex	ASCII	Hex	ASCII	Hex	ASCII	Hex	ASCII	Hex	ASCII
00	NUL	10	DLE	20	SP	30	0	40	@	50	P	60	`	70	p
01	SOH	11	DC1	21	!	31	1	41	A	51	Q	61	a	71	q
02	STX	12	DC2	22	"	32	2	42	B	52	R	62	b	72	r
03	ETX	13	DC3	23	#	33	3	43	C	53	S	63	c	73	s
04	EOT	14	DC4	24	$	34	4	44	D	54	T	64	d	74	t
05	ENQ	15	NAK	25	%	35	5	45	E	55	U	65	e	75	u
06	ACK	16	SYN	26	&	36	6	46	F	56	V	66	f	76	v
07	BEL	17	ETB	27	'	37	7	47	G	57	W	67	g	77	w
08	BS	18	CAN	28	(	38	8	48	H	58	X	68	h	78	x
09	HT	19	EM	29	)	39	9	49	I	59	Y	69	i	79	y
0A	LF	1A	SUB	2A	*	3A	:	4A	J	5A	Z	6A	j	7A	z
0B	VT	1B	ESC	2B	+	3B	;	4B	K	5B	[	6B	k	7B	{
0C	FP	1C	FS	2C	,	3C	<	4C	L	5C	\	6C	l	7C	|
0D	CR	1D	GS	2D	-	3D	=	4D	M	5D	]	6D	m	7D	}
0E	SO	1E	RS	2E	.	3E	>	4E	N	5E	^	6E	n	7E	~
0F	SI	1F	US	2F	/	3F	?	4F	O	5F	_	6F	o	7F	DEL

Among the more convenient features of the code is the placement of the codes for the numbers 0–9. They are placed such that conversion between BCD and ASCII is accomplished by simply OR-ing on the top 3 bits, or AND-ing them off. In addition, translation between upper and lower case just involves adding or subtracting hexadecimal 20. The code also includes all of the more common control codes such as BS (back space), LF (line feed), CR (carriage return), and ESC (escape)

Although ASCII was among the first computer codes generated, it has stood the test of time and most, if not all, computers use it in one form or another. It is also used extensively in small LCD and video controller chips, thermal printers and keyboard encoder chips. It has even left its mark on serial communications, in that most serial ports offer the option of 7-bit serial transmission.

Error Detection

One of the things that most engineers ask when first exposed to ASCII is what to do with the eighth bit in an 8-bit system. It seems a waste of data memory to just leave it empty, and it doesn't make sense that older computer systems wouldn't use the bit in some way. It turns out that the eighth bit did have a use. It started out in serial communications where corruption of data in transit was not uncommon. When serially transmitted, the eighth bit was often used for error detection as a *parity* bit.

The method involved including the parity bit which, when exclusive OR-ed with the other bits, would produce either a one or a zero. Even parity was designed to produce a zero result, and odd parity produced a one. By checking each byte as it came in, the receiver could detect single-bit errors, and when an error occurred, request a retransmission of the data. This is the same parity bit that is still used in serial ports today. Users are given the option to use *even* or *odd*, and can even choose *no* parity, which turns off the error checking.

Parity works fine for 7-bit ASCII data in an 8-bit system, but what about 8-, 16-, and 32-bit data? When computer systems began passing larger and larger blocks of data, a better system was needed—specifically, one that didn't use up 12.5% of the bandwidth—so several other error-checking systems were developed. Some are able to determine multibit errors in a group of data bytes, while other simpler systems can only detect single-bit errors. Other, more complex, methods are even able to detect and correct bit errors in one or more bytes of data. While this area of design is indeed fascinating, it is also well beyond the scope of this book.

For our use here, we will concentrate on two of the simpler systems, the *check sum*, and the *cyclic redundancy check* or *CRC*.

The check sum is the simpler of the two systems and, just as it sounds, it is simply a one- or two-byte value that holds the binary sum of all the data. It can detect single-bit errors, and even some multibit errors, but it is by no means a 100% check on the data.

A CRC, on the other hand, uses a combination of shifts and boolean functions to combine the data into a check value. Typically a CRC shifts each byte of data in the data block into the CRC value one bit at a time. Each bit, before it is shifted into the CRC value, is combined with feedback bits taken from the current value of the CRC. When all of the bits in the data block have been shifted into the CRC value, a unique CRC value has been generated that should detect single and more of the multibit errors. The number, type, and combination of bit errors that can be detected is determined by several factors. These include both the number of bits in the CRC and the specific combination of bits fed back from the CRC value during the calculation. As mentioned previously, an in-depth description of CRC systems, and even a critique of the relative merits of the different types of CRC algorithms is a subject sufficient to fill a book, and as such is beyond the scope of this text. Only this cursory explanation will be presented here. For more information on CRC systems, the reader is encouraged to research the subject further.

One final note on CRCs and check sums. Because embedded designs must operate in the real world, and because they will be subject to EMI, RFI, and a host of other disruptive forces, CRCs and check sums are also typically used to validate the contents of both program and data memory. Periodically running a check sum on the program memory, or a CRC check of the data in data memory is a convenient "sanity check" on the system. So, designers working in noisy environments with high functional and data integrity requirements should continue their research into these valuable tools of the trade.

Data Structures

In a typical high-level application, once the format for the data in a program has been determined, the next step is to define a data structure to hold the information. The structure will determine what modifying functions, such as assignment and math functions, are available. It will determine what other formats the data can be converted into, and what user interface possibilities exist for the data.

In an embedded design, a data structure not only defines storage for data, it also provides a control conduit for accessing control and data registers of the system peripherals. Some peripheral functions may only need byte-wide access, while others may require single bit control. Still others may be a combination of both. In any case, it is essential that the right type of data structure be defined for the type of data to be stored or the type of control to be exercised over the peripheral.

Therefore, a good understanding of the data structure's inner workings is important both for efficiency in data storage and for efficient connections to the system's peripherals. Of specific interest is:

1. What type of information can be stored in the data structure?
2. What other functions are compatible with the data structure?
3. Can the data structures be used to access peripheral control and data registers?
4. How does the date structure actually store the information in memory?
5. How do existing and new functions access the data?

A good understanding of the data structures is important both for efficiency in data storage and for an efficient conduit to the system's peripherals. Knowing how a language stores information can also be proactive in the optimization process, in that it gives the designer insight into the consequences of using a particular data type as it applies to storage and access overhead. This information may allow the designer to choose wisely enough to avoid the need for custom routines altogether.

The following sections covering data structures will try to answer all five of these questions as they apply to each of the different data structures.

Simple Data Types

The term "simple data type" refers to variables that store only one instance of data and store only one format of data at a time. More complex data types, which hold more than one instance of data or hold more than one type of data, will be covered in the next section titled *Complex Data Types*.

```
BIT        variable_name
```

Declaration 2.1

The simplest data type is the **boolean** or **BIT**. This data type has only two possible states, 1 or 0. Alternately, TRUE or FALSE, and YES or NO can also be used with some compilers. It is typically used to carry the result of a boolean logical expression or the binary status of a peripheral or comparison. It can even be used as part of another data type to hold the sign of a value. In each case, the variable provides a simple on/off or yes/no functionality or status.

When BIT is used as a variable, it is assigned a value just like any other variable. The only difference with the BIT data structure is that it can also be assigned the result of a comparison using combinations of boolean logic and the standard comparison operators, < > and =.

Note: A helpful debugging trick is to assign the result of a comparison to a BIT variable and then use the variable in the conditional statement. This allows the designer to monitor the status of the BIT variable and determine the path of execution without having to step through the entire code block step by step.

Code Snippet 2.1

```
Flag = (Var_A > Var_B) & (Var_A < Var_C);
if Flag then printf(Var_A);
```

To use the BIT data structure as a conduit to a peripheral control register, the bit must be defined to reside at the corresponding address and bit of the peripheral function to be controlled. As this is not universally supported in C compilers, compilers that do support the feature may have different syntax. So, this is yet another point that must be researched in the user's manual for the compiler. If the compiler does not allow the user to specify both the address and bit location, there is an alternate method using the STRUCTURE statement and that will be covered in the *Complex Data Structures* section of this chapter.

Due to the boolean's simple data requirements, BIT is almost always stored as a single bit within a larger data word. The compiler may choose to store the binary value alone within a larger data word, or it may combine multiple bits and other small data structures for more efficient storage. The designer also has the option to force the combination of BITs and other small data structures within a larger data word for convenience, or for more efficient access to control bits within a peripheral's control register. Additional information on this process is presented in the STRUCTURE data structure following.

To access a BIT, the compiler may copy the specific data bit to be accessed into a holding location and then shift it to a specific location. This allows the high-level language to optimize its math and comparison routines for a single bit location within a data word, making the math and comparison routines more efficient. However, this does place some overhead on the access routines for the BIT's data structure.

Other compilers, designed for target microcontrollers with instructions capable of setting, clearing, manipulating, and testing individual bits within a data word, avoid this overhead by simply designing their boolean and comparison routines to take advantage of the BIT instructions.

To access the BIT directly in memory, the designer needs two pieces of information, the address of the data word containing the BIT, and the location of the BIT within the data word. The address of the byte containing the BIT is typically available through the variable's label. The specific BIT within the byte may not be readily available, and may change as new variables are added to the design. For these reasons, it is generally best to only use manual access of a BIT defined using either a compiler function that allows the designer to specify the bit location, or a STRUCTURE

Using a STRUCTURE to define the location of a BIT is also useful in that it can be used to force the compiler to group specific variables together. It can also be used to force a group of commonly used BITs into common bit locations for faster access. Finally, defining a BIT within a STRUCTURE and a UNION, gives the designer the option to access the BITs as either individual values or as a group for loading default states at start-up.

One point that should be noted concerning this data type is that not all high-level language compilers recognize it. And, many compilers that do recognize the data type may not agree on its name or syntax, so the designers should review the user's guide for any compiler they intend to use, as there may be differences in the syntax used or restrictions on the definition of this data type.

Declaration 2.2 →

```
SIGNED CHAR       variable_name
UNSIGNED CHAR     variable_name
```

The **CHAR** data type was originally designed to hold a single ASCII character, thus the name CHAR, which is short for character. CHARs are still commonly used for holding single ASCII characters, either for individual testing or as part of an output routine, or even grouped with other CHARs to form an array of characters called a STRING. However, over time, it has also come to be a generic variable type for 8-bit data. In fact, most if not all modern high-level languages allow the use of CHAR variables in math operations, conditional statements, and even allow the definition of a CHAR variable as either signed or unsigned.

In embedded programming, the CHAR is equally as important as the boolean/BIT data type because most peripheral control registers will be one or more bytes in length and the CHAR variable type is a convenient way to access these registers. Typically, a control register for a peripheral will be defined as a CHAR for byte-wide access, allowing the entire register to be set with one assignment. The CHAR may also be tied to a STRUCTURE of BITs using a UNION definition to allow both bit-wise control of the functions, as well as byte-wise access for initialization. More information on both the UNION and the STRUC-TURE will be presented in later sections of this chapter.

An important point to note is that this variable may be assumed to be signed or unsigned by the C compiler if the words SIGNED or UNSIGNED are not included in the definition of the variable. The only ANSI requirement is that the compiler be consistent in its definitions. Therefore, it is best to specify the form in the definition of the variable to avoid problems migrating between compilers.

Manually accessing a CHAR variable at the language level is very simple, as most compilers recognize the data structure as both a character variable, and a signed or unsigned binary value. Access at the assembly language level is also simple as the name given to the variable can be used as an address label to access the data memory. Because the CHAR represents the smallest data structure short of a BIT, the format used to store the data in memory is also simple. The 8-bit value is simply stored in the lower 8 bits of the data memory word. Because the data is stored as a single byte, no additional information, beyond the address, is required.

Declaration 2.3

```
INT                 variable_name
UNSIGNED INT        variable_name
```

INT, short for integer, is the next larger data type. It is typically used to hold larger signed and unsigned binary values, and while the BITs and CHARs have consistent and predefined data lengths, the length of an INT is largely dependent on the specific implementation of the high-level compiler. As a result, the actual number of bits in an INT can vary from as few as 16 bits, to whatever the upper limit of the compiler is. The only limitation on the size of an INT is that it must be larger than a CHAR and less than or equal to the size of a LONG. So, to determine the actual size of an INT in a specific compiler, it is necessary to consult the user's manual for the compiler being used.

Because of an INT's somewhat indeterminate length, it can present a problem for efficiently storing larger data. Some compilers may not allocate sufficient bits to hold an application's data, while others may allocate too many bits, resulting in wasted data storage. This can be a very serious problem if the application using the data is to be shared across several different compilers and processors. To alleviate this problem, the designer has three basic options:

1. The large groups of data can be broken into individual bytes and stored as an array of unsigned CHARs, and then recreated in an INT when needed. This minimizes the storage requirements to the minimum number of required bytes, but it also complicates any math or comparison operation that may be required.

2. The INT can be defined as LONGs within a STRUCTURE, allowing the designer to specify the number of bits to be used for the variable. This eliminates the math problem, but the compiler

will incur additional overhead, when it automatically converts the data into a standard-length LONG prior to performing the math, and will then incur additional overhead converting it back when the math is complete.

3. The best solution is to simply get to know the compilers to be used and define the variables appropriately for each implementation. The variable type casting will then force the compiler to use the appropriate math and comparison functions, resulting in a much simpler design, while incurring only a minimal processing overhead.

As with the CHAR variable type, the name given to the variable acts as a label and can be used as a pointer to the data in assembly language. However, the number of bytes reserved for the variable and the order in which the bytes are stored in data memory may differ from compiler to compiler. So, once again, it is up to the designers to do their homework and research the exact storage format used.

One of the important statements in the previous paragraph is often missed: "the order in which the bytes are stored in data memory may differ." Specifically, does the compiler store the MSB in the first or last data memory location allocated to the variable? There are two formats that can be used: *big endian* and *little endian*. In the big endian format, the MSB is stored in the first data memory address (lowest memory address) and the LSB is stored in the last data memory address (highest memory address). In little endian, the reverse is true; the LSB is in the first memory address and the MSB in the last. So, to correctly access an INT in assembly, it is necessary not only to determine the number of bytes stored but also which storage format is used. This information is also typically found in the manual. However, if it is not explicitly stated, a simple test routine can answer the question. The test routine defines an INT variable and loads the value 4660 into the variable. Then, by examining data memory, the format can be determined. If the data in the lower memory address is the hexadecimal value 12 followed by the hex value 34, then the format is big endian; if the first byte is 0x34, then the format is little endian.

Due to the generally variable length and format of the INT, it is not a good choice for accessing peripheral registers containing control bits or data. INTs can be, and often are, used for this purpose, but the practice can cause portability problems, including unexpectedly truncated data, the inclusion of data bits from adjacent peripherals, and even scrambled data. The practice is only recommended if the portability of the resulting routines is not a goal of the project.

Declaration 2.4

```
LONG               variable_name
UNSIGNED LONG      variable_name
```

LONG, short for long integer, is the next larger data type. It is typically used to hold very large signed and unsigned binary values, and while the BITs and CHARs have consistent and predefined data lengths, the length of a LONG is again, dependent on the specific implementation of the high-level compiler. As a result, the actual number of bits in a LONG can vary from as few as 16 bits, up to whatever the upper limit of the compiler defines for data types. The only limitation on the size of a LONG variable is that it must be at least as large, or larger, than an INT. Typically, a LONG is twice the size of an INT, but this is not specified by the ANSI[2] standard. So, to determine the actual size of an INT in a specific compiler, it is necessary to consult the user's manual for the compiler being used.

Because the LONG is somewhat nonstandard in length, it can also present problems for portability and efficiently storing larger data. As a result, the storage options that applied to the INT serve equally well for the LONG.

Storage problems for larger groups of data can be handled by breaking the larger data blocks into individual bytes and storing as an array of unsigned CHARs, and then recreating in a LONG when needed. This minimizes the storage requirements to the minimum number of required bytes, but it also complicates any math or comparison operation that may be required.

The portability problems can be alleviated by simply getting to know the compilers being used, and defining the variables appropriately for each

---

[2] ANSI and the ANSI logo are registered trademarks of the American National Standards Institute

implementation. The variable type casting will then force the compiler to use the appropriate math and comparison functions, resulting in a much simpler design, while incurring only a minimal processing overhead.

The actual length of the variable will also affect manual access to a LONG variable. As with the CHAR, the name given to the variable acts as a label when accessing the data in assembly language. However, the number of bytes stored for the variable and the order in which the bytes are stored in data memory may differ from compiler to compiler. So, once again, it is up to the designers to do their homework and research the exact storage format used.

Due to the generally variable length and format of the LONG, and its excess length, it is almost never used for accessing peripheral registers containing control bits or data. In fact, due to their length, LONG data types will generally only be useful for very specialized data within the program, although a variable requiring the number of bits included in a LONG is generally rare.

One place that LONG variables do find use is for intermediate results in calculations involving INTs, or as accumulation variables that hold the summation of a large number of data samples. While the LONG may seem attractive for this use, it is can have some unforeseen consequences. Remember that the compiler will typically convert all data in a math function to the largest data type prior to performing the operation. This can result in a shortage of temporary data storage during math operations on the LONG variables. As an example, performing a multiply on a 24-bit LONG variable can use up 12 bytes of data storage just for the temporary storage of the upgraded term variables. So, it is generally advisable to resort to either an array of CHARs or, in extreme cases, an array of INTs to store large data values. This allows the designer to more tightly regulate the amount of data storage required. It also limits the amount of temporary data storage required for math, even though it will require a custom, and somewhat complicated, math routine.

Manually accessing a LONG variable uses the same process as accessing an INT; there are just more bytes to access. As with other data types, the variable name will act as a label for the starting data memory address of the data, and the appropriate big/little endian format must be used to access the data in the proper sequence.

Declaration 2.5

```
FLOAT     variable_name
DOUBLE    variable_name
```

FLOAT, short for floating-point, and **DOUBLE**, short for double precision floating-point, are another simple data structure common to embedded C programming. Typically the FLOAT and DOUBLE are used to hold very large or very small signed binary values. They accomplish this by using a system similar to scientific notation in base-ten numbers. The data structure maintains a base value, or mantissa, and an exponent which holds the power of two associated with the MSB of the mantissa. Together, the exponent and mantissa are concatenated into a single data structure.

Most implementations assign 32 bits of storage for the exponent and mantissa of a FLOAT, and 64 bits for the DOUBLE. However, it is important to note that, like the INT and LONG, the exact size of the FLOAT is determined by the compiler implementation and, potentially, configuration options for the compiler. So, to determine the actual size of a FLOAT or DOUBLE in a specific compiler, it is necessary to consult the user's manual for the compiler being used.

Because the actual implementation of both FLOATs and DOUBLEs is dependent upon the standard used by the compiler, and their size and complex nature tends to limit their application in embedded designs, they will not be discussed in any great detail here. Any reader interested in the specifics of FLOAT or DOUBLE data structures can find additional information in either an advanced computer science text or the IEEE specification IEEE 754.

Code Snippet 2.2

```
pointer_name = *variable_name;
pointer_name = &variable_name;
```

Pointers are the last data structure to be covered in this chapter. A pointer, simply stated, is a variable that holds the address of another variable. With it, designers can access data memory independently of a specifically defined variable name. In fact, one of the primary uses of data pointers is to create dynamically allocated data storage, which is essentially an unnamed variable created "on-the-fly" as the program is running. This ability to create storage is quite powerful, although the responsibility of monitoring the amount of available data storage shifts from the compiler to the designer.

Pointers are somewhat unique in that they are typically associated with another data type. The reason for this is because the pointer needs to know the storage format of the data so it can correctly interpret the data. It also needs this information if it is to be used to dynamically allocate variables, so it can reserve the right amount of memory. This is not to say that a pointer can't be used to access one type of data with another type's definition. In fact, this is one of the more powerful capabilities of the pointer type.

The syntax of the pointer data structure is also somewhat unique. The '*' sign is used as a prefix for the variable being accessed, to indicate that the data held in the variable is to be loaded into the pointer. The '&' sign is used as a prefix for the variable being accessed, to indicate that the address of the variable is to be loaded into the pointer. What this means is that both the data and the address of a variable can be loaded into the pointer data structure. Having the ability to access both gives pointers the ability to not only pass addresses around, but also to perform math on the addresses.

Accessing pointers by machine language is typically not needed as most microcontrollers already have the ability to access data through index registers. This, plus the ability to use variable labels as constant values in assembly language provides all the functionality of a pointer. In addition, the number of bits used for a pointer will be dependent upon the addressing modes used by the compiler and the architectural specifics of the microcontroller. So, an explanation of how to access pointers through assembly language will be highly specific to both the microcontroller and the language, and of little additional value, so no attempt will be made to explain access here.

Complex Data Types

Complex data types refer to those variable types that either hold more than one type of data, STRUCTUREs and UNIONs, or more than one instance of a simple data type, ARRAYs. These data types allow the designer to group blocks of data together, either for programming convenience or to allow simplified access to the individual data elements.

One complex data type that will not be covered is POINTERs, mainly because their ability to dynamically allocate data is, in general, not particularly applicable to small embedded applications, where the data storage requirements tend to be static. In addition, the amount of memory available in small microcontrollers is insufficient to implement a heap of any reasonable size, so using pointers would be inefficient at best.

Declaration 2.6

```
STRUCT structure_name {
    variable_type variable_name;
    variable_type variable_name;
    } variable_name;
```

The **STRUCTURE** data type is a composite data structure that can combine multiple variables and multiple variable types into a single variable structure. Any simple variable structure available in the language can typically be included within a structure, and included more than once. The specific number of bits allocated to each variable can also be specified, allowing the designer to tailor the storage capacity of each variable.

Each instance of the various data structures within the STRUCTURE is given a specific name and, when combined with the STRUCTURE's name, can be accessed like any other variable in the system. Names for individual fields within a structure can even be repeated in different STRUCTUREs because the name of the different STRUCTUREs allows the high-level language to differentiate the two variables.

Using this capability, related variables can even be grouped together under a single name and stored in a common location. While the improved organization of storage is elegant and using a common group name improves readability, the biggest advantage of common storage for related variables is the ability to store and retrieve groups of data in a faster, more efficient manner. The importance of this capability will become clearer when context storage and switching are discussed later in the chapter.

The STRUCTURE is also very useful for creating control and data variables linked to the system peripherals, because it can be used to label and access individual flags and groups of bits, within an 8- or 16-bit peripheral control register. The labeling, order, and grouping of the bits is specified when the STRUCTURE is defined, allowing the designer to match up names and bits in the variables to the names and bits specified in the peripheral's control and data registers. In short, the designer can redefine peripheral control and data bits and registers and unique variables accessible by the program.

For example, the following is a map of the control bits for an analog-to-digital converter peripheral. In its control register are bits that specify the clock used by the ADC (ADCS1 & ADCS0), bits that specify the input channel, (CHS3--CHS0), a bit that starts the conversion and signals the completion of the conversion (GO/DONE), and a bit that enables the ADC (ADON).

Definition 2.1

ADCON0 (Analog to Digital Control Register)

Bit 7	Bit 6	Bit 5	Bit 4	Bit 3	Bit 2	Bit 1	Bit0
ADCS1	ADCS0	CHS2	CHS1	CHS0	GO/DONE	CHS3	ADON

To control the peripheral, some of these bits have to be set for each conversion, and others are set only at the initial configuration of the peripheral. Defining the individual bit groups with a STRUCTURE allows the designer to modify the fields individually, changing some, while still keeping others at their initialized values. A common prefix also helps in identifying the bits as belonging to a common register.

Declaration 2.7

```
STRUCT REGDEF{
        UNSIGNED INT        ADON:1;
        UNSIGNED INT        CHS3:1;
        UNSIGNED INT        GODONE:1;
        UNSIGNED INT        CHS:3;
        UNSIGNED INT        ADCS:2;
        } ADCON0;
```

In the example, UNSIGNED INT data structures, of a specified 1-bit length are defined for bits 0 through 2, allowing the designer to access them individually to turn the ADC on and off, set the most significant channel select bit, and initiate and monitor the conversion process. A 3-bit UNSIGNED INT is used to specify the lower 3 bits of the channel selection, and a 2-bit UNSIGNED INT is tied to clock selection. Using these definitions, the controlling program for the analog-to-digital converter can now control each field individually as if they were separate variables, simplifying the code and improving its readability.

Access to the individual segments of the STRUCTURE is accomplished by using the STRUCTURE's name, followed by a dot and the name of the specific field. For example, `ADCON0.GODONE = 1`, will set the GODONE bit within the ADCON0 register, initiating a conversion. As an added bonus, the names for individual groups of bits can be repeated within other STRUCTUREs. This means descriptive names can be reused in the STRUCTURE definitions for similar variables, although care should be taken to not repeat names within the same STRUCTURE.

Another thing to note about the STRUCTURE definition is that the data memory address of the variable is not specified in the definition. Typically, a compiler-specific language extension specifies the address of the group of variables labeled ADCON0. This is particularly important when building a STRUCTURE to access a peripheral control register, as the address is fixed in the hardware design and the appropriate definition must be included to fix the label to the correct address. Some compilers combine the definition of the structure and the declaration of its address into a single syntax, while others rely on a secondary definition to fix the address of a previously defined variable to a specific location. So, it is up to the designer to research the question and determine the exact syntax required.

Finally, this definition also includes a type label "REGDEF" as part of the variable definition. This is to allow other variables to reuse the format of this STRUCTURE if needed. Typically, the format of peripheral control registers is unique to each peripheral, so only microcontrollers with more than one of a given peripheral would be able to use this feature. In fact, due to its somewhat dubious need, some compilers have dropped the requirement for this part of the definition, as it is not widely used. Other compilers may support the convention to only limited degrees, so consulting the documentation on the compiler is best if the feature is to be used.

Access to a STRUCTURE from assembly language is simply a matter of using the name of the structure as a label within the assembly. However, access to the individual bits must be accomplished through the appropriate assembly language bit manipulation instructions.

Declaration 2.8

```
UNION union_name {
    variable_type variable_name;
    variable_type variable_name;
    } variable_name;
```

In some applications, it can be useful to be able to access a given piece of data not only by different names, but also using different data structures. To handle this task, the complex data type **UNION** is used. What a UNION does is create two definitions for a common word, or group of words, in data memory. This allows the program to change its handling of a variable based on its needs at any one time.

For example, the individual groups of bits within the ADCON0 peripheral control register in the previous section were defined to give the program access to the control bits individually. However, in the initial configuration of the peripheral, it would be rather cumbersome and inefficient to set each variable one at a time. Defining the STRUCTRUE from previous example in a UNION allows the designer to not only individually access the groups of bits within the peripheral control register, but it also allows the designer to set all of the bits at once via a single 8-bit CHAR.

Declaration 2.9

```
UNION    UNDEF{
        STRUCT REGDEF{
            SHORT          ADON;
            SHORT          CHS3;
            SHORT          GODONE;
            UNSIGNED CHAR       CHS:3;
            UNSIGNED CHAR       ADCS:2;
            } BYBIT;
        UNSIGNED CHAR  BYBYTE;
        } ADCON0 @ 0x1F;
```

In the example, the original STRUCTURE definition is now included within the definition of the UNION as one of two possible definitions for the common data memory. The STRUCTURE portion of the definition has been given the sub-name "BYBIT" and any access to this side of the definition will require its inclusion in the variable name. The second definition for the same words of data memory is an unsigned CHAR data structure, labeled by the sub-name "BYBYTE."

To access the control register's individual fields, the variable name becomes a combination of the UNION and STRUCTURE's naming convention; `ADCON0.BYBIT.GODONE = 1`. Byte-wide access is similarly accessed through the UNION's name combined with the name of the unsigned CHAR: `ADCON0.BYBYTE = 0x38`.

Declaration 2.10

```
data_type variable_name[max_array_size]
```

The **ARRAY** data structure is nothing more than a multielement collection of the data type specified in the definition. Accessing individual elements in the array is accomplished through the index value supplied within the square brackets. Other than its ability to store multiple copies of the specified data structure, the variables that are defined in an array are indistinguishable from any other single element instance of the same data structure. It is basically a collection of identical data elements, organized into an addressable configuration.

To access the individual data elements in an array, it is necessary to provide an index value that specifies the required element. The index value can be thought of as the address of the element within the group of data, much as a house address specifies a home within a neighborhood. One unique feature of the index value is that it can either be a single value for a 1-dimensional array, or multiple values for a multidimensional array. While the storage of the data is not any different for a 1-dimensional array versus a multidimensional array, having more than one index variable can be convenient for separating subgroups of data within the whole, or representing relationships between individual elements.

By definition, the type of data within an array is the same throughout and can be of any type, including complex data types such as STRUCTUREs and UNIONs. The ARRAY just specifies the organization and access of the data within the block of memory. The declaration of the ARRAY also specifies the size of the data block, as well as the maximum value of all dimensions within the ARRAY.

One exception to this statement that should be noted: Not all compilers support ARRAYs of BOOLEANs or BITs. Even if the compiler supports the data type, ARRAYs of BOOLEANs or BITs may still not be supported. The user's manual should be consulted to determine the specific options available for arrays.

Accessing an array is just a matter of specifying the index of the data to be accessed as part of the variables; note:

Code Snippet 2.3

```
ADC_DATA[current_value] = 34;
```

In this statement, the element corresponding to the index value in current_value is assigned the value 34. Current_value is the index value, 34 is the data, and ADC_DATA is the name of the array. For more dimensions in an ARRAY, more indexes are added, surrounded by square brackets. For instance:

Code Snippet 2.4

```
ADC_DATA[current_value][date,time];
```

This creates a two-dimensional array with two index values required to access each data value stored in the array.

Accessing an array via assembly language becomes a little more complex, as the size of the data type in the array will affect the absolute address of each element. To convert the index value into a physical data memory address, it is necessary to multiply the index by the number of bytes in each element's data type, and then add in the first address of the array. So, to find a specific element in an array of 16-bit integers, assuming 8-bit data memory, the physical memory address is equal to:

Equation 2.1

```
(Starting address of the ARRAY) + (2 * (index value))
```

The factor of 2, multiplied by the index value, accounts for the 2-byte size of the integer, and the starting address of the ARRAY is available through the ARRAY's label. Also note that the index value can include 0, and its maximum value must be 1 less than the size of the array when it was declared.

Accessing multidimensional ARRAYs is even more complex, as the dimensions of the array play a factor in determining the address of each element. In the following ARRAY the address for a specific element is found using this equation:

Equation 2.2

```
(starting address of the ARRAY)+(2*index1)+(2*index
    2*(max_index1+1))
```

The starting address of the array and index1 are the same as the previous example, but now both the maximum size of index1 and the value in index2 must be taken into account. By multiplying the maximum value of index1, plus 1, by the second index, we push the address up into the appropriate block of data. To demonstrate, take a 3 by 4 array of 16-bit integers defined by the following declaration:

Declaration 2.11

```
Int K_vals[3][4] = {  0x0A01, 0x0A02, 0x0A03, 0x0B01, 0x0B02, 0x0B03,
                      0x0C01, 0x0C02, 0x0C03, 0x0D01, 0x0D02, 0x0D03}
```

This will load all 12, 16-bit, locations with data, incrementing through the first index variable. And then incrementing the second index variable each time the first variable rolls over. So, if you examine the array using X as the first index value, and Y as the second, you will see the data arrayed as follows:

Table 2.3

X→	0	1	2
Y			
0	0x0A01	0x0A02	0x0A03
1	0x0B01	0x0B02	0x0B03
2	0x0C01	0x0C02	0x0C03
3	0x0D01	0x0D02	0x0D03

There are a couple of things to note about the arrangement of the data: One, the data loaded when the array was declared was loaded by incrementing through the first index and then the second. Two, the index runs from 0 to the declared size–1. This is because zero is a legitimate index value, so declaring an array as K_val[3] actually creates 3 locations within the array indexed by 0, 1, and 2.

Now, how was the data in the array actually stored in data memory? If we do a memory dump of the data memory starting at the beginning address of the array, and assume a big endian format, the data should appear in memory as follows:

Memory 2.1

```
0x0100:   0x0A 0x01 0x0A 0x02 0x0A 0x03 0x0B 0x01
0x0108:   0x0B 0x02 0x0B 0x03 0x0C 0x01 0x0C 0x02
0x0110:   0x0C 0x03 0x0D 0x01 0x0D 0x02 0x0D 0x03
```

So, using the previous equation to generate an address for the element stored at [1][3], we get:

```
Address = 0x0100 + (byte_per_var*1) + (byte_per_
  var*3*3)
Address = 0x0100 + (2*1) + (2*3*3)
Address = 0x0114
```

From the dump of data memory, the data at 0x0114 and 0x0115 is 0x0D and 0x02, resulting in a 16-bit value of 0x0D02 which matches the value that should be in K_vals[1][3].

Communications Protocols

When two tasks in a multitasking system want to communicate, there are three potential problems that can interfere with the reliable communication of the data. The receiving task may not be ready to accept data when the sending task wants to send. The sending task may not be ready when the receiving task needs the data. Or the two tasks may be operating at significantly different rates, which means one of the two tasks can be overwhelmed in the transfer. To deal with these timing related problems, three different communications protocols are presented to manage the communication process.

The simple definition of a protocol is "a sequence of instructions designed to perform a specific task." There are diplomatic protocols, communications protocols, even medical protocols, and each one defines the steps taken to achieve a desired result, whether the result is a treaty, transfer of a date, or treating an illness. The power of a protocol is that it plans out all the steps to be taken, the order in which they are performed, and the way in which any exceptions are to be handled.

The communications protocols presented here are designed to handle the three different communications timing problems discussed previously. Broadcast is designed to handler transfers in which the sender is not ready when the receiver wants data. Semaphore is designed to handle transfers in which the receiver is not ready when the sender wants to send data. Buffer is designed to handle transfers in which the rates of the two tasks are significantly different.

Simple Data Broadcast

A simple broadcast data transfer is the most basic form of communications protocol. The transmitter places its information, and any updates, in a common globally accessible variable. The receiver, or receivers, of the data then retrieve the information when they need it. Because the receiver is not required to acknowledge its reception of the data, and the transmitter provides no indication of changes in the data, the transfer is completely asynchronous. A side effect of this form of transfer is that no event timing is transferred with the data; it is purely a data transfer.

This protocol is designed to handle data that doesn't need to include event information as part of the transfer. This could be due to the nature of the data, or because the data only takes on significance when combined with other events. For example, a system that time stamps the reception of serial communications into a system. The current time would be posted by the real time clock, and updated as each second increments. However, the receiver of the current time information is not interested in each tick of the clock, it only needs to know the current time, when a new serial communication has been received. So, the information contained in the variables holding the current time are important, but only when tied to secondary event of a serial communication. While a handshaking protocol could be used for this transfer, it would involve placing an unreasonable overhead on the receiving task in that it would have to acknowledge event tick of the clock.

Because this transfer does not convey event timing, there are some limitations associated with its use:

1. The receiving tasks must be able to tolerate missing intermediate updates to the data. As we saw in the example, the receiver not only can tolerate the missing updates, it is more efficient to completely ignore the data until it needs it.

2. The sending task must be able to complete all updates to the data, before the information becomes accessible to the receiver. Specifically, all updates must be completed before the next time the receiving task executes; otherwise, the receiving task could retrieve corrupted data.

3. If the sending task cannot complete its updates to the date before a receiving task gains access to the data, then:

a. The protocol must be expanded with a flag indicating that the data is invalid, a condition that would require the receiver to wait for completion of the update.

b. Or, the receiver must be able to tolerate invalid data without harm.

As the name implies, a broadcast data transfer is very much like a radio station broadcast. The sender regularly posts the most current information in a globally accessible location, where the receiver may retrieve the data when it needs it. The receiver then retrieves the data when its internal logic dictates. The advantage of this system is that the receiver only retrieves the data when it needs it and incurs no overhead to ignore the data when it does not need the data. The down side to this protocol is simple: the sender has no indication of when the receiver will retrieve the data, so it must continually post updates whether they are ultimately needed or not. This effectively shifts the overhead burden to the transmitter. And, because there is no handshaking between the sender and receiver, the sender has no idea whether the receiver is even listening. So, the transfer is continuous and indefinite.

If we formalize the transfer into a protocol:

- The transmitter posts the most recent current data to a global variable accessible by the receiver.

- The receiver then retrieves the current data, or not, whenever it requires the information.

- The transmitter posts updates to the data, as new information become available.

Because neither party requires any kind of handshaking from the other and the timing is completely open and the *broadcast protocol* is limited to only transferring data, no event timing is included. A receiver that polls the variable quickly enough may catch all the updates, but there is nothing in the protocol to guarantee it. So the receiving task only really knows the current value of the data and either does not know or care about its age or previous values.

The first question is probably, "Why all this window dressing for a transfer using a simple variable?" One task stores data in the holding variable and another retrieves the data, so what's so complicated? That is correct—the mechanism is simple—but remember the limitations that went along with the protocol. They are important, and they more than justify a little window dressing:

1. The transmitting task must complete any updates to a broadcast variable before the receiver is allowed to view the data.

2. If the transmitting task cannot complete an update, it must provide an indication that the current data is not valid, and the receiving task must be able to tolerate this wait condition.

3. Or, the receiver must be tolerant of partially updated data.

These restrictions are the important aspect of the Broadcast Transfer and have to be taken into account when choosing a transfer protocol, or the system could leak data.

Event-Driven Single Transfer

Data transfer in an event-driven single transfer involves not only the transfer of data but also creates a temporary synchronization between the transmitter and the receiver. Both information and timing cross between the transmitter and receiver.

For example, a keyboard-scanning task detects a button press on the keyboard. It uses an event-driven single transfer to pass the code associated with the key onto a command-decoding task. While the code associated with the key is important, the fact that it is a change in the status of the keyboard is also important. If the event timing were not also passed as part of the transfer, the command decoding task would not be able to differentiate between the initial press of the key and a later repeat of the key press. This would be a major problem if the key being pressed is normally repeated as part of the system's operations. So, event-driven single transfers of data require an indication of new data from the transmitter.

A less obvious requirement of an event-driven single transfer is the acknowledgment from the receiver indicating that the data has been retrieved. Now, why does the transmitter need to know the receiver has the data? Well, if the transmitting routine sends one piece of data and then immediately generates another to send, it will need to either wait a sufficiently long period of time to guarantee the receiver has retrieved the first piece of data, or have some indication from the receiver that it is safe to send the second piece of data. Otherwise, the transmitter runs the risk of overrunning the receiver and losing data in the transfer. Of the two choices, an acknowledge from the receiver is the more efficient use of processor time, so an acknowledge is required as part of any protocol to handle event-driven single transfers.

What about data—is it a required part of the transfer? Actually, no, a specific transfer of data is not necessary because the information can be implied in the transfer. For example, when an external limit switch is closed, a monitoring task may set a flag indicating the closure. A receiving task acknowledges the flag by clearing it, indicating it acknowledges the event. No format data value crossed between the monitoring and receiving tasks because the act of setting the flag implied the data by indicating that the limit switch had closed.

So, the protocol will require some form of two-way handshaking to indicate the successful transfer of data, but it does not actually have to transfer data. For that reason, the protocol is typically referred to as a *semaphore protocol*, because signals for both transfer and acknowledgment are required.

The protocol for handling event-driven single transfers should look something like the following for a single transfer:

- The transmitter checks the last transfer and waits if not complete.

- The transmitter posts the current data to a global variable, accessible by the receiver (optional).

- The transmitter sets a flag indicating new data is available.

- The transmitter can either wait for a response or continue with other activities.

- The receiver periodically polls the new data flag from the transmitter.

- If the flag is set, it retrieves the data (optional), and clears the flag to acknowledge the transfer.

There are a few limitations to the protocol that should be discussed so the designer can accurately predict how the system will operate during the transfer.

1. If the transmitter chooses to wait for an acknowledgement from the receiver, before continuing on with other activities:

    a. Then the transmitter can skip the initial step of testing for an acknowledge prior to posting new data.

    b. However, the transmitter will be held idle until the receiver notices the flag and accepts the data.

2. If, on the other hand, the transmitter chooses to continue on with other activities before receiving the acknowledgement:

    a. The transmitter will not be held idle waiting for the receiver to acknowledge the transmitter.

    b. However, the transmitter may be held idle at the initial step of testing for an acknowledge prior to most new data.

It is an interesting choice that must be made by the designer. Avoid holding the transmitter idle and risk a potential delay of the next byte to be transferred, or accept the delay knowing that the next transfer will be immediate. The choice is a trade-off of transmitter overhead versus a variable delay in the delivery of some data.

Other potential problems associated with the semaphore protocol can also appear at the system level and an in-depth discussion will be included in the appropriate chapters. For now, the important aspect to remember is that a semaphore protocol transfers both data and events.

Event-Driven Multielement Transfers

In an event-driven multielement transfer, the requirement for reliable transfer is the same as it is for the Event driven single transfer. However, due to radically different rates of execution, the transmitter and receiver can not tolerate the synchronization required by the semaphore protocol. What is needed is a way to slow down the data from the transmitter, so the receiver can process it, all without losing the reliability of a hand-shaking style of transfer.

As an example, consider a control task sending a string of text to a serial output task. Because the serial output task is tied to the slower transfer rate of the serial port, its execution will be significantly slower than the control task. So, either the control task must slow down its execution to accommodate the serial task, or some kind of temporary storage is needed to hold the message until the serial task is ready to send it. Given the control task's work is important and it can't slow down to the serial task's rate, then the storage option is the only one that makes sense in the application.

So, the protocol will require at a minimum; some form of data storage, a method for storing the data, and a method for retrieving it. It is also assumed that the storage and retrieval methods will have to communicate the number of elements to be transferred as well.

A protocol could be set up that just sets aside a block of data memory and a byte counter. The transmitting task would load the data into the memory block and set the byte counter to the number of data elements. The receiving task can then retrieve data until its count equals the byte counter. That would allow the transmitting task to run at its rate loading the data, and allow the receiver to take that data at a rate it can handle. But what happens if the transmitting task has another block of data to transfer, before the receiving task has retrieved all the data?

A better protocol is to create what is referred to as a *circular buffer*, or just buffer protocol. A buffer protocol uses a block of data memory for storage, just as the last protocol did. The difference is that a buffer also uses two address pointers to mark the locations of the last store and retrieve of data in the data block. When a new data element is added to the data memory block, it is added in the location pointed to by the storage pointer and the pointer is incremented. When a data element is retrieved, the retrieval pointer is used to access the data and then it is incremented. By comparing the pointers, the transmitting and receiving tasks can determine:

1. Is the buffer empty?
2. Is there data present to be retrieved?
3. Is the buffer is full?

So, as the transmitter places data in the buffer, the storage pointer moves forward through the block of data memory. And as the receiver retrieves data from the buffer, the retrieval pointer chases the storage pointer. To prevent the system from running out of storage, both pointers are designed to "wraparound" to the start of the data block when they pass the end. When the protocol is operating normally, the storage pointer will jump ahead of the retrieval pointer, and then the retrieval pointer will chase after it. Because the circular buffer is essentially infinite in length, because the pointers always wraparound, the storage space will be never run out. And the two pointers will chase each other indefinitely, provided the transmitter doesn't stack up so much data that the storage pointer "laps" the retrieval pointer.

So, how does the buffer protocol look from the pointer of view of the transmitting task and the receiving task. Let's start with the transmit side of the protocol:

- The transmitter checks to see if the buffer is full, by comparing the storage pointer to the retrieval pointer.
- If the buffer is not full, it places the data into the buffer using the storage pointer and increments the pointer.
- If the transmitter wishes to check on the receiver's progress, it simply compares the storage and retrieval pointers.

From the receiver's point of view:

- The receiver checks the buffer to see if data is present by comparing the storage and retrieval pointers.
- If the pointers indicate data is present, the receiver retrieves the data using the retrieval pointer and increments the pointer.

So, the two tasks have handshaking through the two pointers, to guarantee the reliable transfer of data. But, using the data space and the pointers allows the receiving task to receive the data at a rate it can handle, without holding up the transmitter.

Implementing a buffer protocol can be challenging though, due to the wraparound nature of the pointers. Any increment of the pointers must include a test for the end of the buffer, so the routine can wrap the pointer back around to the start of the buffer. And, the comparisons for buffer full, buffer empty, and data present can also become complicated due to the wraparound.

In an effort to alleviate some of this complexity, the designer may choose to vary the definition of the storage and retrieval pointers to simplify the various comparisons. Unfortunately, no one definition will simplify all the comparisons, so it is up to the designer to choose which definition works best for their design. The following shows all four possible definitions for the storage and retrieval pointers, plus the comparisons required to determine the three buffer conditions.

Table 2.4

Pointer definitions	Comparisons	Meaning
Storage > last element stored	IF (Storage == Retrieval)	then buffer is empty
Retrieval > last element retrieved	IF (Storage+1 == Retrieval)	then buffer is full
	IF (Storage <> Retrieval)	then data present
Storage > last element stored	IF (Storage+1 == Retrieval)	then buffer is empty
Retrieval > next element retrieved	IF (Storage == Retrieval)	then buffer is full
	IF (Storage+1 <> Retrieval)	then data present
Storage > next element stored	IF (Storage == Retrieval+1)	then buffer is empty
Retrieval > last element retrieved	IF (Storage == Retrieval)	then buffer is full
	IF (Storage <> Retrieval+1)	then data present
Storage > next element stored	IF (Storage == Retrieval)	then buffer is empty
Retrieval > next element retrieved	IF (Storage+1 == Retrieval)	then buffer is full
	IF (Storage <> Retrieval)	then data present

It is interesting that the comparisons required to test each condition don't change with the definition of the pointers. All that does change is that one or the other pointer has to be incremented before the comparison can be made. The only real choice is which tests will have to temporarily increment a pointer to perform its test, the test for buffer full, or the test for buffer empty/data available. What this means for the designer is that the quicker compare can be delegated to either the transmitter (checking for buffer full), or the receiver (checking for data present). Since the transmitter is typically running faster, then options one or four are typically used.

Also note that the choices are somewhat symmetrical; options one and four are identical, and options two and three are very similar. This makes sense, since one and four use the same sense for their storage and retrieval pointers, while the pointer sense in two and three are opposite and mirrored.

One point to note about buffers, because they use pointers to store and retrieve data and the only way to determine the status of the buffer is to compare the pointers, the buffer-full test always returns a full status when the buffer is one location short of being full. The reason for this is because the comparisons for buffer empty and buffer full turn out to be identical, unless the buffer-full test assumes one empty location.

If a buffer protocol solves the problem of transferring data between a fast and slow task, then what is the catch? Well, there is one and it is a bear. The basic problem is determining how big to make the storage space. If it is too small, then the transmitter will be hung up waiting for the receiver again because it will start running into buffer-full conditions. If it is too large, then data memory is wasted because the buffer is under-utilized.

One final question concerning the buffer protocol is how is the size of the data storage block determined? The size can be calculated based on the rates of data storage, data retrieval, and the frequency of use. Or the buffer can be sized experimentally by starting with an oversized buffer and then repeatedly testing the system while decreasing the size. When the transmitting tasks starts hitting buffer-full conditions, the buffer is optimized. For now, just assume that the buffer size is sufficient for the designs need, and a more in-depth explanation of the two methods will be presented in Chapter 5.

Mathematics

In embedded programming, mathematics is the means by which a program models and predicts the operation of the system it is controlling. The math may take the form of thermodynamic models for predicting the best timing and mixture in an engine, or it may be a simple time delay calculation for the best toasting of bread. Either way, the math is how a microcontroller takes its view of the world and transforms that data into a prediction of how to best control it.

For most applications, the math libraries supplied with the compiler will be sufficient for the calculations required by our models and equations. However, on occasion, there will be applications where it may be necessary to "roll our own" routines, either for a specialized math function, or just to avoid some speed or data storage inefficiencies associated with the supplied routines. Therefore, a good understanding of the math underlying the libraries is important, not only to be able to replace the routines, but also to evaluate the performance of the supplied functions.

Binary Addition and Subtraction

Earlier in the chapter, it was established that both base ten and binary numbering system use a digit position system based on powers of the base. The position of the digit also plays a part in the operation of the math as well. Just as base-ten numbers handle mathematics one digit at a time, moving from smallest power to largest, so do binary numbers in a computer. And just like base-ten numbers, carry and borrow operations are required to roll up over- or under-flows from lower digits to higher digits. The only difference is that binary numbers carry up at the value 2 instead of ten.

So, using this basic system, binary addition has to follow the following rules:

Table 2.5

If the carry_in from the next lower digit = 0

▶   0 + 0 + carry_in   results in 0 & carry_out = 0

▶   1 + 0 + carry_in   results in 1 & carry_out = 0

▶   0 + 1 + carry_in   results in 1 & carry_out = 0

▶   1 + 1 + carry_in   results in 0 & carry_out = 1

Table 2.6

If the carry_in from the next lower digit = 1

▶   0 + 0 + carry_in   results in 1 & carry_out = 0

▶   1 + 0 + carry_in   results in 0 & carry_out = 1

▶   0 + 1 + carry_in   results in 0 & carry_out = 1

▶   1 + 1 + carry_in   results in 1 & carry_out = 1

Using these rules in the following example of binary addition produces a result of 10101100. Note the carry_in values are in **bold**:

Example 2.7

```
111 111 <--carry bits
  00110101
 +01110111
         0   1 + 1                 =   0 with carry_out
        0    1 + 0 + carry_in      =   0 with carry_out
       1     1 + 1 + carry_in      =   1 with carry_out
      1      0 + 0 + carry_in      =   1
     0       1 + 1                 =   0 with carry_out
    1        1 + 1 + carry_in      =   1 with carry_out
   0         1 + 0 + carry_in      =   0 with carry_out
  1          0 + 0 + carry_in      =   1
  10101100
```

Converting the two values to decimal, we get 53 + 119, for a total of 172. 172 in binary is 1010110, so the math checks.

Binary subtraction operates in a similar manner, using the borrow instead of carry. Building a similar table of rules for subtraction yields the following:

Table 2.7

If the borrow_in from the next lower digit = 0
- ▶ 0 – 0 – borrow in results in 0 & borrow_out = 0
- ▶ 1 – 0 – borrow in results in 1 & borrow_out = 0
- ▶ 0 – 1 – borrow in results in 1 & borrow_out = 1
- ▶ 1 – 1 – borrow in results in 0 & borrow_out = 0

Table 2.8

If the borrow_in from the next lower digit = 1
- ▶ 0 – 0 – borrow in results in 1 & borrow_out = 1
- ▶ 1 – 0 – borrow in results in 0 & borrow_out = 0
- ▶ 0 – 1 – borrow in results in 0 & borrow_out = 1
- ▶ 1 – 1 – borrow in results in 1 & borrow_out = 1

Using these rules for subtraction in the following example produces a result of 00111110. Note the borrow values are in **bold**:

Example 2.8

```
111111   <--borrow
 10110101
-01110111
        0   1 - 1               = 0
       1   0 - 1               = 1 with borrow_out
      1   1 - 1 - borrow_in = 1 with borrow_out
     1   0 - 0 - borrow_in = 1 with borrow_out
    1   1 - 1 - borrow_in = 1 with borrow_out
   1   1 - 1 - borrow_in = 1 with borrow_out
  0   0 - 1 - borrow_in = 0 with borrow_out
 0        1 - 0 - borrow_in = 0
 00111110
```

Converting the two values to decimal, we get 181 – 119, for a difference of 62. 62 in binary is 00111110, so, again, the math checks.

And, as expected, binary addition and subtraction are not any different than addition and subtraction in base ten. The carry_out carries up a value of 1 to the next digit, and a borrow_out carries up a value of –1 to the next digit. This makes sense—addition and subtraction are universal concepts, and should be independent of the base of the number system.

Binary Multiplication

In addition, we added each digit together, one at a time, and carried the overflow up to the next digit as a carry. In multiplication, we multiply each digit together, one at a time, and carry the overflow up to the next digit as a carry as well. The only difference is that the carry may be greater than 1.

For multipliers with more than one digit, we again handle each one separately, multiplying the digit through all the digits of the multiplicand, and then add the results from each digit together to get a result, making sure to align the digits with the digit in the multiplier. For example:

Example 2.9

```
    123  Multiplicand
   x321  Multiplier
```

```
    123   (1 x 123 x 1)      the x1 is due to the position of the
                             1 in the multiplier
   2460   (2 x 123 x 10)     the x10 is due to the position of the
                             2 in the multiplier
 +36900   (3 x 123 x 100)    the x100 is due to the position of the
                             3 in the multiplier
```

```
  37483  Result
```

Thus is the essence of long multiplication—straightforward and simple, if somewhat tedious. So, it should come as no surprise that the process is no different for binary multiplication. Each bit in the multiplier, 1 or 0, is multiplied by each of the bits in the multiplicand. And when all the bits have been multiplied, we add together the result, making sure that we keep each interim result lined up with its multiplier bit. Just as straightforward and simple, although a little less tedious as we only have to multiply by 1 or 0.

So, if we convert 6 and 11 into binary and multiply them together, we should get the binary equivalent of 66.

Example 2.10

```
   1011  (11 in decimal)
  x0110  (6 in decimal)
00000000  (0 x 1011, the original value x 1)
00010110  (1 x 10110, the original value x 2)
00101100  (1 x 101100, the original value x 4)
+00000000  (0 x 1011000, the original value x 8)
01000010
```

And, 01000010 in decimal is 66, so once again the math checks out.

Before we move on to division, let's take a minute and check out some interesting points in binary multiplication.

1. The digit by digit multiply is only multiplying by 1 or 0, so the process of multiplying each bit of the multiplier with each bit of the multiplicand is very simple. In fact, algorithms for binary multiply typically don't bother with the bit-by-bit multiply; they just check the multiplier bit and if it is set, they shift over the multiplicand and add it into the result.

2. The act of shifting the multiplicand left to align with the multiplier, for each bit in the multiplier, would be a waste of time. It is simpler to just create a temporary variable to hold the shifted form of the multiplier from the last bit, and then shift it once for the next. That way the temporary variable only has to be shifted once for each bit of the multiplier.

3. The bits in the multiplier will have to be tested one at a time, from the LSB to the MSB, to perform the multiplication. If we can use a temporary variable to hold a shift copy of the multiplicand, why not use a temporary variable to hold a shifted copy of the multiplier that shifts to the right? That way the bit tested in the multiplier is always the LSB.

4. The result of the multiply was nearly twice the size of the multiplier and multiplicand. In fact, if the multiplier and multiplicand were both 1111, it would have been twice the size. So, to prevent losing any bits in the result to roll over, the multiply algorithm will have to have a result at least twice the size of input variables, or have a number of bits equal to the total bits in both the input variables, if they are different sizes.

Using these insights, an efficient binary multiply routine can be created that is fairly simple. It is just a matter of shifting and adding inside a loop:

Algorithm 2.1

```
char A        ; multiplicand
char B        ; multiplier
int  C        ; 16-bit result
int  temp_a ; 16-bit temp holding variable for
                multiplicand
char temp_b ; 8-bit temp holding variable for
                multiplier

C = 0
Temp_a = A
Temp_b = B
FOR I = 0 to 7                    ; multiplier is 8 bits
      IF (LSB of B = 1) THEN C = C + temp_a
      SHIFT temp_a LEFT 1    ;multiplicand * 2
      SHIFT temp_b RIGHT 1   ; multiplier / 2
NEXT I
```

For each pass through the loop, the LSB of the multiplier is tested. If the bit is set, then the multiplicand is added to the result. If the bit is clear, the multiplicand is not added to the result. In either case, the temporary copy of the multiplicand is multiplied by 2 and the temporary copy of the multiplier is divided by 2 for the next pass through the loop. The loop repeats until all of the multiplicand bits have been tested.

Binary Division

Binary division is also a simplified version of base 10 long division. Remember the techniques for base 10 division from school? Take the divisor and see if it divides into the first digit of the dividend and if it does, put the number of times it does above the line. Then multiply that result by the divisor and subtract it from the dividend. Pass the remainder down to the next line and repeat the process until the remainder is less than the divisor. At that point, you have a result and any left-over remainder.

Example 2.11

```
                           0128  ← result
         Divisor →  12 ) 1546  ← dividend
                         0000  (0 x 12 x 1000)
                         1546
                         1200  (1 x 12 x 100)
                          346
                          240  (2 x 12 x 10)
                          106
                           96  (8 x 12 x 1)
                           10  ← remainder
```

Binary division operates in the same way; the divisor is left shifted until its LSB is in the same digit position as the MSB of the dividend, and the divisor is subtracted from the dividend. If the result is positive, the corresponding bit in the result is set, the divisor is right shifted one position, and the process is repeated until the result is less than the remainder. As an example, let's take 15 and divide it by 5. 15 is 1111 in binary, and 5 is 0101. Performing the divide:

Example 2.12

```
                                     0011        Result
         Divisor      0101 ) 0001111             Dividend
                             0101000             (0 x 0101 x 1000)
                            -0010100
                             0001111
                             0010100             (0 x 0101 x 0100)
                            -0010100
                             0001111
                            -0001010             (1 x 0101 x 0010)
                             0000101
                            -0000101             (1 x 0101 x 0001)
                                   0             Remainder
```

We end up with a result of 0011, or 3 in decimal, with a 0 remainder. Since 15 divided by 5 is equal to 3 with no remainder, the math checks.

If we examine the division process, we find some of the same interesting points that we found in examining the multiply process:

1. Prior to beginning the divide, the divisor had to be left-shifted until its LSB was in the same digit position as the dividend's MSB. This means the algorithm will require a temporary variable for the divisor.

2. The difference between the dividend and the shifted devisor will also have to be held in a temporary variable.

3. To accommodate the initial subtractions of the divisor, the dividend had to be padded with additional zeros. So, the minimum length of the temporary variable used for the dividend must be at least equal to the total number of bits in the dividend and the divisor, −1. Remember that the first subtraction is with the LSB of the divisor in the same position as the MSB or the dividend.

4. The temporary variable used to hold the dividend will hold the remainder at the end of the operation.

5. The bit set in the result for each successful subtraction of the divisor is the same digit position as the LSB of the divisor.

Using these insights, an efficient binary multiply routine can be created that is fairly simple. It is just a matter of shifting, testing and subtracting with a bit set. The resulting algorithm is similar to the multiplication algorithm:

Algorithm 2.2

```
char A         // divisor
char B         // dividend
char C         // result
char R         // remainder
int  temp_a    // 16-bit temp holding variable for divisor
int  temp_b    // 16-bit temp holding variable for dividend

C = 0
temp_a = SHIFT A LEFT 7                    // left shift divisor 7x
temp_b = B                                 // dividend
FOR I = 0 to 7                             // loop repeats 8x
       SHIFT C LEFT 1                      // shift to next bit in R
       temp_b = temp_b - temp_a
       if (borrow = 0)
              then
                     C = C + 1;
                     ; set the bit
              else
                     temp_b = temp_b + temp_a // undo subtract
       endif
       SHIFT temp_a RIGHT 1                // shift the divisor 1
NEXT I
R = temp_b
```

At the start of the routine, the divisor and dividend are copied into their temporary variables, and the divisor is left-shifted 7 times. This leaves the divisor LSB in the same digit position as the MSB of the dividend. The divisor is subtracted from the dividend and the result is checked for a borrow; remember that the borrow indicated that the divisor is larger than the dividend, resulting in a negative difference. If the borrow is set, then the divisor is added back into the dividend to undo the subtraction. If the borrow is clear, then the dividend can be subtracted, and the corresponding bit in the result is set. The divisor is right-shifted, and the loop repeats for all 8 bits in the dividend.

Note that the bit set in the result is always the LSB, and the result is shifted one position to the left at the start of each loop. But, from the section above, we expected to set the result bits from the MSB down to the LSB, corresponding with the LSB of the divisor. Why the change? The algorithm could be done as it is described previously, but it would require another temporary variable to hold a single bit corresponding to the LSB of the divisor. The bit would be shifted with the divisor, and if the divisor was subtracted, we would OR the bit into the result. However, by setting the LSB and shifting left each time the divisor is shifted right, we accomplish the same result, and it doesn't require an additional temporary variable for a single bit.

Numeric Comparison

In the previous example of division, we compared the divisor to the dividend on each pass through the loop to determine if the divisor was less than or equal to the dividend. We did this with a subtraction and a test of the borrow flag. If the result of the subtraction was negative, then the divisor was greater than the dividend. But what about greater than, equal to, less than or equal to, or just plain not equal—how are those comparisons performed? The answer is that we still do a subtraction, but we just have to test for the right combination of positive, negative, or zero.

Fortunately, microcontrollers are well-equipped to perform these tests because whenever a microcontroller performs a subtraction, status flags in the microcontroller's status register record information about the result. Typically, this information includes both a borrow and zero flags. The borrow flag indicates whether the result of the operation was positive or negative and the zero flag tells us if the result of the operation was zero.

So, if we look at the results of a subtraction, by testing the flags we should be able to determine every combination of relationships between the two values:

- If the result of the subtraction is zero, then the two values are equal.

- If the borrow flag is set, then the larger value was subtracted from a smaller value.

- If the borrow is clear, then the smaller was subtracted from the larger, unless the zero flag is also set, in which case the values are equal.

Fairly simple, but unfortunately, there is a little more to it than just less than, greater than, and equal. There is also greater than or equal, less than or equal, and just not equal. The microcontroller could just perform the subtraction and test for all of the possible combinations of flags, but if both flags have to be tested for every condition that could be inefficient. Some conditions will require that both flags be tested, and others will require only one test. Assuming that the tests exhibit some symmetry, it should be possible to swap the order of the variables in the subtraction to give us a set of operations that can determine the relationship with only one test. So, let's build a table showing both possible ways the subtraction can be performed for each of the tests and see if we can find a single test for each condition.

Table 2.9   *Subtraction-Based Comparisons*

Relationship	Subtraction	Result	Tests required
A > B	B – A	Negative	Borrow = true
	A – B	Positive & non-zero	Borrow = false and Zero = false
A => B	B – A	Negative or zero	Borrow = true or Zero = true
	A – B	Positive	Borrow = false
A = B	B – A	Zero	Zero = true
	A – B	Zero	Zero = true
A <= B	B – A	Positive	Borrow = false
	A – B	Negative or zero	Borrow = true or Zero = true
A < B	B – A	Positive & non-zero	Borrow = false and Zero = false
	A – B	Negative	Borrow = true
A!= B	B – A	Non-zero	Zero = false
	A – B	Non-zero	Zero = false

From the table, we can determine that:

- For A > B, subtract A from B and test for Borrow = true.

- For A => B, subtract B from A and test for Borrow = false.

- For A = B, subtract either variable from the other and test for Zero = true.

- For A <= B, subtract A from B and test for Borrow = false.

- For A < B, subtract B from A and test for Borrow = true.

- For A != B, subtract either variable from the other and test for Zero = false.

As predicted, by swapping the order of the variables in some of the subtractions, we can simplify the tests down to a single bit test for each of the possible comparisons.

Conditional Statements

Now that we have the math of the comparison figured out, what about the conditionals statements that use the comparison? If we assume a C-like programming language, the conditional statements include IF/THEN/ELSE, SWITCH/CASE, DO/WHILE, and FOR/NEXT. While some of the statements are related, each has its own unique function and requirements.

The IF/THEN/ELSE, or IF statement, is the most basic conditional statement. It makes a comparison and, based on the result, changes the flow of execution in the program. The change can be to include an additional section of the program, or to select between two different sections. The comparison can be simple or compound. The statements can even be nested to produce a complex decision tree. In fact, the IF statement is the basis for all of the conditional statements, including the SWITCH/CASE, DO/WHILE, and FOR/NEXT.

For now, let's start with just the basic IF conditional statement. In a typical IF, a comparison is made using the techniques described in the last section. If the result of the comparison is true, the block of instructions associated with the THEN part of the statement is executed. If the result of the comparison is false, the block of instructions associated with the ELSE part of the statement is executed. Note, the ELSE portion of the statement is optional in most high-level languages. If the ELSE is omitted, then a false result will cause the program to fall through the instruction with no action taken. The implementation of the statement typically takes the following form:

Code Snippet 2.5

```
IF (comparison)
    THEN
            {Section_a}
    ELSE
            {Section_b}
ENDIF                        ; note some languages use {}
                             around the two
                             ; sections in place of ENDIF
```

A common variation of the basic IF is to combine two or more statements into a more complex comparison. This is commonly referred to as Nested IF statements, and may involve new IF statements in either, or both, the THEN or ELSE side of the statement. By nesting the IF statements, several different comparisons can be obtained:

- Complex combinations, involving multiple variables, can be tested for a single combination.

- A single variable can be compared to multiple values.

- Or multiple variables can be compared against multiple values.

Let's start with the simpler comparison, comparing multiple variables for a single combination. This comparison can be implemented by nesting multiple IF statements, the first IF comparing the first variable against its value and the THEN portion of the statement, another IF comparing the second variable against its value, and so on for all the variables and values.

Code Snippet 2.6

```
IF (Var_A > 5)
    THEN IF (Var_B < 3)
            THEN IF (Var_C <> 6)
                    THEN
                            {Section_a}
ENDIF
IF (Var_A <= 5) THEN {Section_b}
IF (Var_B >= 3) THEN {Section_b}
IF (Var_C == 6) THEN {Section_b}
```

However, this is an inefficient use of program memory because each statement includes the overhead of each IF statement. The ELSE condition must be handled separately with multiple copies of the Section B code.

The better solution is to put all the variables and the values in a single compounded IF statement. All of the variables, compared against their values, are combined using boolean operators to form a single yes or no comparison. The available boolean operators are AND (&&), OR (||), and NOT (!). For example:

Code Snippet 2.7

```
IF (Var_A > 5) && (Var_B < 3) && (Var_C <> 6)
    THEN
            {Section_a}
    ELSE
            {Section_b}
    ENDIF
```

This conditional statement will execute Section_a if; Var_A > 5 <u>and</u> Var_B < 3, <u>and</u> Var_C is not equal to 6. Any other combination will result in the execution of Section_b. So, this is a smaller, more compact, implementation that is much easier to read and understand in the program listing.

The next IF statement combination to examine involves comparing a single variable against multiple values. One of the most common examples of this type of comparison is a WINDOW COMPARISON. In a window comparison, a single variable is compared against two values which form a window, or range, of acceptable or unacceptable values. For instance, if the temperature of a cup of coffee is greater than 40 degrees C, but less than 50 degrees C, it is considered to have the right temperature. Warmer or colder, it either is too cold or too hot to drink. Implementing this in a IF statement would result in the following:

Code Snippet 2.8

```
IF (Temperature > 40) && (Temperature < 50)
    THEN
        {Drink}
    ELSE
        {Don't_Drink}
    ENDIF
```

The compound IF statement checks for both a "too hot" and "too cool" condition, verifying that the temperature is within a comfortable drinking temperature range. The statement also clearly documents what range is acceptable and what is not.

Another implementation of comparing a single value against multiple values is the ELSE IF combination. In this configuration, a nested IF is placed in the ELSE portion of the statement, creating a string of comparisons with branches out of the string for each valid comparison. For instance, if different routines are to be executed for each of several different values in a variable, an ELSE IF combination can be used to find the special values and branch off to each one's routine. The nested IF statement would look like the following:

Code Snippet 2.9

```
IF (Var_A = 5)
    THEN
        {Routine_5}
    ELSE IF (Var_A = 6)
        THEN
            {Routine_6}
        ELSE IF (Var_A = 7)
            THEN
                {Routine_7}
            ELSE
                {Other_Routine}
```

And,

- If Var_A is 5, then only Routine_5 is executed.
- If Var_A is 6, then only Routine_6 is executed.
- If Var_A is 7, then only Routine_7 is executed.
- If Var_A is not 5, 6, or 7, then only the Other_Routine is executed.

Now, if each statement checks for its value, why not just have a list of IF statements? What value does nesting the statements have? There are three reasons to nest the IF statements:

1. Nesting the IF statements saves one IF statement. If the comparison was implemented as a list of IF statements, a window comparison would be required to determine when to run the Other_Routine. It is only run if the value is not 5, 6, or 7.

2. Nesting the statements speeds up the execution of the program. In the nested format, if Routine_5 is executed, then when it is done, it will automatically be routed around the rest of the IF statements and start execution after the last ELSE. In a list of IF statements, the other three comparisons would have to be performed to get past the list of IF statements.

3. If any of the routines modify Var_A, there is the possibility that one of the later comparisons in the last might also be true, resulting in two routines being executed instead of just the one intended routine.

So, nesting the ELSE IF statements has value in reduced program size, faster execution speed, and less ambiguity in the flow of the program's execution.

For more complex comparisons involving multiple variables and values, IF/THEN/ELSE statements can be nested to create a decision tree. The decision tree quickly and efficiently compares the various conditions by dividing up the comparison into a series of branches. Starting at the root of the tree, a decision is made to determine which half of the group of results is valid. The branches of the first decision then hold conditional statements that again determine which ¼ set of solutions are valid. The next branch of the second decision then determines which 1/8 set of solutions is valid, and so on, until there is only one possible solution left that meets the criteria. The various branches resemble a tree, hence the name "decision tree."

To demonstrate the process, assume that the letters of a name—Samuel, Sally, Thomas, Theodore, or Samantha—are stored in an array of chars labeled NAME[]. Using a decision tree, the characters in the array can then be tested to see which name is present in the array. The following is an example of how a decision tree would be coded to test for the three names:

Code Snippet 2.10

```
IF (NAME[0] == 'S')
      THEN IF (NAME[2] == 'm')
                 THEN IF (NAME[3] == 'a')
                             THEN Samantha_routine();
                             ELSE Samuel_routine();
                 ELSE Sally_routine
      ELSE IF (NAME[2] == 'o')
                 THEN Thomas_routine();
                 ELSE Theodore_routine();
```

The first IF statement uses the letter in location 0 to differentiate between S and T to separate out Thomas and Theodore from the list of possible solutions. The next IF in both branches uses the letter is location 2 to differentiate between M and L to separate out Sally from the list of possible solutions, and to differentiate between Thomas and Theodore. The deepest IF uses the letter in location 3 to differentiate between Samantha and Samuel. So, it only takes two comparisons to find Thomas, Theodore, or Sally, and it only three comparisons to find either Samantha or Samuel.

If, on the other hand, the comparison used a list of IF statements rather than a decision tree, then each IF statement would have been more complex, and the number of comparisons would have increased. With each statement trying to find a distinct name, all of the differentiating letters must be compared in each IF statement. The number of comparisons required to find a name jumps from a worst case of three (for Samantha and Samuel), to four and five for the last two names in the IF statement list. To provide a contrast, the list of IF statements to implement the name search is shown below:

Code Snippet 2.11

```
IF (NAME[0] == 'S') && (NAME[2] == 'm') && (NAME[3]
    == 'a')
    THEN Samantha_routine;
IF (NAME[0] == 'S') && (NAME[2] == 'm') && (NAME[3]
    == 'u')
    THEN Samuel_routine;
IF (NAME[0] == 'S') && (NAME[2] == 'a')
    THEN Sally_routine;
IF (NAME[0] == 'T') && (NAME[2] == 'o')
    THEN Thomas_routine;
IF (NAME[0] == 'T') && (NAME[2] == 'e')
    THEN Theodore_routine;
```

As predicted, it will take four comparisons to find Thomas, and five to find Theodore, and the number of comparisons will grow for each name added to the list. The number of differentiating characters that will require testing will also increase and names that are similar to those in the list increase. A decision tree configuration of nested IF statements is both smaller and faster.

Another conditional statement based on the IF statement is the SWITCH/CASE statement, or CASE statement as it is typically called. The CASE statement allows the designer to compare multiple values against a single variable in the same way that a list of IF statements can be used to find a specific value. While a CASE statement can use a complex expression, we will use it with only a single variable to determine equality to a specific set of values, or range of values.

In its single variable form, the CASE statement specifies a controlling variable, which is then compared to multiple values. The code associated with the matching value is then executed. For example, assume a variable (Var_A) with five different values, and for each of the values a different block of code must be executed. Using a CASE statement to implement this control results in the following:

⟶
Code Snippet 2.12

```
SWITCH (Var_A)
{
        Case 0:   Code_block_0();
            Break;
        Case 1:   Code_block_1();
            Break;
        Case 2:   Code_block_2();
            Break;
        Case 3:   Code_block_3();
            Break;
        Case 4:   Code_block_4();
            Break;
        Default:  Break;
}
```

Note that each block of code has a break statement following it. The break causes the program to break out of the CASE statement when it has completed. If the break were not present, then a value of zero would have resulted in the execution of Code block 0, followed by Code block 1, then Code block 2, and so on through all the blocks in order. For this example, we only wanted a single block to execute, but if the blocks were a sequence of instructions and the variable was only supplying the starting point in the sequence, the case statement could be used to start the sequence, with Var_A supplying the starting point.

Also note the inclusion of a Default case for the statement; this is a catch-all condition which will execute if no other condition is determined true. It is also a good error recovery mechanism when the variable in the SWITCH portion of the statement becomes corrupted. When we get to state machines, we will discuss further the advantages of the Default case.

Loops

Often it is not enough to simply change the flow of execution in a program. sometimes what is needed is the ability to repeat a section until a desired condition is true, or while it is true. This ability to repeat until a desired result or do while a condition is true is referred to as an iteration statement, and it is very valuable in embedded programming. It allows designers to write programs that can wait for desired conditions, poll for a specific event, or even fine tune a calculation until a desired result occurs. Building these conditional statements requires a combination of the comparison capabilities of the IF statement with a simple GOTO to form a loop.

Typically there are three main types of iterating instructions, the FOR/NEXT, the WHILE/DO and the DO/WHILE. The three statements are surprisingly similar; all use a comparison function to determine when to loop and when not to, and all use an implied GOTO command to form the loop. In fact, the WHILE/DO and the DO/WHILE are really variations of each other, with the only difference being when the comparison is performed. The FOR/NEXT is unique due to its ability to automatically increment/decrement its controlling variable.

The important characteristic of the WHILE/DO statement, is that it performs its comparison first. Basically, WHILE a condition is true, DO the enclosed loop. Its logic is such that if the condition is true, then the code inside the loop is executed. When the condition is false, the statement terminates and begins execution following the DO. This has an interesting consequence: if the condition is false prior to the start of the instruction, the instruction will terminate without ever executing the routine within the loop. However, if the condition is true, then the statement will execute the routine within the loop until the condition evaluates as false. The general syntax of a DO/WHILE loop is shown below:

Code Snippet 2.13

```
WHILE (comparison)
    Routine();
DO
```

DO is a marker signifying the end of the routine to be looped, and the WHILE marks the beginning, as well as containing the comparison to be evaluated. Because the comparison appears at the beginning of the routine to be looped, it should be remembered that the condition is evaluated before the first execution of the routine and the routine is only executed if the condition evaluates to a true.

The mirror of the WHILE/DO is the DO/WHILE statement. It is essentially identical to the WHILE/DO, with the exception that it performs its comparison at the end. Basically, DO the enclosed loop, WHILE a condition is true. Its logic is such that, if the condition is true, then the code inside the loop is executed. When the condition is false, the statement terminates and begins execution following the WHILE. This has the alternate consequence that, even if the condition is false prior to the start of the instruction, the instruction will execute the routine within the loop at least once before terminating. If the condition is true, then the statement will execute the routine within the loop until the condition evaluates as false. The general syntax of a DO/WHILE loop is shown below:

Code Snippet 2.14

```
DO
    Routine();
WHILE (comparison)
```

DO is a marker signifying the beginning of the routine to be looped, and the WHILE marks the end, as well as containing the comparison to be evaluated. Because the comparison appears at the end of the routine to be looped, it should be remembered that the condition is evaluated after the first execution of the routine.

So, why have two different versions of the same statement? Why a DO/WHILE *and* a WHILE/DO? Well, the DO/WHILE could more accurately be described as a REPEAT/UNTIL. The ability to execute the routine at least once is desirable because it may not be possible to perform the comparison until the routine has executed. Some value that is calculated, or retrieved by, the routine may be needed to perform the comparison in the WHILE section of the command. The WHILE/DO is desirable for exactly the opposite reason—it may be catastrophic to make a change unless it is determined that a change is actually needed. So, having the option to test before or test after is important, and is the reason that both variations of the commands exist.

The third type of iteration statement is the FOR/NEXT, or FOR statement. The FOR statement is unique in that it not only evaluates a condition to determine if the enclosed routine is executed, but it also sets the initial condition for the variable used in the conditions, and specifies how the variable is indexed on each iteration of the loop. This forms essentially a fully automatic loop structure, repeating any number of iterations of the loop until the termination condition is reached. For example, a FOR loop could look like the following:

Code Snippet 2.15

```
FOR (Var_A=0; Var_A<100; Var_A=Var_A+5)
    routine();
```

In the example, a variable Var_A is initially set to zero at the beginning of the loop. The value in Var_A is compared to 100, and if it is less than 100, then the routine is executed. After execution of the routine is complete, the variable is incremented by 5 and the comparison is repeated. The result is that the routine is executed, and the variable incremented by 5, over and over until the comparison is false.

Within the general format of the FOR statements are a couple of options:

1. The initial value of the variable doesn't have to be zero. The value can be initialized to any convenient value for a specific calculation in the routine within the loop.

2. The increment value is similarly flexible. In fact, the increment value can be negative, resulting in a decrement of the value, or the increment value can be dynamic, changing on each pass through the loop.

3. The termination condition may also be dynamic, changing for each pass through the loop.

4. The variable used to control the loop is also accessible within the loop, allowing the routine to length, shorten, or even stop the loop by incrementing, decrementing or assigning a value to the variable.

5. If all three terms are left out of the FOR statement, then an infinite loop is generated which will never terminate.

Other Flow Control Statements

Three other program flow control statements are important in later discussions, GOTO, CALL, and RETURN. The GOTO statement is just as the name suggests. It is an unconditional jump from one place in the program to another. The CALL is similar, except it retains the address of the next instruction, following the CALL instruction, in a temporary location. This return address is then used when the RETURN statement is reached to specify the jump-back location.

The use of the GOTO statement is often criticized as an example of poor programming. If the program were properly designed, then looping and conditional statements are sufficient for proper programming. Unfortunately, in embedded programming there are conditions and events beyond the designer's control. As a result, it is sometimes required to break out of the program flow and either restart the program or rearrange its execution to correct a fault. So, while the GOTO is not a statement that should be used lightly, it is a statement that will be needed for certain fault recovery programming.

The CALL and RETURN are more acceptable to mainstream programming, as they are the means of creating subroutines. When a section of programming is used in multiple places in the program, it is a more efficient use of program memory to build a small separate routine and access it through CALL and RETURN statements.

Although the CALL and RETURN statements are useful, their use should be tempered with the knowledge that each CALL will place two or more bytes of data onto a data structure called the STACK. The purpose of the STACK is to store temporary values that don't have a specific storage location, such as the return address of a CALL. The issue with using the STACK is that:

1. Data memory is often limited with small microcontrollers, and any function that increases data memory usage runs the risk of over-writing an existing variable.

2. The number of locations within the STACK is sometimes limited in small microcontrollers, and unnecessary calls may result in the loss of the oldest return address stored there.

3. Interrupt functions also use the STACK to store return addresses, making it difficult to gauge the exact number of locations in use at any given time.

So, limiting the number of subroutines built into a program is only prudent.

One of the reasons often given for including a large number of subroutines in a program is the ability of subroutines to compress functionality, making the program more readable to anyone following the designer. If the purpose of a subroutine is to alleviate complexity in the listing, then subroutines can still be used, they just have to include the INLINE statement in front of the CALL. What the INLINE statement does is force the language compiler to disregard the CALL/RETURN statements and compile the routines from the subroutine in line with the routines calling the subroutine. In this way, the readability enhancement of the subroutine is still achieved, while eliminating the impact on the amount of data memory available in the STACK. However, it should be noted that the use of the INLINE instruction is not a common practice. Typically, a macro performs the same function and is a more commonly used construct. So, for compatibility and general form, the INLINE statement should only be used if the designer is comfortable with its use and is aware of any impact its use might have on the resulting code.

State Machines

Control systems that manage electrical or mechanical systems must often be able to generate, or respond to, sequential events in the system. This ability to use time as part of the driver equation is in fact one of the important abilities of a microcontroller that makes it such a good control for electrical and mechanical systems. However, implementing multiple sequences can become long and involved if a linear coding style is used.

A simple construct, called a *state machine*, simplifies the task of generating a sequence by breaking the sequence into a series of steps and then executing them sequentially. While this sounds like an arbitrary definition of a linear piece of code, the difference is that the individual sections, or steps in the sequence, are encoded within a SWITCH/CASE statement. This breaks the sequence into logical units that can be easily recognized in the software listing and, more importantly, it allows other functions to be performed between the individual steps. It does this by only executing one step each time it is called. Repeatedly calling the state machine results in the execution of each step in the sequence. To retain the state machine's place in the sequence, a storage variable is defined that determines which step in the sequence is to be executed next. This variable is referred to as the *state variable*, and it is used in the SWITCH/CASE statement to determine which step, or state, in the state machine is to be executed when the state machine is called.

For this system to work, the state variable must be incremented at the completion of each state. However, it is also true that the sequence of states may need to change due to changes in the condition of the system. Given that the state variable determines which state is executed, it follows that to change the sequence of states, one must simply load the state variable with a new value corresponding with the new direction the sequence must go. As we will see in this book, this simple construct is very powerful, and is in fact the basis for multitasking.

So, the short definition of a state machine is a collection of steps (states) selected for execution based on the value in a state variable. Further, manipulation of the value in the state variable allows the state machine to emulate all the conditional statements previously presented in this chapter.

One of the advantages of the state machine-based design is that it allows the easy generation of a sequence of events. Another advantage of state machine-based design is its ability to recognize a sequence of events. It does this by utilizing the conditional change of the state variable, much as described in the previous paragraph. The only difference is that the state variable does not normally change its value, unless a specific event is detected. As an analogy, consider a combination lock: to open the lock, the numbers have to be entered in a specific sequence such as 5, 8, 3, 2. If the numbers were entered 2, 3, 5, 8, the lock would not open, so the combination is not only the numbers but their order.

If we were to create a state machine to recognize this sequence, it would look something like the following:

Code Snippet 2.16

```
State = 0;
SWITCH (State)
{
   CASE 0: IF (in_key()==5)   THEN state = 1;
           Break;
   CASE 1: IF (in_key()==8)   THEN State = 2;
                              Else State = 0;
           Break;
   CASE 2: IF (in_key()==3)   THEN State = 3;
                              Else State = 0;
           Break;
   CASE 3: IF (in_key()==2)   THEN UNLOCK();
                              Else State = 0;
           Break;
}
```

Provided that the values returned by in_key() are in the order of 8, 5, 3, 2, the state variable will step from 0 to 3 and the function UNLOCK() will be called. The state variable is only loaded with the value of the next state when the right value is received in the right state. If any of the values are out of sequence, even though they may be valid for another state, the state variable will reset to 0, and the state machine will start over. In this way, the state machine will step through its sequence only if the values are received in the same sequence as the states in the state machine are designed to accept.

So, state machines can be programmed to recognize a sequence of events, and they can be programmed to generate a sequence of events. Both rely on the history of the previous states and the programmable nature of the state-to-state transitions.

Implementing a state machine is just a matter of:

1. Creating a state variable.

2. Defining a series of states.

3. Decoding the state variable to access the states.

4. Tying actions to the states.

5. Defining the sequence of the states, and any conditions that change the sequence.

For example, consider a state machine designed to make peanut and jelly sandwiches. The sequence of events is:

1. Get two slices of bread.
2. Open peanut butter jar.
3. Scoop out peanut butter.
4. Smear on first slice of bread.
5. Open jelly jar.
6. Scoop out jelly.
7. Smear on second slice of bread.
8. Invert second slice of bread.
9. Put second slice on first slice of bread.
10. Eat.

OK, the first thing to do is create a state variable; let's call it PBJ. It has a range of values from 1 to 10, and it probably defines as a CHAR. Next, we have to define the sequence of steps in the process, and create a means to decode the state variable.

If we take each of these instructions and build them into a CASE statement to handle decoding the state variable, then all it needs is the appropriate updates to the state variable and the state machine is complete.

Algorithm 2.3

```
SWITCH(PBJ)
{
      case 1:    Get two slices.
                 PBJ = 2
                 break
      case 2:    Open peanut butter jar.
                 PBJ = 3
                 break
      case 3:    Scoop out peanut butter.
                 PBJ = 4
                 break
      case 4:    Smear on first slice of bread.
                 PBJ = 5
                 break
      case 5:    Open jelly jar.
                 PBJ = 6
                 break
      case 6:    Scoop out jelly.
                 PBJ = 7
                 break
      case 7:    Smear on second slice of bread.
                 PBJ = 8
                 break
      case 8:    Invert second slice of bread.
                 PBJ = 9
                 break
      case 9:    Put second slice on first slice of bread.
                 PBJ = 10
                 break
      case 10:   Eat
                 break
      Default:   break
}
```

The calling routine then simply calls the subroutine 10 times and the result is an eaten peanut butter and jelly sandwich.

Why go to all this trouble? Wouldn't it be simpler and easier to just write it as one long function? Well, yes, the routine could be done as one long sequence with the appropriate delays and timing. But this format has a couple of limitations. One, making a PB and J sandwich would be all the microcontroller could do during the process. And, two, making one kind of a PB and J sandwich would be all the routine would be capable of doing. There is an important distinction in those two sentences; the first states that the microcontroller would only be able to perform one task, no multitasking, and the second states that all the program would be capable of would be one specific kind of PB and J sandwich, no variations.

Breaking the sequence up into a state machine means we can put other functions between the calls to the state machine. The other calls could cover housekeeping details such as monitoring a serial port, checking a timer, or polling a keyboard. Breaking the sequence up into a state machine also means we can use the same routine to make a peanut butter only sandwich simply by loading the state variable with state 8, instead of state 5 at the end of state 4. In fact, if we include other steps such as pouring milk and getting a cookie, and include some additional conditional state variable changes, we now have a routine that can make several different varieties of snacks, not just a PB and J sandwich.

The power of the state machine construct is not limited to just variations of a sequence. By controlling its own state variable, the state machine can become a form of specialized virtual microcontroller—basically a small, software-based controller with a programmable instruction set. In fact, the power and flexibility of the state machine will be the basis for the multitasking system described later in the book.

Before we dive into some of the more advanced concepts, it is important to understand some of the basics of state machine operation. The best place to start is with the three basic types of state machines: *execution-indexed*, *data-indexed*, and the *hybrid* state machine.

The *execution-indexed state machine* is the type of state machine that most people envision when they talk about a state machine, and it is the type of state machine shown in the previous examples. It has a CASE statement structure with routine for each CASE, and a state variable that controls which state is executed when the state machine is called. A good example of an Execution-indexed state machine is the PB&J state machine in the previous example. The function performed by the state machine is specified by the value held in the state variable.

The other extreme is the *data-indexed state machine*. It is probably the least recognized form of a state machine, even though most designers have created several, because it doesn't use a SWITCH/CASE statement. Rather, it uses an array variable with the state variable providing the index into the array. The concept behind a data-indexed state machine is that the sequence of instructions remains constant, and the data that is acted upon is controller by the state variable.

A *hybrid state machine* combines aspects of both the data-indexed and the execution-indexed to create a state machine with the ability to vary both its execution and the data it operates on. This hybrid approach allows the varied execution of the execution indexed with the variable data aspect of the data-indexed state machine.

We have three different formats, with different advantages and disadvantages. Execution indexed allows designers to vary the actions taken in each state, and/or respond to external sequences of events. Data indexed allows designers to vary the data acted upon in each state, but keep the execution constant. And, finally, the hybrid combines both to create a more efficient state machine that requires both the varied execution of the execution-indexed and the indexed data capability of the data-indexed state machine. Let's take a closer look at the three types and their capabilities.

Data-Indexed State Machines

Consider a system that uses an analog-to-digital converter, or ADC, to monitor multiple sensors. Each sensor has its own channel into the ADC, its own calibration offset/scaling factors, and its own limits. To implement these functions using a data-indexed state machine, we start by assigning a state to each input and creating an array-based storage for all the values that will be required.

Starting with the data storage, the system will need storage for the following:

1. Calibration offset and scaling values.

2. Upper and lower limit values.

3. The final, calibrated values.

Using a two-dimensional array, we can store the values in the following format. Assume that S_var is the state value associated with a specific ADC channel:

- ADC_Data[0][S_var] variable in the array holding the calibration offset values

- ADC_Data[1][S_var] variable in the array holding the calibration scaling values

- ADC_Data[2][S_var] variable in the array holding the upper limit values

- ADC_Data[3][S_var] variable in the array holding the lower limit values

- ADC_Data[4][S_var] variable in the array holding the ADC channel select command value

- ADC_Data[5][S_var] variable in the array holding the calibrated final values

The actual code to implement the state machine will look like the following:

Code Snippet 2.17

```
Void ADC(char S_var, boolean alarm)
{
    ADC_Data[4][S_var] = (ADC*ADC_Data[1][S_
      var])+ADC_Data[0][S_var];
    IF (ADC_Data[4][S_var]>ADC_Data[2][S_var]) THEN
      Alarm = true;
    IF (ADC_Data[4][S_var]<ADC_Data[3][S_var]) THEN
      Alarm = true;
    S_var++;
    IF (S_var > max_channel) then S_var = 0;
    ADC_control = ADC_Data[5][S_var];
    ADC_convert_start = true;
}
```

In the example, the first line converts the raw data value held in ADC into a calibrated value by multiplying the scaling factor and adding in the offset. The result is stored into the ADC_Data array. Lines 2 and 3 perform limit testing against the upper and lower limits store in the ADC_Data array and set the error variable if there is a problem. Next, the state variable S_var is incremented, tested against the maximum number of channels to be polled, and wrapped around if it has incremented beyond the end. Finally, the configuration data selecting the next channel is loaded into the ADC control register and the conversion is initiated—a total of seven lines of code to scan as many ADC channels as the system needs, including both individual calibration and range checking.

From the example, it seems that data-indexed state machines are fairly simple constructs, so how do they justify the lofty name of state machine? Simple—by exhibiting the ability to change its operation based on internal and external influences. Consider a variation on the previous example. If we add another variable to the data array and place the next state information into that variable, we now have a state machine that can be reprogrammed "on the fly" to change its sequence of conversions based on external input.

- ADC_Data[6][S_var] variable in the array holding the next channel to convert

Code Snippet 2.18

```
Void ADC(char S_var, boolean alarm)
{
    ADC_Data[4][S_var] = (ADC*ADC_Data[1][S_
        var])+ADC_Data[0][S_var];
    IF (ADC_Data[4][S_var]>ADC_Data[2][S_var]) THEN
        Alarm = true;
    IF (ADC_Data[4][S_var]<ADC_Data[3][S_var]) THEN
        Alarm = true;
    S_var = ADC_Data[6][S_var];
    ADC_control = ADC_Data[5][S_var];
    ADC_convert_start = true;
}
```

Now the sequence of channels is controlled by the array ADC_Data. If the system does not require data from a specific channel, it just reprograms the array to route the state machine around the unneeded channel. The state machine could also be built with two or more next channels, with the actual next channel determined by whether a fault has occurred, or an external flag is set, or a value reported by one of the channels has been exceeded.

Don't let the simplicity of the state machine deceive you; there is power and flexibility in the data-indexed state machine. All that is required is the imagination to look beyond the simplicity and see the possibilities.

Execution-Indexed State Machines

Execution-indexed state machines, as described previously, are often mistakenly assumed to be little more than a CASE statement with the appropriate routines inserted for the individual states. While the CASE statement, or an equivalent machine language construct, is at the heart of an execution-based state machine, there is a lot more to their design and a lot more to their capabilities.

For instance, the capability to control its own state variable lends itself to a wide variety of capabilities that rival normal linear coding. By selectively incrementing or loading the state variable, individual states within the state machine can implement:

- Sequential execution.

- Computed GOTO instructions.

- DO/WHILE instructions.

- WHILE/DO instructions.

- FOR/NEXT instructions.

- And even GOSUB/RETURN instructions.

Let's run through some examples to demonstrate some of the capabilities of the execution-indexed state machine type.

First of all, to implement a sequence of state steps, it is simply a matter of assigning the value associated with the next state in the sequence, at the end of each state. For example:

Code Snippet 2.19

```
SWITCH(State_var)
{
    CASE 0:     State_var = 1;
                Break;
    CASE 1:     State_var = 2;
                Break;
    CASE 2:     State_var = 3;
                Break;
}
```

Somewhere in each state, the next state is loaded into the state variable. As a result, each execution of the state machine results in the execution of the current state's code block and the advancement of the state variable to the next state. If the states are defined to be sequential values, the assignment can even be replaced with a simple increment. However, there is no requirement that the states be sequential, or that the state machine must sequence down the case statement on each successive call to the state machine. It is perfectly valid to have the state machine step through the case statement in whatever pattern is convenient, particularly if the pattern of values in the state variable is convenient for some other function in the system, such as the sequence of energized windings in a brushless motor. The next state can even be defined by the values in an array, making the sequence entirely programmable.

Computed GOTO instructions are just a simple extension of the basic concept used in sequential execution. The only difference is the assignment is made from the result of a calculation. For example:

Code Snippet 2.20

```
SWITCH(State_var)
{
        CASE 0:     State_var = 10 * Var_a;
            Break;
        CASE 10:  Function_A;
            State_var = 0;
            Break;
        CASE 20:  Function_B;
            State_var = 0;
            Break;
        CASE 30:  Function_C
            State_var = 0;
            Break;
}
```

Based on the value present in Var_a, the state machine will execute one of three different states the next time it is called. This essentially implements a state machine that cannot only change its sequence of execution based on data, but can also change its execution to one of several different sequences based on data.

Another construct that can be implemented is the IF/THEN/ELSE statement. Based on the result of a comparison in one of the states, the state machine can step to one of two different states, altering its sequence. If the comparison in the conditional statement is true, then the state variable is loaded with the new state value associated with the THEN part of the IF statement and the next time the state machine is executed, it will execute the new state. If the comparison results in a false, then the state variable is loaded with a different value and the state machine executes the state associated with the ELSE portion of the IF statement. For example:

Code Snippet 2.21

```
SWITCH(State_var)
{
    CASE 0:  IF (Var_A > Var_B) THEN State_var = 1;
                                ELSE State_var = 2;
             Break;
    CASE 1:  Var_B = Var_A
             State_var = 0;
             Break;
    CASE 2:  Var_A = Var_B
             State_var = 0;
             Break;
}
```

In the example, whenever the value in Var_A is larger than the value in Var_B, the state machine advances to state 1 and the value in Var_A is copied into Var_B. The state machine then returns to state 0. If the value in Var_B is greater than or equal to Var_A, then Var_B is copied into Var_A, and the state machine returns to state 0.

Now, having seen both the GOTO and the IF/THEN/ELSE, it is a simple matter to implement all three iterative statements by simply combining the GOTO and the IF/THEN/ELSE. For example, a DO/WHILE iterative statement would be implemented as follows:

Code Snippet 2.22

```
CASE 4:   Function;
          State_var = 5;
          Break;
CASE 5:   IF (comparison)    THEN State_var = 4;
                             ELSE State_var = 6;
          Break;
CASE 6:
```

In the example, state 4 holds the (DO) function within the loop, and state 5 holds the (WHILE) comparison. And, a WHILE/DO iterative statement would be implemented as follows:

Code Snippet 2.23

```
CASE 4:   IF (comparison)    THEN State_var = 5;
                             ELSE State_var = 6;
          Break;
CASE 5:   Function;
          State_var = 4;
          Break;
CASE 6:
```

In this example, state 4 holds the (WHILE) comparison, and state 5 holds the (DO) function within the loop. A FOR/NEXT iterative statement would be implemented as follows:

Code Snippet 2.24

```
CASE 3:   Counter = 6;
          State_var = 4;
          Break;
CASE 4:   IF (Counter > 0)   THEN State_var = 5;
                             ELSE State_var = 6;
          Break;
CASE 5:   Function;
          Counter = Counter - 1;
          State_var = 4;
          Break;
CASE 6:
```

In the last example, the variable (Counter) in the FOR/NEXT is assigned its value in state 3, is compared to 0 in state 4 (FOR), and is then incremented and looped back in state 5 (NEXT).

These three iterative constructs are all simple combinations of the GOTO and IF/THEN/ELSE described previously. Building them into a state machine just required breaking the various parts out into separate states, and appropriately setting the state variable.

The final construct to examine in an execution-indexed state machine is the CALL/RETURN. Now, the question arises, why do designers need a subroutine construct in state machines? What possible use is it?

Well, let's take the example of a state machine that has to generate two different delays. State machine delays are typically implemented by repeatedly calling a do-nothing state, and then returning to an active state. For example, the following is a typical state machine delay:

Code Snippet 2.25

```
CASE 3:  Counter = 6;
         State_var = 4;
         Break;
CASE 4:  IF (Counter == 0) THEN State_var = 5;
         Counter = Counter - 1;
         Break;
CASE 5:
```

This routine will wait in state 4 a total of six times before moving on to state 5. If we want to create two different delays, or use the same delay twice, we would have to create two different wait states. However, if we build the delay as a subroutine state, implementing both the CALL and RETURN, we can use the same state over and over, saving program memory. For example:

Code Snippet 2.26

```
CASE 3:  Counter = 6;
         State_var = 20;
         Back_var = 4
         Break;
           |        |
           |        |
CASE 12: Counter = 10;
         State_var = 20;
         Back_var = 13
         Break;
           |        |
           |        |
CASE 20: IF (Counter == 0) THEN State_var = Back_var;
         Counter = Counter - 1;
         Break;
```

In the example, states 3 and 12 are calling states and state 20 is the subroutine. Both 3 and 12 loaded the delay counter with the delays they required, loaded Back_var with the state immediately following the calling state (return address), and jumped to the delay state 20 (CALL). State 20 then delayed the appropriate number of times, and transferred the return value in Back_var into the state variable (RETURN).

By providing a return state value, and setting the counter variable before changing state, a simple yet effective subroutine system was built into a state machine. With a little work and a small array for the Back_var, the subroutine could even call other subroutines.

Hybrid State Machines

Hybrid state machines are a combination of both formats; they have the CASE structure of an execution-based state machine, as well as the array-based data structure of a data-indexed state machine. They are typically used in applications that require the sequential nature of an execution-based state machine, combined with the ability to handle multiple data blocks.

A good example of this hybrid requirement is a software-based serial transmit function. The function must generate a start bit, 8 data bits, a parity bit and one or more stop bits. The start, parity, and stop bits have different functionality and implementing them within an execution-based state machine is simple and straightforward. However, the transmission of the 8 data bits does not work as well within the execution-based format. It would have to be implemented as eight nearly identical states, which would be inefficient and a waste of program memory. So, a second data-driven state machine, embedded in the first state machine, is needed to handle the 8 data bits being transmitted. The following is an example of how the hybrid format would be implemented:

⟶

Code Snippet 2.27

```
SWITCH(Ex_State_var)
{
    CASE 0:                                 // waiting for new character
                IF (Data_avail == true) THEN Ex_State_var = 1;
                Break;

    CASE 1:                                 // begin with a start bit
                Output(0);
                Ex_State_var = 2;
                DI_State_var = 0;
                Break;

    CASE 2:                                 // sending bits 0-7
                If ((Tx_data & (2^DI_State_var))) == 0)
                        Then    Output(0);
                        Else    Output(1);
                DI_State_var++;
                If (DI_State_var == 8) Then Ex_State_var = 3;
                Break;

    CASE 3:                                 // Output Parity bit
                Output(Parity(Tx_data));
                Ex_State_var = 4;
                Break;

    CASE 4:                                 // Send Stop bit to end
                Output(1);
                Ex_State_var = 0
}
```

Note that the example has two state variables, Ex_State_var and DI_State_var. Ex_State_var is the state variable for the execution-indexed section of the state machine, determining which of the four cases in the SWITCH statement is executed. DI_State_var is the state variable for the data-indexed section of the state machine, determining which bit in the 8-bit data variable is transmitted on each pass through state 2. Together the two types of state machine produce a hybrid state machine that is both simple and efficient.

On a side note, it should be noted that the Ex_State_var and DI_State_var can be combined into a single data variable to conserve data memory. However, this is typically not done due to the extra overhead of separating the two values. Even if the two values are combined using a Structure declaration, the compiler will still have to include additional code to mask off the two values.

Multitasking

In this last section of Chapter 2, we finally get to the subject that defines this book, multitasking. Multitasking is the ability to execute multiple separate tasks in a fashion that is seemingly simultaneous. Note the phrase "seemingly simultaneous." Short of a multiple processor system, there is no way to make a single processor execute multiple tasks at the same time. However, there is a way to create a system that seems to execute multiple tasks at the same time. The secret is to divide up the processor's time so it can put a segment of time on each of the tasks on a regular basis. The result is the appearance that the processor is executing multiple tasks, when in actuality the processor is just switching between the tasks too quickly to be noticed.

As an example, consider four cars driving on a freeway. Each car has a driver and a desired destination, but no engine. A repair truck arrives, but it only has one engine. For each car to move toward its destination, it must use a common engine, shared with the other cars on the freeway. (See Figure 2.1.)

Now in one scenario, the engine could be given to a single car, until it reaches its destination, and then transferred to the next car until it reaches its destination, and so on until all the cars get where they are going. While this would accomplish the desired result, it does leave the other cars sitting on the freeway until the car with the engine finishes its trip. It also means that the cars would not be able to interact with each other during their trips.

A better scenario would be to give the engine to the first car for a short period of time, then move it to the second for a short period, then the third, then the fourth, and then back to first, continuing the rotation through the cars over and over. In this scenario, all of the cars make progress toward their destinations. They won't make the same rate of progress that they would if they had exclusive use of the engine, but

Figure 2.1   *Automotive Multitasking.*

they all do move together. This has a couple of advantages; the cars travel at a similar rate, all of the cars complete their trip at approximately the same time, and the cars are close enough during their trip to interact with each other.

This scenario is in fact, the common method for multitasking in an operating system. A task is granted a slice of execution time, then halted, and the next task begins to execute. When its time runs out, a third task begins executing, and so on.

While this is an over-simplification of the process, it is the basic underlying principle of a multitasking operating system: multiple programs operating within small slices of time, with a central control that coordinates the changes. The central control manages the switching between the various tasks, handles communications between the tasks, and even determines which tasks should run next. This central control is in fact the multitasking operating system. If we plan to develop software that can multitask without an operating system, then our design must include all of the same elements of an operating system to accomplish multitasking.

Four Basic Requirements of Multitasking

The three basic requirements of a multitasking system are: context switching, communications, managing priorities. To these three functions, a fourth—timing control—is required to manage multitasking in a real-time environment. Functions to handle each of these requirements must be developed within a system for that system to be able to multitask in real time successfully.

To better understand the requirements, we will start with a general description of each requirement, and then examine how the two main classes of multitasking operating systems handle the requirements. Finally, we'll look at how a stand-alone system can manage the requirements without an operating system.

Context Switching

When a processor is executing a program, several registers contain data associated with the execution. They include the working registers, the program counter, the system status register, the stack pointer, and the values on the stack. For a program to operate correctly, each of these registers must have the right data and any changes caused by the execution of the program must be accurately retained. There may also be addition data, variables used by the program, intermediate values from a complex calculation, or even hidden variables used by utilities from a higher level language used to generate the program. All of this information is considered the program, or task, context.

When multiple tasks are multitasking, it is necessary to swap in and out all of this information or context, whenever the program switches from one task to another. Without the correct context, the program that is loaded will have problems, RETURNs will not go to the right address, comparisons will give faulty results, or the microcontroller could even lose its place in the program.

To make sure the context is correct for each task, a specific function in the operating system, called the *Context Switcher*, is needed. Its function is to collect the context of the previous task and save it in a safe place. It then has to retrieve the context of the next task and restore it to the appropriate registers. In addition to the context switcher, a block of data memory sufficient to hold the context of each task must also be reserved for each task operating.

When we talk about multitasking with an operating system in the next section, one of the main differentiating points of operating systems is the event that triggers context switcher, and what effect that system has on both the context switcher and the system in general.

Communications

Another requirement of a multitasking system is the ability of the various tasks in the system to reliably communicate with one another. While this may seem to be a trivial matter, it is the very nature of multitasking that makes the communications between tasks difficult. Not only are the tasks never executing simultaneously, the receiving task may not be ready to receive when the sending task transmits. The rate at which the sending task is transmitting may be faster than the receiving task can accept the data. The receiving task may not even accept the communications. These complications, and others, result in the requirement for a *communications system* between the various tasks. Note: the generic term "intertask communications" will typically be used when describing the data passed through the communications system and the various handshaking protocols used.

Managing Priorities

The *priority manager* operates in concert with the context switcher, determining which tasks should be next in the queue to have execution time. It bases its decisions on the relative priority of the tasks and the current mode of operation for the system. It is in essence an arbitrator, balancing the needs of the various tasks based on their importance *to the system* at a given moment.

In larger operating systems, system configuration, recent operational history, and even statistical analysis of the programs can be used by the priority manager to set the system's priorities. Such a complicated system is seldom required in embedded programming, but some method for shifting emphasis from one task to another is needed for the system to adapt to the changing needs of the system.

Timing Control

The final requirement for real-time multitasking is *timing control*. It is responsible for the timing of the task's execution. Now, this may sound like just a variation on the priority manager, and the timing control does interact with the priority manager to do its job. But, while the priority manager determines which tasks are next, it is the timing control that determines the order of execution, setting when the task executes.

The distinction between the roles can be somewhat fuzzy. However, the main point to remember is that the timing control determines *when* a task is executed, and it is the priority control that determines *if* the task is executed.

Balancing the requirements of the timing control and the priority manager is seldom simple nor easy. After all, real-time systems often have multiple asynchronous tasks, operating at different rates, interacting with each other and the asynchronous real world. However, careful design and thorough testing can produce a system with a reasonable balance between timing and priorities. In fact, much of the system-level design in Chapters 3 and 4 will deal specifically with determining and managing these often-conflicting requirements.

Operating Systems

To better understand the requirements of multitasking, let's take a look at how two different types of operating systems handle multitasking. The two types of operating system are *preemptive* and *cooperative*. Both utilize a context switcher to swap one task for another; the difference is the event that triggers the context switch. A *preemptive* operating system typically uses a timer-driven interrupt, which calls the context switcher through the interrupt service routine. A *cooperative* operating system relies on subroutine calls by the task to periodically invoke the context switcher. Both systems employ the stack to capture and retrieve the return address; it is just the method that differs. However, as we will see below, this creates quite a difference in the operation of the operating systems.

Of the two systems, the more familiar is the preemptive style of operating system. This is because it uses the interrupt mechanism within the microcontroller in much the same way as an interrupt service routine does.

When the interrupt fires, the current program counter value is pushed onto the stack, along with the status and working registers. The microcontroller then calls the interrupt service routine, or ISR, which determines the cause of the interrupt, handles the event, and then clears the interrupt condition. When the ISR has completed its task, the return address, status and register values are then retrieved and restored, and the main program continues on without any knowledge of the ISR's execution.

The difference between the operation of the ISR and a preemptive operating system is that the main program that the ISR returns to is not the same program that was running when the interrupt occurred. That's because, during the interrupt, the context switcher swaps in the context for the next task to be executed. So, basically, each task is operating within the ISR of every other task. And just like the program interrupted by the ISR, each task is oblivious to the execution of all the other tasks.

The interrupt driven nature of the preemptive operating system gives rise to some advantages that are unique to the preemptive operating system:

- The slice of time that each task is allocated is strictly regulated. When the interrupt fires, the current task loses access to the microcontroller and the next task is substituted. So, no one task can monopolize the system by refusing to release the microcontroller.

- Because the transition from one task to the next is driven by hardware, it is not dependent upon the correct operation of the code within the current task. A fault condition that corrupts the program counter within one task is unlikely to corrupt another current task, provided the corrupted task does not trample on another task's variable space. The other tasks in the system should still operate, and the operating system should still swap them in and out on time. Only the corrupted task should fail. While this is not a guarantee, the interrupt nature of the preemptive system does offer some protection.

- The programming of the individual tasks can be linear, without any special formatting to accommodate multitasking. This means traditional programming practices can be used for development, reducing the amount of training required to bring on-board a new designer.

However, because the context switch is asynchronous to the task timing, meaning it can occur at any time during the task execution, complex operations within the task may be interrupted before they complete, so a preemptive operating system also suffers from some disadvantages as well:

- Multibyte updates to variables and/or peripherals may not complete before the context switch, leaving variable updates and peripheral changes incomplete. This is the reason preemptive operating systems have a communications manager to handle all communications. Its job is to only pass on updates and changes that are complete, and hold any that did not complete.

- Absolute timing of events in the task cannot rely on execution time. If a context switch occurs during a timed operation, the time between actions may include the execution time of one or more other tasks. To alleviate this problem timing functions must rely on an external hardware function that is not tied to the task's execution.

- Because the operating system does not know what context variables are in use when the context switch occurs, any and all variables used by the task, including any variables specific to the high-level language, must be saved as part of the context. This can significantly increase the storage requirements for the context switcher.

While the advantages of the preemptive operating system are attractive, the disadvantages can be a serious problem in a real-time system.

The communications problems will require a communications manager to handle multibyte variables and interfaces to peripherals. Any timed event will require a much more sophisticated timing control capable of adjusting the task's timing to accommodate specific timing delays. And, the storage requirements for the context switcher can require upwards of 10–30 bytes, per task—no small amount of memory space as 5 to 10 tasks are running at the same time. All in all, a preemptive system operates well for a PC, which has large amounts of data memory and plenty of program memory to hold special communications and timing handlers. However, in real-time microcontroller applications, the advantages are quickly outweighed by the operating system's complexity.

The second form of multitasking system is the *Cooperative* operating system. In this operating system, the event triggering the context switch is a subroutine call to the operating system by the task currently executing. Within the operating system subroutine, the current context is stored and the next is retrieved. So, when the operating system returns from the subroutine, it will be to an entirely different task, which will then run until it makes a subroutine call to the operating system. This places the responsibility for timing on the tasks themselves. They determine when they will release the microcontroller by the timing of their call to the operating system, thus the name cooperative. This solves some of the more difficult problems encountered in the preemptive operating system:

- Multibyte writes to variables and peripherals can be completed prior to releasing the microcontroller, so no special communications handler is required to oversee the communications process.

- The timed events, performed *between* calls to the operating system, can be based on execution time, eliminating the need for external hardware-based delay systems, *provided* a call to the operating system is not made between the start and end of the event.

- The context storage need only save the current address and the stack. Any variables required for statement execution, status, or even task variables do not need to be saved as all statement activity is completed before the statement making the subroutine call is executed. This means that a cooperative operating system has a significantly smaller context storage requirement than a preemptive system. This also means the context switcher does not need intimate knowledge about register usage in the high-level language to provide context storage.

However, the news is not all good; there are some drawbacks to the cooperative operating system that can be just as much a problem as the preemptive operating system:

- Because the context switch requires the task to make a call to the operating system, any corruption of the task execution, due to EMI, static, or programming errors, will cause the entire system to fail. Without the voluntary call to the operating system, a context switch cannot occur. Therefore, a cooperative operating system will typically require an external watchdog function to detect and recover from system faults.

- Because the time of the context switch is dependent on the flow of execution within the task, variations in the flow of the program can introduce variations into the system's long-term timing. Any timed events that span one or more calls to the operating system will still require an external timing function.

- Because the periodic calls to the operating system are the means of initiating a context switch, it falls to the designer to evenly space the calls throughout the programming for all tasks. It also means that if a significant change is made in a task, the placement of the calls to the operating system may need to be adjusted. This places a significant overhead on the designer to insure that the execution times allotted to each task are reasonable and ap-proximately equal.

As with the preemptive system, the cooperative system has several advantages, and several disadvantages as well. In fact, if you examine the lists closely, you will see that the two systems have some advantages and disadvantages that are mirror images of each other. The preemptive system's context system is variable within the tasks, creating comple-tion problems. The cooperative system gives the designer the power to determine where and when the context switch occurs, but it suffers in its handling of fault conditions. Both suffer from complexity in relation to timing issues, both require some specialized routines within the operating system to execute properly, and both require some special design work by the designer to implement and optimize.

State Machine Multitasking

So, if preemptive and cooperative systems have both good and bad points, and neither is the complete answer to writing multitasking software, is there a third alternative? The answer is yes, a compromise system designed in a cooperative style with elements of the preemptive system.

Specifically, the system uses state machines for the individual tasks with the calls to the state machine regulated by a hardware-driven timing system. Priorities are managed based on the current value in the state variables and the general state of the system. Communications are handled through a simple combination of handshaking protocols and overall system design.

The flowchart of the collective system is shown in Figure 2.2. Within a fixed infinite loop, each state machine is called based on its current priority and its timing requirements. At the end of each state, the state machine executes a return and the loop continues onto the next state machine. At the end of the loop, the system pauses, waiting for the start of the next pass, based on the timeout of a hardware timer. Communications between the tasks are handled through variables, employing various protocols to guarantee the reliable communications of data.

As with both the preemptive and cooperative systems, there are also a number of advantages to a state machine-based system:

- The entry and exit points are fixed by the design of the individual states in the state machines, so partial updates to variables or peripherals are a function of the design, not the timing of the context switch.

- A hardware timer sets the timing of each pass through the system loop. Because the timing of the loop is constant, no specific delay timing subroutines are required for the individual delays within

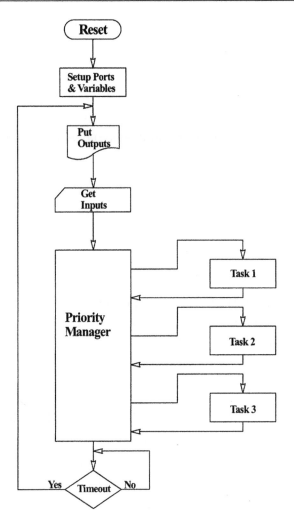

Figure 2.2   *State Machine Multitasking.*

the task. Rather, counting passes through the loop can be used
to set individual task delays.

- Because the individual segments within each task are accessed via
  a state variable, the only context that must be saved is the state
  variable itself.

- Because the design leaves slack time at the end of the loop and
  the start of the loop is tied to an external hardware timer, reasonable changes to the execution time of individual states within the
  state machine do not affect the overall timing of the system.

- The system does not require any third-party software to implement, so no license fees or specialized software are required to generate the system.

- Because the designer designs the entire system, it is completely scalable to whatever program and data memory limitation may exist. There is no minimal kernel required for operation.

However, just like the other operating systems, there are a few disadvantages to the state machine approach to multitasking:

- Because the system relies on the state machine returning at the end of each state, EMI, static, and programming flaws can take down all of the tasks within the system. However, because the state variable determines which state is being executed, and it is not affected by a corruption of the program counter, a watchdog timer driven reset can recover and restart uncorrupted tasks without a complete restart of the system.

- Additional design time is required to create the state machines, communications, timing, and priority control system.

The resulting state machine-based multitasking system is a collection of tasks that are already broken into function-convenient time slices, with fixed hardware-based timing and a simple priority and communication system specific to the design. Because the overall design for the system is geared specifically to the needs of the system, and not generalized for all possible designs, the operation is both simple and reliable if designed correctly.

The balance of this book will concentrate on the design methodology required to create the minimal set of task state machines, timing controls, priority management, and communications required to meet the specific needs of almost any embedded system.

3

System-Level Design

In this chapter, we will start the actual software design process. Because we are using a top-down approach to the design, it follows that this chapter will deal primarily with the top level of the design. This level of design is referred to as the *system level*. At this level, the general organization of the software will be developed, including definition of the tasks, layout of the communications, determination of the overall system timing, and the high-level definition of the priority structure.

These four areas—tasks, communications, timing, and priorities—will be a recurring theme in this book. This should not be surprising, considering they are the four basic requirements for multitasking. The development of the system tasks includes context switching, but for our purposes, it is expanded to include: the creation of the tasks; the development of a communications plan to handle all the communications between tasks; a timing control system to insure that each task is active at the right time to accomplish its function; and, finally, a priority manager to shift execution time to those tasks that are important to the system at any given moment.

To begin the system-level design, the designer needs a clear understanding of what the final software design must accomplish. The source of this information is the *system requirements document*, or simply the requirements document. The requirements document should contain the functions required, their timing, their communications needs, and their priorities.

If the requirements document does not contain all of these answers, and it typically doesn't, then it is up to the designer to obtain this information. The answer may come through asking questions of the department that generated the document, such as Marketing. Some of the information may be implied through a reference to another document, such as an industry standard on RS-232 serial communications. And, in some cases, the designer may simply have to choose.

Wherever the answers come from, they should end up in the requirements document. As part of the design, this document will be a living entity throughout the design process. As the requirements change, either through external requests from other departments or through compromises that surface in the design, the changes must be documented and must include an explanation of the reason for the change. In this way, the requirements document not only defines what the system should be, but also shows how it evolved during the development.

Some may ask, "Why go to all this trouble? Isn't commenting in the listing sufficient?" Well, yes, the commenting is sufficient to explain how the software works, but it does not explain why the software was designed in a certain way. It can't explain that the allocation of the tasks had to be a certain way to meet the system's priorities. It can't explain that halfway through the design additional functions were added to meet a new market need. And it can't explain why other design options were passed over because of conflicts in the design. Commenting the listing conveys the how and what, while the requirements document conveys the why.

One note on documentation: over the course of this chapter and the next several important pieces of information will be generated. This information will, of course, be available in the requirements document. However, an effective shorthand technique is to also list the information in a *design notes* file. This file should be kept simple; a text file is typically best. In this file, all of the notes, decisions, questions, and answers should be noted.

Personally, I keep a text file open in the background to hold my design notes when I dissect a requirements document. That way, I can note important information as I come across it. Another good reason to keep a design notes text file is that it is an excellent source of documentation for commenting. Whether generating a header comment for a software function or source information for a user's guide, all a designer has to do is copy and paste applicable information out of the design notes file. This saves time and eliminates errors in typing and memory. It also tends to produce more verbose header comments.

Dissecting the Requirements Document

While this may sound a little gruesome, it is accurate. The designer must carve up the document and wring out every scrap of information to feed the design process. In the following sections, we will categorize the information, document it in a couple of useful shorthand notations, and check the result for any vague areas or gaps. Only when the designer is sure that all the information is present and accounted for, should the design continue on. If not, then the designer runs the risk of having to start over. The five most frustrating words a designer ever hears are "What I really meant was."

So what is needed in a requirements document? Taking a note from the previous section, the four basic requirements are:

- *Tasks*: This includes a list of all the functions the software will be required to perform and any information concerning algorithms.

- *Communications*: This includes all information about data size, input, output, or temporary storage and also any information about events that must be recognized, and how.

- *Timing*: This includes not only the timing requirements for the individual tasks, but also the overall system timing.

- *Priorities*: This includes the priorities for the system, priorities in different system modes, and the priorities within each task.

Together, these four basic requirements for the system define the development process from the system level, through the component level, down to the actual implementation. Therefore, they are the four areas of information that are needed in a requirements document.

So, where to start? As the saying goes, "Start at the beginning." We start with the system tasks, which means all the functions that are to be performed by the tasks. And that means building a *function list*.

To aid in the understanding of the design process, and to provide a consistent set of examples, we will use the design of a simple alarm clock as an example. The following is a short description of the design and the initial requirement document:

Document 3.1

```
Requirements Document

The final product is to be a 6-digit alarm clock
   with the following features:
1. 6-digit LED display, showing hours : minutes :
   seconds. The hours can be in either a 12 hour or
   24 hour format. In the 12 hour format a single
   LED indicator specifying AM / PM is included.
2. 6 controls, FAST_SET, SLOW_SET, TIME_SET, ALARM_
   SET, ALARM_ON, SNOOZE.
3. The alarm shall both flash the display, and emit
   a AM modulated audio tone.
```

Function List

The first piece of documentation to build from the requirements document is a comprehensive *function list*. The function list should include all of the software functions described in the requirements document, any algorithms that may be specified or implied, and the general flow of the functions operation.

Reviewing the requirements document above, the following preliminary list of functions was compiled.

→

List 3.1

```
Preliminary Function List
1. Display functions to output data onto the
   displays
   a. 12-hour display function for time
   b. 24-hour display function for time
   c. 12-hour display function for alarm
   d. 24-hour display function for alarm
   e. Display flashing routine for the alarm
2. An input function to monitor and debounce the
   controls
   a. Control input monitoring function
   b. Debounce routine
3. A Command decoder function to decode the com-
   mands entered by the controls
4. An alarm function to check the current time and
   generate the alarm when needed.
   a. Turn alarm on / off
   b. Snooze
   c. Generate alarm tone
   d. Set alarm
5. Real-time clock
   a. Increment time at 1Hz
   b. Set Time
```

Function List Questions

1. Display function questions

    1.1. Are displays scanned or driven in parallel?

    1.2. How is 12 / 24 hour operation selected?

2. Input function questions

    2.1. How do the control inputs work?

3. A command decoder questions

    3.1. What are the commands?

    3.2. How do the commands work?

4. An alarm function questions

    4.1. How does the user turn the alarm on and off?

    4.2. How does the user know the alarm is on or off?

    4.3. How does the snooze function work?

    4.4. How is the alarm set?

    4.5. What frequency is the alarm tone?

5. Real-time clock questions
    5.1. What is the time reference for 1 Hz?
    5.2. How does the time reference operate?
    5.3. What happens if the power fails?
    5.4. How is the time set?

How can something as simple as an alarm clock generate so many functions and so many questions? I know how an alarm clock works, so why can't I just start writing code? While the designer may have a very good idea of how an alarm clock works, the purpose of this exercise is to get a very good idea of how marketing thinks the alarm clock should work, so we can design the alarm clock they want. Remember those five terrifying words, "what I really meant was."

Note: The designer should not be concerned if some of the functions appear to be repeated, such as the functions for time set, alarm set, and the function to flash the display, for example. Duplicates will be removed when the functions are combined into the various system tasks. In addition, duplicate listings indicate that the functionality may be split across a couple functions, so they also serve to indicate some of the function design choices that are yet to be made. Don't delete them until after the design decision is made.

The questions raised are also important:

■   How will the LED display system be implemented in hardware? How are the controls implemented? How does the time reference operate and what will the software have to do?

The group designing the hardware will have the answer to these questions.

■   How is the time and alarm time set? How is snooze initiated? How is 12/24 hour operation selected?

The answer to these questions will have to be answered by the group envisioning the product's look and feel.

As part of the function list, the designer should also include information about any algorithms used by a function. For example, the algorithm for converting data into a 7-segment format, any math routines for the 60 second/minute roll over, and even the algorithm for calculating the new alarm time when a snooze is activated. All of these will be a factor in the development of the different tasks in the system and should be recorded.

One final piece of information to note is the flow of the functions. Flow deals with the order in which things happen in a function. It can be simple and linear. For example: Increment seconds, if seconds = 60 then seconds = 0 and increment minutes. Or, it can be complex and require a graphical flow chart to accurately depict its functionality.

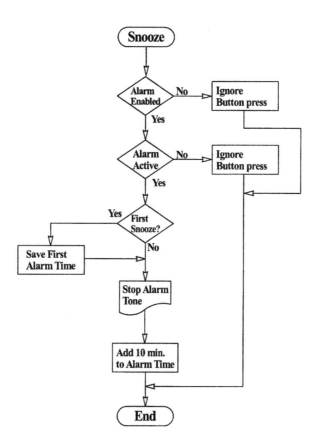

Figure 3.1 *Flow Chart of Snooze Function.*

Either way, it needs to be clearly defined so the designer has a clear idea of how the function works, with a list of any exceptions.

Note that there is nothing wrong with drawing pictures, and flow charts are very useful for graphically depicting the flow of a function. The use of pseudocode is another useful tool for describing how a function operates. Designers should not feel reluctant to drag out a large piece of paper and start drawing. If electronic copies of the documentation are required, the drawings can always be scanned and stored in a digital form.

Finally, when this section on the requirements document started, it was stated that any answers to questions should be included in a revision of the requirements document. So, including answers from all the groups, the document is rewritten with the new information:

Document 3.2

REQUIREMENTS DOCUMENT

The final product is to be a 6-digit alarm clock with the following features:
1. A scanned 6-digit numeric LED display.
    a. Time display is in either 24-hour or 12-hour AM/PM format with hours, minutes, and seconds displayed.
    b. Single LED enunciators are included for both ALARM ON and PM time.
    c. No indicator is used for AM or 24-hour operation.
    d. No indication of snooze operation is required.
    e. The alarm function can flash the display.
    f. Battery operation can blank the display.
2. 6 controls, FAST_SET, SLOW_SET, TIME_SET, ALARM_SET, ALARM_ON, SNOOZE.
    a. All controls, except ALARM_ON are push buttons. Combinations of button presses initiate the various commands. ALARM_ON is a slide switch.
    b. See below for command function information.
3. A Command decoder function to decode the commands entered by the controls.
    a. See below for detailed command operation.
4. An alarm function.
    a. Alarm time shall be displayed in hours and minutes with the seconds display blank when in the alarm set mode. The format shall match the current time display.
    b. The maximum number of snooze commands is not limited.

Document 3.2
(continued)

    c. The display shall flash in time to the tone.
    d. Turning the alarm on and off, setting the alarm time, and initiating snooze is described in the Command function section of the document.
    e. The alarm tone shall be 1 kHz, modulated at a 1 Hz rate (50% duty cycle).
5. The clock shall use the 60-Hz power cycle as a time-keeping reference for the real-time clock function.
    a. If 5 consecutive 60-Hz cycles are missed, the clock shall revert to the microcontroller clock.
    b. A battery back-up system shall be included that requires no action from the microcontroller to operate.
    c. While on battery operation, the display and alarm functions shall be disabled. If the alarm time passes during battery operation, then the alarm shall sound when 60-Hz power is restored.
    d. When the microcontroller detects 5 consecutive 60-Hz cycles, it shall revert to the power line time base.
    e. See below for setting the time and selecting 12/24-hour operation.

The new document, while verbose, is also much less ambiguous concerning the functionality of the system. Most of the questions have been answered and a significant amount of information has been added. The edits to the document are by no means complete, since there is information concerning communications, timing, and priorities yet to be examined. If you look carefully at the revised document, none of the questions concerning the operation of the commands have been answered. However, at this point most of the functionality of the various software functions has been clarified.

It is now time to answer the questions concerning the user interface, or command structure, of the system. In the previous section, questions concerning this information were asked but not answered. The reason is that the user interface, while contributing to the list of functions, is a sufficiently unique subject that it warrants special attention. Therefore, it is the next section to be covered.

The User Interface

A good user interface can make a product useful and a joy to use, while a bad user interface can be a source of frustration and pain. Although the science of developing a good user interface is sufficiently complex to fill several books this size, a fairly simple analysis of the proposed system can typically weed out most of the more common problems and inefficiencies. Additionally, the technique described in this section clearly documents the command structure and clearly shows any missing information. Even if the interface has been used extensively in older systems, it never hurts to revisit the evaluation, if only to get a clear picture of the command flow.

The first step is to storyboard, or flow chart, the command structure. This is accomplished by graphically showing the step-by-step sequence required to perform a command entry. For instance, setting the time on our alarm clock:

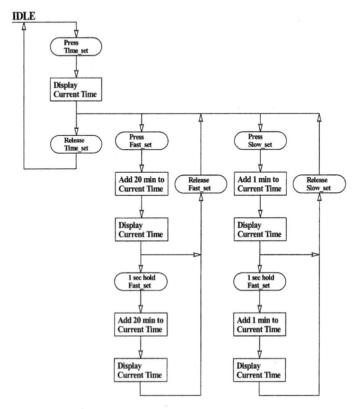

Figure 3.2 *Command Structure Flow Chart of Time_Set.*

In the example, round bubbles are used to indicate inputs from the users and rectangular boxes indicate responses from the system. Arrows then indicate the flow of the process, with the point of the arrow indicating the next event in the sequence. Some arrows have two or more points, indicating that two or more different directions are possible. For example, after the current time has been displayed by the system, the user has the option to release the TIME_SET button and terminate the command, or press either the FAST_SET or SLOW_SET buttons to change the current time.

At the top of the diagram is a line labeled IDLE and this is where the time set command sequence begins and ends. IDLE has been defined for this diagram to be the normal state of the system with the alarm disabled. Other system modes with mode-specific command sequences could include ALARM_ON, SNOOZE, and ALARM_ACTIVE. By using a specific system mode as a starting point, the diagram is indicating that the command is only available or recognized in that specific mode. If the label was ALL, then the command would be available in all system modes. Combinations of modes, such as ALARM_ON and ALARM_ACTIVE, can also be specified to indicate that a command is only available in the listed modes. However, most commands are typically available in all modes of the system, with only special-purpose commands restricted to a specific mode. For example, the ALARM_SET command would be available whether the alarm is enabled or disabled, while the SNOOZE command is only useful when the alarm is active, so it makes sense to only allow it for that specific mode.

Each command diagram should be complete, in that it shows all legitimate actions available for the command. It can also be useful to diagram sequences that generate an error, as this clarifies the error-handling functions in the user interface. In our example of an alarm clock, the system's response to an improper input is simply to ignore it. More complex systems may not have this luxury and may need a specific response to the unwanted input. To separate legitimate actions from errors, it is typically sufficient to draw the arrows for error conditions in red and the legitimate course of action in black. For diagrams that will be copied in black and white, a bold line to indicate improper input can also be used.

In more complex systems, the storyboards for a command structure can become large and cumbersome. To avoid this problem, the designer can replace sections of the diagram with a substitution box indicating additional information is available in a subdiagram. See the dashed line box surrounding the "Press FAST_SET" and "Add 20 min to current time" boxes in Figure 3.2. This is particularly useful if a commonly used edit sequence, used in multiple places in the diagram, can be replaced with a single subdiagram. The only prudent limitation on the practice is that the substituted section should only have one entrance and one exit. Some systems may in fact be so complex that an overall command storyboard may be required, with the individual commands listed as subdiagrams.

When all the storyboards are complete, they should be shown to the group that designed the system so they can clarify any misunderstandings. This is best done at the beginning, before several hundred lines of software are written and debugged.

Once all of the storyboards are complete, take each storyboard and note down how many key presses are required to set each function, worst case. For the clock time set example, the worst-case number of key presses is 83, 1 for the initial press and hold of the TIME-SET button, 23 presses of the FAST_SET to set hours, and 59 presses of the SLOW_SET to set minutes. Next, calculate the time required to perform that number of button presses. Assume that a key can be pressed repeatedly at a rate of 2–3 presses per second. For the clock this means that the worst-case time required to set the time is 42 seconds if each key press is made individually, and as much as 83 seconds if the auto-repeat feature is used.

Now, for the complete command structure, list the commands based on the frequency that each command is likely to be used, with most often used at the top of the list, and least often used at the bottom. Next to each command sequence name, list the worst-case number of key presses required to perform the command and the estimated time required. See the following list for the commands used in the alarm clock:

Table 3.1

Frequency of Use	Function Name	Button Presses	Time
Most infrequent	Set Time	83	42/83 sec
Infrequent	Set Alarm	83	42/83 sec
Frequent	Enable Alarm	Slide Switch	1 sec
Frequent	Disable Alarm	Slide Switch	1 sec
Very frequent	Snooze	1	½ sec

The times and number of key presses should be the inverse of the frequency of use. Specifically, the most common commands should have the least number of key presses and the fastest time to perform, and the least-often used commands should have the largest number of key presses and the longest time to set. If any command is out of sequence, then the flow of that command should be reconsidered, so that it falls in line with the other commands. From the example, Set Time and Set Alarm time are the longest to set and the least frequently used. The Snooze command is the most frequently used and the fastest to activate.

Another criterion for menu-based command structures is the depth of the menu that holds a command. Commonly used commands should be at the top level, or at the most, one level deep in the command structure. Commands deeper in the menu structure should have progressively less frequent use. See the following example menu structure:

Structure 3.1

```
ROOT Menu
    Delete
    Edit  →  Copy
             Paste
             Search  →  Find
             Replace
    File  →  Open
             Save
             Close
             New  →  Blank Template
                     Select Template
```

In this example, the most-often used command is Delete and it is at the top of the menu. Edit commands and File commands come next, with the New file commands buried the deepest in the menu. Typically, a user can remember one or two levels of a menu structure, provided that each level has only three or four functions. Any deeper, and they will typically have to consult a manual (unlikely), or dig through the menus to find the function they want. While designers might wish that users used the manuals more often, making this a requirement by burying commonly used commands at the bottom of a complex menu structure will only drive customers to your competitors.

Another obvious, but nonetheless often overlooked, requirement is that related commands should be in a common subdirectory, and the relationship of the commands should be viewed from the user's point of view, not the designers. Just because Paste and Replace have similar functions does not mean that the user will look for them in the same submenu. The correct choice is to group the commands as shown, by their use by the user, rather than their inner workings.

One hallmark of a good user interface is reusing buttons for similar functions in different commands. For instance, in the clock example, there was a FAST_SET and SLOW_SET button. They are used to set the current time, so it makes sense that the same buttons would also be used to set the Alarm time. Keeping common functions with the same buttons allows the user to stereotype the button's function in their minds and aids in their understanding of the command structure. With this in mind, it would be a major failing in a user interface to change the function of the control, unless *and only unless*, the second function is an extension of the control's original function. For instance, changing from 12 hour to 24 hour by pressing FAST_SET and SLOW_SET buttons together is acceptable because it is an extension of the buttons' original functions. Using the SNOOZE button in combination with the ALARM_SET button is just confusing for the user.

Once the user interface has been clearly defined, the requirements document should be updated to include the storyboards and any changes that may have come out of the analysis. Any changes or additions to the function list, necessitated by the user interface, should also be made at this time.

USER INTERFACE OPTIONS

So far, we have discussed interfaces based on just displays and buttons. Another method for entry is to use a rotary encoder as an input device. Designers today tend to forget that the original controls on tube radios were all knobs and dials. For all their simplicity, they did provide good resolution and responsive control, plus most users readily identify with the concept of turning a knob. Because they use only a two-bit Grey code to encode their movement, their interface is simple and the output is not tied to the absolute position of the rotary encoder, making them ideal for setting multiple values.

Imagine the simplicity of setting the alarm clock in the previous example using a rotary encoder. Simply hold down the set button and turn the dial until the right time appears on the display. Because the knob can move in two directions and at a rate determined by the user, it gives them additional control that a simple two-button interface does not.

Another trick with a rotary encoder is to tie the increment and decrement stop size to the rate of rotation, giving the control an exponential control resolution. Several quick flips of the knob can run the value up quickly by incrementing the value using a large increment. Then slower, more precise, rotations adjust the value with a smaller increment, allowing the user to fine-tune the value.

Another handy rotary input device is the simple potentiometer combined with an analog-to-digital converter input. This is a single input with many of the same features as the rotary encoder, plus the potentiometer is also nonvolatile, meaning it will not lose its setting when the power is removed. It does present a problem in that it cannot turn through multiples of 360 degrees indefinitely, but depending on the control function, this may not be a problem.

At the end of this phase of the dissection, the designer should have a revised function list. Any missing information in the requirements document should have been identified and answers found. A clear description of the user interface and command structure should have been generated, with storyboards. Any cumbersome or complicated sequences in the command structure should have been identified and rewritten to simplify the interface. And, finally, the requirements document should have been updated to include the new information. As always, any general notes on the system, with any applicable algorithms or specific information concerning the design, should also have been compiled.

The revised documents should look like the following:

Document 3.3

```
Revised Function list
1) Display functions to output data onto the displays
   a)  12-hour display function for time
   b)  24-hour display function for time
   c)  12-hour display function for alarm
   d)  24-hour display function for alarm
   e)  Display flashing routine for the alarm
   f)  PM indicator display function
   g)  Alarm on indicator display function
   h)  Function to scan LED displays
2) An input function to monitor and debounce the controls
   a)  input function to monitor buttons
   b)  Debounce routine
   c)  Auto repeat routine
   d)  60-Hz monitoring routine
   e)  60-Hz Fail / Recovery monitoring routine
3) A Command decoder function to decode the commands
   entered by the controls
   a)  An alarm function to check the current time and
       generate the alarm when needed.
   b)  Snooze function to silence alarm for 10 minutes.
   c)  Alarm on / off toggling routine
   d)  Initiate Snooze
   e)  Generate alarm tone routine
   f)  Set alarm function
       i)  Routine to increment alarm by 1 min
       ii) Routine to increment alarm by 20 min
   g)  Set Time function
       i)  Routine to increment Time by 1 min
       ii) Routine to increment Time by 20 min
   h)  Toggle 12/24 hour mode
```

Document 3.3
(continued)

4) Real-time clock routine
    a) Time increment routine based on 60-Hz power line
        time base
    b) Time increment routine based on internal clock
        time base
    c) Display blanking routine for operation from
        internal clock time base

DESCRIPTION OF THE USER INTERFACE
    Display
        6-digit scanned LED display
        1 indicator for PM operation in 12-hour mode
        1 indicator to show alarm is active

    Controls (inputs)
        1 slide switch to enable / disable the alarm
        1 push button for ALARM_SET
        1 push button for TIME_SET
        1 push button for FAST_SET
        1 push button for SLOW_SET
        1 push button for SNOOZE

    Time base inputs
        60-Hz line time base
        System clock

Command
Structure 3.1

DESCRIPTION OF THE COMMAND STRUCTURE
    To set Time
        Hold the TIME_SET button
        (display will show current time with seconds
        blank)
            Press SLOW_SET to increment time by 1 min
            Hold SLOW_SET to auto-increment time by
                1 min at 1-HZ rate
            Press FAST_SET to increment time by 20 min
            Hold FAST_SET to auto-increment time by
                20 min at 1-HZ rate
            (in 12-hour mode, time will roll over at
                12:59)
            (in 24-hour mode, time will roll over at
                23:59)
            Release the TIME_SET button to return to
                normal operation
            (Seconds will appear and start incrementing
                from 0)

```
To set alarm time
    Hold the ALARM_SET button
    (display will show current alarm time with sec-
    onds blank)
        Press SLOW_SET to increment alarm time by 1
          min
        Hold SLOW_SET to auto-increment alarm time
          by 1 min at 1-HZ rate
        Press FAST_SET to increment alarm time by 20
          min
        Hold FAST_SET to auto-increment alarm time
          by 20 min at 1-HZ rate
        (in 12-hour mode, time will roll over at
          12:59)
        (in 24-hour mode, time will roll over at
          23:59)
        Release the ALARM_SET button to return to
          normal operation
        (display will show current time)

To turn alarm on
    Slide alarm control switch to on
    (alarm indicator will light)

To turn alarm off
    Slide alarm control switch to off
    (alarm indicator will go blank)

To activate snooze mode, alarm must be active
    Press the SNOOZE button
    (alarm will be remain enabled)
    (tone will stop for for 10 min and then sound
    again)

To toggle 12 hour / 24 hour mode
    Release ALARM_SET and TIME_SET buttons
    Hold the FAST_SET button
    Press the SLOW_SET button
    (12/24 hour mode will toggle)
    (if result is 24-hr mode, time is displayed in
    24-hr format on press)
    (if result is 12-hr mode, time is displayed in
    12-hr format on press)
```

As no major changes have been made to the requirements document since the last section, the document will not be repeated here.

Communications

The next area of information to extract from the requirements document relates to communication pathways, both within the system and between the system and any external systems—specifically, information concerning the volume and type of data that will have to be handled by each pathway. This gives the designer a basis to plan out the communications system and to estimate the necessary data memory space required. Some of this information will be specified in the form of communications protocols between the system and external entities such as terminals, remote systems, or autonomous storage. Some of the information will be dictated by the operation of the peripherals in the system, such as timers, A-to-D converters, and the system's displays. And, some of the requirements will be dictated by the operations of the tasks themselves. As with the function list, we will have to play detective and determine what information is present, what is missing, and what is implied.

What kind of information are we looking for? We will have two forms of storage: dynamic and static. Dynamic storage handles a flow of information—for example, a serial peripheral that receives messages from another system. The task managing the peripheral will require storage for the message until it can be passed to a control task for processing. Because the peripheral may continue to receive new information while it is processing the old message, the storage will typically be larger to hold both the current message and the new one being received. This storage is therefore considered dynamic because the amount of data stored changes with time. The data storage is also not constant. While messages are being received, then the storage holds data. If all the messages received by the peripheral task have been processed, the storage is empty. Static storage, on the other hand, has a fixed storage requirement because the information is continuous, regardless of the current activity of its controlling task—for example, the variable structures that hold the current time and alarm time information in our clock example. The data may be regularly updated, but it doesn't change in size, and there is always valid data in the variables, so static storage is constant in size and continuously holds data.

All data pathways within a system will fall into one of these two categories. What we as designers need to do at this point in the design is find the various pathways, determine if the storage is static or dynamic, and make a reasonable estimate concerning the amount of storage required.

A good place to start is the peripherals that introduce information to the system. These include serial communications ports, button inputs, A-to-D converters (ADCs), even timers. These peripherals constitute sources of data for the system as their data is new to the system and not derived from other existing data. To determine whether their requirements are static or dynamic, we will have to determine what the information is and how the system will ultimately use it. Let's take a couple of examples, and determine which are static or dynamic:

Example 3.1 ——————▶ An A-to-D that captures sensor data from several sources. In this example the A-to-D continuously samples multiple sources, voltage, current, temperature, and pressure. It then scales the resulting value and stores the information in a collection of status variables. This peripheral is collecting a continuous stream of data, but it is not storing the information as a stream of data. Rather, it is updating the appropriate status variable each time a new sample is converted. This is an example of static storage. The memory requirements are simply the collection of status variables, multiplied by their width. The number of variables does not change, and they all contain valid data continuously.

Example 3.2 ——————▶ An A-to-D that captures a continuous stream of samples from a single source for digital signal processing. The data is stored in a large array, with the most current at the top and the oldest at the bottom. While this certainly sounds dynamic, it is actually static. As in the previous example, the amount of data does not change, but simply flows through the array of values. Each time a new value is added, the old value falls off the other end. The amount of storage required is the size of the array holding the collection of values, multiplied by their width. The number of variables does not change, and they all contain valid data continuously.

→
Example 3.3
A command decoder that converts individual button presses into control commands for the system. This certainly sounds static: a button is pressed and a command comes out. However, the storage requirement is actually dynamic. In the definition of static and dynamic storage, it was stated that the amount of valid information in a static system must be constant. Here the output of the system can be a valid command, or the system may be idle with no valid data output. The amount of data changes, even if only from one command to zero commands, so the system is dynamic.

→
Example 3.4
A system that reads data from a disc drive. This system is definitely dynamic, since the data is read from the disc as the information passes under the heads in the drive, so the timing of the data's arrival is dictated by the physics of the spinning disc. The system that uses the information is very probably not synchronized to the spin of the disc, so the system reading the disc will have to buffer up the information to handle the timing discrepancy between the disc and the receiving system. Because the timing is asynchronous, there is no way to predict the amount of time between the reception of the data and its subsequent transmission to the receiving system. So, the amount of data stored at any given moment is variable, ranging from zero to the maximum size of the disc file, and that makes this storage requirement dynamic.

OK, so some data is static, and we can readily determine the storage requirements for these functions, but how do we determine the maximum size of dynamic storage? The answer lies in the rate at which the information enters the system. In a typical system, such as a serial port, there will be three potential data rates.

1. *The maximum rate*: Typically this is determined by the electrical characteristics of the peripheral, the maximum conversion rate of the A-to-D, the baud rate of a serial port, or the roll-over time of a timer. It represents the theoretical maximum possible rate at which data can be sent, and it should be used to set the timing requirements of the task that will manage the peripheral.

2. *The average rate*: Typically this is an indicator of the average data load on the system. For a serial port, this will be the number of

packets sent in a typical second, multiplied by the average size of the packets. It is not the fastest rate at which the peripheral will have to operate, but it does indicate how much data the system will have to handle on a regular basis.

3. *The peak rate*: This rate is the worst-case scenario, short of the maximum rate defined for the peripheral. It indicates the maximum *amount* of data that will be transmitted in a given second. The word amount is the important distinction between the peak rate and the maximum rate. The maximum rate assumes a continuous flow of data forever. The peak rate indicates the amount of data sent, minus all the delays between packets, and characters in the flow of data. So, the peak rate, by definition, must be less than the maximum rate, and it represents the maximum data load on the system.

So, the maximum rate determines the speed at which the task managing the peripheral must operate, and the average and peak rates determine the average and worst-case data load on the system. How does this determine the amount of storage required? To answer the question, consider the example of a system that must receive serial data from another system.

Data from an external system is transmitted in the following format: 9600 baud, with 8-bit data, no parity, and 1 stop bit. Further, the data will be received in packets of 10 bytes, at an average rate of two packets every second.

So, to store the data received from the serial port, it is pretty obvious the temporary data storage structure will be an 8-bit CHAR. And, given a baud rate of 9600, with 8-bit data, 1 start bit, and 1 stop bit, the maximum rate at which 8-bit CHARs will be generated is 960 characters per second. That means that the receiving task will have to be called at least 960 times a second to keep up with the data. So far, so good, the maximum data rate is 960 characters a second.

Equation 3.1 ⟶

$$960 = (9600\text{baud}/(8 \text{ bit data} + 1 \text{ start bit} + 1 \text{ stop bit})).$$

However, how big a buffer will be needed to handle the data? Well, the packet size is 10 bytes, so a packet requires 10 bytes of storage. Given that the average rate at which a packet can be received is 2 per second, then the system will have to process 20 characters a second. And the minimum storage would have to be 20 CHARs, 10 for the current packet, plus 10 more to hold the accumulating data in the second packet.

OK, the system needs a minimum of 20 CHARs to buffer the incoming data. However, what happens if the peak rate is five packets per second? Now we need more storage; a minimal 20 CHAR buffer will be overrun. How much more storage should actually be allocated? At the moment, we don't have sufficient information to determine the exact storage needs, either average or peak. This is because we don't know the rate at which the system will actually process the packets. However, a good guess can be made using the average and peak rate numbers. If the average rate is two packets per second, then the maximum time the system will have to process a packet is limited to ½ a second. If the peak rate is five packets per second, and the system can process packets at a rate of two per second, then the buffer storage will have to be at least 41 CHARs. Five incoming packets each second, less one processed packet during the first half of the second, gives four packets of storage. At 10 CHARs per packet, plus one extra for the pointers, that's 41 CHARs. So, a good maximum size guess is 41 bytes for the storage.

One side note to consider, before we leave the discussion on buffer size and packet rates, if the control task is fast enough to process the data as it is received, why even user a buffer? Why not just process the data as it is received? Using this method would seem to be very appealing because it is both faster, and less wasteful of data memory. Unfortunately, there is an opportunity cost that is not readily apparent. If the control task is preoccupied with processing the data as it is received, it will not be able to handle other important conditions that may arise while the packet is in process. The response to other system conditions will quite literally by blocked by the reception of the data packet until it is complete. Using the buffer to queue up the complete packet allows the control task to handle the packet all at once, freeing it up to handle other important events as they occur. So, the buffer system in effect trades off data storage for more efficient use of the control task's execution time.

Another point to consider: if the control task does not use a buffer system and processes the data on a CHAR by CHAR basis, it can potentially be hung up if the data stream from the communications peripheral is interrupted in mid-packet. In fact, if the control task does not include some kind of time out timer, the control task may not notice even notice the interruption and hang the entire system waiting for a character that will never arrive.

At this point, the information that should be collected is:

1. What the data is, and its probable variable size.

2. Whether the storage requirement is static or dynamic.

3. Where the data comes from, and goes to.

4. The approximate amount of storage required for the storage.

5. And all information concerning the rate at which the data will appear.

Decisions concerning the actual format of the data storage and the final amount of data memory allocated will be left until later in the design, when more information concerning processing time is available. Until then, just note the information for each pathway in the system.

Having retrieved the specifications for data entering the system, the next step is to gather requirements for data leaving the system. And, again, the exits, like the entrances, will be through the peripherals and can be either static or dynamic.

In the previous section, we determined that static variables were fixed in length and continuously held valid data. The same is true for output peripherals—for example, the LED displays in our clock example. The task that scans the information onto the displays will get its information from one of two static variables that hold the current time and alarm time for the system. The data feed for the peripheral task has a constant size and continuously holds valid data, so the storage for the display is static.

However, if the peripheral is a serial output port, then the storage is no longer static because the amount of data is probably variable in length, and once transmitted, it probably no longer be valid either. Therefore the output queue for a serial output task is probably dynamic. But be careful, it could be that the serial output task simply grabs data from fixed variables in the system, converts them into ASCII characters, and sends them out. In this case, storage for the serial port task may be static because it is constant in length and always holds valid data. Careful examination of the requirements document is required to make a proper determination.

As in the previous section, a determination of the amount of data memory needed to hold any dynamic storage will also have to be made. Unfortunately, there may not be any explicit peak and average data rates to base the calculation on. Instead, we will have to examine the requirements placed on the peripheral and make a best guess as to what the average and peak rates are for the peripheral.

For example, consider a serial port that will be used to return information in response to queries from another system. Like the previous section, we will assume a 9600 baud rate, with 8-bit data, no parity, and one stop bit. This fixes the maximum rate of data transmission to 960 characters a second. The trick is now to determine what the average and peak data rates will be.

Well, if the data is sent in response to queries, then we can estimate the worst-case needs using a little common sense and some math. For example, assume the largest response packet is 15 characters long. If the maximum rate that new packets can be generated is limited by the peak rate at which packets can be received, then the peak rate for new outgoing packets is 5 per second (from the previous section). Given 15 CHARs per query, then the outgoing rate is 5 packets per second, or 75 characters per second. That means that a reasonable guess for data storage is 75 CHARS.

The final section of communications-related data to retrieve from the requirements document is any significant data storage requirements not covered in the previous sections. It can include on-chip copies of information stored in a nonvolatile memory; scratchpad memory for translating, compressing, or de-compressing files of data; or temporary storage of data to be moved to a secondary memory. Specifically, large blocks of data that hasn't been accounted for in the input or output peripheral data pathways.

As in previous sections, the data here can be static or dynamic as well. Static presents little challenge, as it is a permanent allocation. However, dynamic storage will again depend on the timing of the tasks sending and receiving the data, so we will again need to know the maximum, average, and peak rates at which the data will be transmitted. And, like the dynamic storage for the output peripherals, we will typically have to infer the rates from other specifications.

Let's take a simple example: temporary storage for nonvolatile values stored in an external EEPROM memory. Having nonvolatile storage for calibration constants, identification data, even a serial number, is often a requirement of an embedded design. However, the time to retrieve the information from the external memory can unnecessarily slow the response of the system. Typically, nonvolatile memory requires additional overhead to access. This may involve the manipulation of address and data registers within an on-chip nonvolatile storage peripheral, or even communications with the memory through a serial bus. In either case, retrieving the data each time it is needed by the system would be inefficient and time consuming. The faster method is to copy the data into faster internal data memory on power-up and use the internal copies for all calculations.

And that is where the amount of internal memory becomes an issue, because:

1. It means that internal data memory must be allocated for the redundant storage of the information.

2. It means that the data will have to be copied from the external memory, and possibly de-compressed, before the system can start up.

3. It means that all updates to the constants must also be copied out to the external memory, after being compressed, when the change is made.

This adds up to several blocks of data: data memory to hold the on-chip copies of the calibration constants; more data memory will be needed for any compression/decompression of the data during retrieval, or storage of updates; and, finally, data memory to buffer up the communications strings passed back and forth to the external memory.

OK, so a few shadow variables will be needed for efficiency. And, certainly some buffer space for communications with the external memory is reasonable, but who builds a compression / decompression algorithm into a small embedded system? Well, it may be a requirement that data tables are compressed to maximize data storage in an external nonvolatile memory, such as a data logger counting tagged fish migrating in a stream. If the data logger is a 10-mile hike from the nearest road, and compression extends the time between downloads, then it makes sense to compress the data. If on-chip storage is limited, then packing bits from several variables into each byte saves the cost (in both dollars and time) required to augment the storage with external memory.

Decompression may also be required for communications with an external peripheral. Take the example of an RTC, or real-time clock, peripheral. Its design is based on a silicon state machine, and the interface is a simple serial transfer. Given the chip is completely hardware in nature, it follows that the data will typically use a format that is convenient for the state machine and the interface, and not necessarily a format that is convenient for the microcontroller talking to it. So, to retrieve the current data and time from the peripheral, it is certainly possible that the microcontroller will have to parse the required data from a long string of bits before they can be stored in the internal variables. It may also be necessary to translate the data from binary integers into BCD values for display.

All of these functions require data storage, some of it dynamic with an as yet undetermined length, and some of it static with a predictable length. Our purpose here is to gather as much information concerning the communications needs of the system and determine the likely storage requirements.

If we examine our clock project in light of these requirements, we come up with the following notes for our design file:

```
INPUT PERIPHERAL
    Buttons: These inputs generate dynamic values a
    single bit in length. There are 6 inputs, with a
    maximum rate of 3 presses per second, an average of
    1 press per second, and a peak rate of 3 per sec-
    ond. That means a storage requirement of 18 bits
    for a worst case.

    60 Hz: This input is the 60-Hz line clock for the
    system. Its rate does not change under normal oper-
    ating conditions, so the maximum, average, and peak
    rates are the same. That leaves us with 1 bit of
    storage.

OUTPUT PERIPHERAL
    Display: The display always has the same number of
    bytes, 7. One for each digit of the display, plus
    1 to keep track of the display currently being
    driven. So, the storage requirement is static. An
    additional bit is needed for blanking the display
    during the Alarm_active time.

    Audio alarm: The alarm control is a single bit,
    with a maximum, average, and peak rate of 2 kHz, so
    a single static bit of storage. Note: The rate is
    determined by doubling the frequency of the tone, a
    1-kHz tone requires a bit rate of 2-kHz. Also, the
    rate was not in the requirements document, so the
    question was asked and marketing determined a 1-kHz
    tone was appropriately annoying to wake some one.

OTHER SIGNIFICANT STORAGE
    Storage for the current time is needed, so six static
    4-bit variables to hold hours, minutes, and seconds.

    Storage for the current alarm time is needed, so four
    static 4-bit variables to hold hours and minutes.

    Storage for the snooze offset alarm time is needed,
    so another four static 4-bit variables to hold the
    offset hours and minutes.
```

Notes

Storage for the following system set commands;
SLOW_SET_TIME, FAST_SET_TIME, SLOW_SET_ALARM_TIME,
and FAST_SET_ALARM_TIME
These four dynamic variables have the same timing
as the FAST_SET and SLOW_SET inputs, so 3 bits per
variable or 12 bits total.

Storage for the following static system variables;
ALARM_ENABLED, ALARM_SET_ACTIVE, ALARM_ACTIVE,
SNOOZE_ACTIVE
It is assumed that the button routine will directly
set these status variables based on the inputs.

It should be noted that these requirements are just estimates at this point in the design, and they are subject to change as the design evolves.

Timing Requirements

While the topic of timing has already been raised in the previous section, in this section the discussion will be expanded to include the execution and response time of the software functions.

When discussing timing in embedded software, there are typically two types of timing requirements, *rate of execution* and *response time*. Rate of execution deals with the event-to-event timing within a software function. It can be the timing between changes in an output, time between samples of an input, or some combination of both. The important thing is that the timing specification relates to the execution timing of the function only—for example, a software serial input routine that simulates a serial port. The rate of execution is related to the baud rate of the data being received. If the baud rate is 9600 baud, then the routine must be called 9600 times a second to accurately capture each bit as it is received.

Response time, on the other hand, is the time between when a trigger event occurs and the time of the first response to the event within the function. The trigger is, by definition, an event external to the function, so the response-timing requirement is a constraint on the software system that manages and calls the software functions. Specifically, it determines how quickly the main program must recognize an event and begin executing the appropriate software routine to handle it. Using the same software serial port routine as an example, the initial trigger for the routine is the falling edge of the start bit. To accurately capture the subsequent flow of data bits, the routine will have to sample near the center of each bit. So, at a maximum, the response time must be less than ¼ bit time; this will place the sample for the first bit within ¼ bit time of 50%. If the sample placement must be more accurate, then the response time must be correspondingly faster.

Both the rate of execution and response timing requirements should be specified in the requirements document, even if they are not critical. Listing the requirement at least indicates what timing the designer has chosen to meet in the design. It will also become important later in this chapter when we determine the system timing.

Note, that for some software functions, the specifications maybe missing. It could an omission in the document or the specification may be hidden within the specification of another function. Either way, it once again falls to the designer to play detective and determine the timing requirements. As an example, consider the control function from our clock example. In the requirements document, there may not be a specific requirement for response time and rate of execution listed for the command decoder function. However, there should be timing specification for the maximum response time to a button command entered by the user. So, if the timing requirement states that the system response to a button press must be less than 200 msecs from the start of the button press, then 200 milliseconds is the maximum time allotted for:

- The response time, plus execution time for the keyboard debounce function responsible for scanning the keyboard, and determining when a valid button press has occurred.

- Plus, the response time allotted to the control task, for the detection of a command.

- Plus, the execution time allotted for processing of the command and making the appropriate change in the system.

- Plus, the maximum time required to display the change of status on the system display.

If we know the button may take as much as 100 ms to stop bouncing and the debounce routine will require a minimum of 50 ms to detect the stable button. And the display task scans through all the displays 60 times a second. Then we can determine that the command function has a maximum of 34 msec to detect and process the command:

$$34 \text{ msec} = 200 \text{ msec} - 100 \text{ msec} - 50 \text{ msec} - (1/60 \text{ Hz})$$

Equation 3.2

So, event through there is not specification for the individual functions in the system, there may be an overall timing specification for the execution of the combination of functions. In fact, this will typically be the case with timing specifications. Timing requirements are most often for a combination of functions rather than the individual functions determined by the designer. This makes sense, as the writers of the requirements document can only specify the performance for the system as a whole, because they will not know what the specific implementation chosen by the designer will look like in the product definition phase. So, designers should take care in their review of the requirements document; sometimes the important information may not be in the most convenient format, and it may in fact be buried within other specifications.

Both timing parameters should also have tolerance requirements listed as well. The response time will typically have a single tolerance value, expressed as a plus percentage / minus percentage. And the execution rate will have at least one and possibly two, depending on the nature of the function.

Because the response time is less complicated, let's start with it first. The response timing tolerance is the amount of uncertainty in the timing of when a functions starts. Typically, it is specified as a plus/minus percentage on the response time, or it can also be specified as just the maximum response time allowed. If it is listed as a ± value, then the response time has both a minimum ($T_{response} - X\%$) and maximum ($T_{response} + X\%$) specification, and the response time is expected to fall within these timing limits. If, on the other hand, the only specification is a maximum response time, the more common form, then the minimum is assumed to be 0 and the maximum is the specified maximum response time. Because the minimum and maximum times are the values important to our design, either form works equally well. The designer need only determine the minimum and maximum and note them down in the design document for the appropriate software function.

The reason for two potentially different tolerances on execution rate is that first tolerance will typically specify the maximum variation for a single worst-case event-event timing, while the second specifies the total variation in the execution timing over a group of events. If only a single tolerance is specified, then it is assumed that it specifies both event-event, and the total variation for a group of events. To clarify, consider a serial port transmit function implemented in software. The routine accepts a byte of data to be sent, and then generates a string of ones and zeros on an output to transmit the start, data, parity, and stop bits. The event-to-event timing tolerance governs the bit-by-bit timing variation in the transitions of the ones and zeros sent. If the port were configured for 9600 baud, then the individual bit timing would be 104 µs. The event-event timing tolerance specifies how much this timing can shift for a single bit period. Some bits may be longer, and others shorter than the optimal 104 µs, but as long as they are within the specification, the receiving system should be able to receive the data.

The overall timing tolerance governs the accumulated average variation in bit timing for the complete byte sent by the routine, basically specifying the maximum variation over the course of the entire transmission. The reason this is important has to do with the idea of stacked tolerances. For example, say each bit time within a serial data transmission is allowed to vary as much as ± 10%. This means that the bit transitions may vary from as short as 94 µs, to as much as 114 µs. This is not a large amount, and for a single bit time, it is typically not critical. However, if the transmitted bits were all long by 10%, the timing error will accumulate and shift the position of the data bits. Over the course of 6 bits, the shift would be sufficient to move the fourth to fifth bit transition so far out that the receiving system would incorrectly think it is sampling the sixth data bit of data. If, on the other hand, the overall average error is kept below 4%, then even though the individual bits may vary by 10%, most of the individual bit timing errors will cancel.

In this scenario, the accumulated error should be sufficiently small to allow the receiver a marginal probability of receiving the valid data.

If we consider the problem from a practical point of view, it makes sense. There will typically be some variation in the timing of output changes. As long as the variation averages out to zero, or some value sufficiently small to be tolerable, then the overall frequency of the output changes will be relatively unaffected by the individual variation. So, note both values in the design notes for future use by the system in the timing analysis later in this chapter.

One other point to note: Check for any exceptions to the timing requirements, specifically any exception tied to a particular action in the function, such as, "The bit timing shall be 9600 baud ±3%, except for the stop bit, which shall be 9600 baud +100/–3". What this requirement tells the designer is that the individual bits in the data stream must vary less than 3%. The one exception is the stop bit which can be as short as the other bits, but may be as long as two complete bits, before the next start bit in the data stream. This is a valuable piece of information that will help in the design of both the timing and priority control sections of the design and, again, it should be noted in the design notes for the project.

Using our alarm clock design as an example, we will first have to glean all the available timing information from the requirements document, and then match it up with our preliminary function list. For those functions that are not specifically named with timing requirements, we will have to apply some deduction and either derive the information from the specifications that are provided, research the requirements in any reference specifications, or query the writers of the document for additional information.

The following is the resulting modification to the requirements document. Note that timing information specified in other sections of the document have been moved to this new section, and additional information has been added as well.

5) TIMING REQUIREMENTS.
  a) Display function timing information
    i)   The display shall scan at a rate greater than 60 Hz per digit (+20%/-0).
    ii) All display changes shall update within 1 digit scan time maximum.
  b) Alarm
    i)   The alarm function will flash the display at a 1-Hz rate (+/-10% event-event, +/-0% overall) Timing of flash shall be synchronous to real-time clock update(+50 msec/-0).
    ii) The alarm tone shall be a 1-kHz tone +/-10% event-event, and overall. Modulation to be at a 1-Hz rate, 50% duty cycle +/-10% event-event, +/-2% overall).
    iii) Alarm shall sound within 200 msec of when alarm time equals current time.
    iv) Alarm shall quiet within 200 msec of snooze detection, or 200 msec of alarm disable.
  a) Commands
    i)   The minimum acceptable button press must be greater than 300 msec in duration, no maximum.
    ii) All button bounce will have damped out by 100 msec after initial button press.
    iii) All commands shall provide a visual feedback (if applicable) within 200 msec of the initial button press.
    iv) For all two-button commands, the first button shall have stopped bouncing a minimum of 100 msec before second button stops bouncing for second button press to register as a valid command.
    v)   Autorepeat function shall have a 1-Hz rate (+/-10% event-event,+/-0% overall) increment shall be synchronous to real-time clock update (+50msec/-0).
  b) Time base
    i)   If 5 consecutive 60-Hz cycles are missed, the clock shall revert to the microcontroller clock within 8 msec of 5th missing rising edge.
    ii) When the microcontroller detects 5 consecutive 60-Hz cycles, it shall revert to the power line time base within 8 msec of 5th rising edge detected.
    iii) The real-time clock function shall have the same accuracy as its timebase (+/-0%). Updates shall be within 16 msec of update event to the real-time clock function.

Applying this new information to the functions listed in our function list should result in the following timing information for the project:

SYSTEM TIMING REQUIREMENTS BY FUNCTION:
1. The LED scanning function rate of execution is 360 Hz +20% / -0% event-event & overall, (6 digits * 60 Hz)
2. Display related functions have a response time of 1 digit scan time maximum (see 1.)
    Functions affected by this timing specification
        12-hour display function for time
        24-hour display function for time
        12-hour display function for alarm
        24-hour display function for alarm
        PM indicator display function
        Alarm on indicator display function
3. The rate of execution for the alarm display flashing routine is (1 Hz rate +/-10% event-event, +/-0% overall)(synchronous to time update +50 msec/-0)
4. The response time for display blanking due to a switchover to the internal time-base is 8 msec maximum, following detection of 5th missing rising edge.
5. All command functions have a response time of 34 msec maximum
    34 msec = 200 msec (spec) - 100 msec (switch bounce) - 50 msec (debounce) - (1/60 Hz)
    Functions affected by this timing specification are Command decoder function plus
        Alarm on/off toggling routine
        Routine to increment alarm by 1 min
        Routine to increment alarm by 20 min
        Routine to increment Time by 1 min
        Routine to increment Time by 20 min
        Toggle 12/24 hour mode
6. No specification for debounce time is given. However, 100 msec is the maximum bounce time, therefore a 50 msec maximum time is chosen for worst-case debounce detection. Both the Control input monitoring function and debounce function must execute in this time.
7. Rate of execution for the Auto repeat function is 1 Hz rate (+/- 10% event-event, +/-0% overall) event synchronous to time update (+50 msec/-0).
8. The response time for the alarm control function is 100 msec following new current time value equal to alarm time (includes tone startup time).

```
9.  The response time for a Snooze function is 50 msec
    maximum (includes tone off time)
    50 msec = 200 msec (spec) - 100 msec (switch
    bounce) - 50 msec (debounce).
10) The execution rate of the alarm tone function rou-
    tine 1-kHz tone +/-10% event-event and overall,
    modulated at a 1-Hz rate, 50% duty cycle +/-10%
    event-event, +/-2% overall).
11) The total response time of the 60-Hz monitoring
    and 60-Hz Fail/Recovery functions must be less
    than 8 msec of either the 5ᵗʰ detected 60-Hz pulse
    or its absence.
12) The rate of execution for the 60-Hz time base and
    internal time base shall be 1 Hz +/-0% overall
    relative to the source time base. Trigger to event
    response time of 16 msec maximum.
```

Once the information is complete, it should be noted in the design notes file for the project. Include any equations used to calculate the timing requirements and any special timing information—for example, the requirement in 3 and 7 requiring synchronous timing to the time update, and the notes in 8 and 9 concerning the inclusion of the startup and off times for the tone generator. At this point all the timing information for the system should be known and documented.

System Priorities

An important topic, related to timing, is the priority requirements for the system. From our discussion earlier, priority handling is different from timing in that timing determines the rate at which a function must be executed, while priority handling is determining if a function should execute. With this in mind, the designer must extract information from the requirements document concerning the operating modes of the system, the priorities within each mode, and when and why those modes change must be determined.

The logical place to start is to determine what operational modes the system has, specifically:

1. Does the system have both an active and passive mode?

2. Does it have an idle mode in which it waits for an external event?

3. Does it have two or more different active modes in which the system has different priorities?

4. Does it have a shut-down mode in which the system is powered but mostly inactive?

5. Does it have a configuration mode in which operational parameters are entered?

6. Is there a fault mode where system errors are handled?

For example, let's generate a priority list for the alarm clock we are designing. From the requirements document, we know:

- The alarm can be either enabled or disabled.

- If enabled, the alarm can either have gone off, or not. Let's call these pending/active.

- If the alarm is active, then it can be temporarily silenced by a snooze command.

- Both the current time and alarm time can be set by button commands.

- If the power fails, the display is blank, time is kept, and alarm functions are inhibited.

If we assign different modes to the various combinations of system conditions, we get the following preliminary list of system modes:

- **Timekeeping mode:** Current time display, alarm is disabled, no commands are in progress, and normal power.

- **Time set mode:** Current time display, alarm is disabled, normal power, and time set commands are in operation.

- **Alarm pending mode:** Current time display, alarm is enabled, normal power, no commands in progress, and alarm is not active.

- **Alarm set mode:** Alarm time display, normal power, alarm set commands are in operation, and alarm is not active.

- **Alarm active mode:** Flashing display of current time, alarmed is enabled, alarm is active, no commands in progress, and normal power.

- **Snooze mode**: Current display time, alarm is enabled, snooze is in progress, and normal power.

- **Power fail mode**: Display is blank, internal time base in operation, alarm is inhibited, and battery supplied power.

Note that each of the system modes is unique in its operation. Some modes are differentiated by the fact that commands are active, others because of the status of the alarm. In fact three of the modes are different states within the alarm function. It doesn't really matter at this point in the design if we have five system modes, or thirty. What we want to determine is all the factors that affect how the system operates. When we get to the priority handler design section of this chapter, we will expand or contract the system mode list as needed to fit the design. For now we just need to generate a reasonable list of modes to hang some additional information on.

If we compare the preliminary list of modes to the previous criteria, we should notice that there is one mode missing, the error mode. We will need a mode to handle error conditions, such as the initial power up, when the system does not know the current time. If we establish this error mode, and define its behavior, we might have something like the following:

- **Error mode**: Display flashing 12:00, alarm is inhibited, no command is in progress, and normal power.

Once the preliminary list of system modes has been established, the next step is to determine which functions are important in each mode. Each mode will have some central operation, or group of operations, that are important and others that are not so important. This translates into some software functions having a higher priority than other functions. In fact, some functions may have such a low priority that they may not even be active. So, using the description of the modes as a guide, we can take the list of functions and determine if each has a high, medium, or low priority in a given mode. Those that are not needed in a specific mode are left off the list. So, once again using our alarm clock as an example, the following preliminary priority list can be compiled:

List 3.2

Priority List
1. Timekeeping mode
    1.1. High Priority
           60-Hz monitoring function
           Time increment function based on 60-Hz
             power line time base
    1.2. Medium Priority
           Function to scan LED displays
           12-hour display function for time
           24-hour display function for time
           PM indicator display function
    1.3. Low Priority
           60-Hz Fail/Recovery monitoring function
           Control input monitoring function
           Debounce function
           Toggle 12/24 hour mode
           Alarm on/off toggling function

2. Time set mode
    2.1. High Priority
           Control input monitoring function
           Debounce function
           Auto repeat function
           Set Time function
           Routine to increment Time by 1 min
           Routine to increment Time by 20 min
    2.2. Medium Priority
           Function to scan LED displays
           12-hour display function for time
           24-hour display function for time
           PM indicator display function
    2.3. Low Priority
           60-Hz monitoring function
           60-Hz Fail/Recovery monitoring function

3. Alarm pending mode
    3.1. High Priority
           60-Hz monitoring function
           Time increment function based on
             60-Hz power line time base
           Alarm control function
    3.2. Medium Priority
           Function to scan LED displays
           12-hour display function for time
           24-hour display function for time
           PM indicator display function

List 3.2
(continued)

3.3. Low Priority
    60-Hz Fail/Recovery monitoring function
    Control input monitoring function
    Debounce function
    Toggle 12/24 hour mode
    Alarm on/off toggling function

4. Alarm set mode
4.1. High Priority
    Time increment function based on 60-Hz
      power line time base
    Control input monitoring function
    Debounce function
    Auto repeat function
    Alarm control function
    Set alarm function
    Routine to increment alarm by 1 min
    Routine to increment alarm by 20 min
4.2. Medium Priority
    Function to scan LED displays
    12-hour display function for alarm
    24-hour display function for alarm
    PM indicator display function
4.1. Low Priority
    60-Hz monitoring function
    60-Hz Fail/Recovery monitoring function

5. Alarm active mode
5.1. High Priority
    60-Hz monitoring function
    Time increment function based on 60-Hz
      power line time base
    Generate alarm tone function
    Alarm control function
5.2. Medium Priority
    Function to scan LED displays
    Display flashing function for the alarm
    12-hour display function for time
    24-hour display function for time
    PM indicator display function
5.3. Low Priority
    60-Hz Fail/Recovery monitoring function
    Control input monitoring function
    Debounce function
    Toggle 12/24 hour mode
    Alarm on/off toggling function
    Snooze function

List 3.2
(continued)

6. Snooze mode
   6.1. High Priority
        60-Hz monitoring function
        Time increment function based on 60-Hz
          power line time base
        Snooze function
        Alarm control function
   6.2. Medium Priority
        Function to scan LED displays
        12-hour display function for time
        24-hour display function for time
        PM indicator display function
   6.3. Low Priority
        60-Hz Fail/Recovery monitoring function
        Control input monitoring function
        Debounce function
        Toggle 12/24 hour mode
        Alarm on/off toggling function

7. Power fail mode
   7.1. High Priority
        Time increment function based on 60Hz
          power line time base
        60-Hz monitoring function
   7.2. Medium Priority
        Function to scan LED displays
        Display blanking function for operation
          from internal clock time base
   7.3. Low Priority
        60-Hz Fail/Recovery monitoring function
        Time increment function based on internal
          clock time base

8. Error mode
   8.1. High Priority
        60-Hz monitoring function
   8.2. Medium Priority
        Function to scan LED displays
        12-hour display function for time
   8.3. Low Priority
        60-Hz Fail/Recovery monitoring function
        Control input monitoring function
        Debounce function

The eight modes are listed with the functions that are important in each mode. The priorities of each function, in each mode, are also established and those functions that are not required are left off the list indicating that they are not used in that particular mode. The result is a clear list of system modes and priorities. The only thing missing are the specific conditions that change the mode. These transitions are generally due to external conditions, such as a command entry or power failure. Transitions can also be due to internal events, such as the alarm time. Whatever the reason, the transition and the event triggering the transition need to be determined and noted. The following are the events triggering a transition in the alarm clock design:

Table 3.2

Original Mode	Next Mode	Trigger Event
Powered down	Error	Initial power up
Error	Time set	Press of the TIME SET button
Error	Alarm set	Press of the ALARM SET button
Timekeeping	Time set	Press of the TIME SET button
Timekeeping	Alarm set	Press of the ALARM SET button
Time set	Timekeeping	Release of the TIME SET button
Alarm set	Timekeeping	Release of the ALARM SET button
Timekeeping	Alarm pending	Alarm control switch to enabled
Alarm pending	Timekeeping	Alarm control switch to disabled
Alarm active	Timekeeping	Alarm control switch to disabled
Alarm pending	Alarm active	Alarm time = current time
Alarm active	Snooze	Snooze command
Snooze	Alarm active	Alarm time + snooze time = current time
{all modes}	Power fail	Fifth consecutive missing 60-Hz pulse
Power fail	Timekeeping	Fifth consecutive 60-Hz pulse
{all modes}	Error	Error condition

With these additions, the system modes and priorities are sufficiently defined for the design.

The only functions that haven't been specified are those functions that fall into the category of *housekeeping functions*. These functions have no specific timing or priority; rather, they are just executed when execution time is available. This could be because their typical timing is infrequent compared to other higher priority functions, or it could be that they are run as a sort of preventive maintenance for the system. Typical examples of this kind of function can include the following:

1. Periodic checks of the voltage of the battery used for battery backup.
2. Periodic checks of the ambient temperature.
3. Periodic verification of a data memory checksum.
4. Functions so low in priority that any other functions are run before they are.
5. Functions that may have a higher priority in other modes, but do not in the current mode.

Any function that is not in the system list of priorities could be included in the list of housekeeping functions, so it can be included in the priority control system. Note that it is perfectly acceptable to have no housekeeping functions. And it is also acceptable to have functions in the list that are only present in some system modes. The only purpose of the list is to guarantee that all functions get execution time, some time during the operation of the system. For our example with the alarm clock, there are no housekeeping functions beyond those with low priority in the various system modes.

Error Handling

The final section of information to glean from the requirements document is error handling—specifically, what set of errors is the system designed to recognize and how will the system handle the errors. Some errors may be recoverable, such as syntax error in an input, out of paper in a printer, or a mechanical jam. Other errors are more serious and may not be recoverable, such as low battery voltage, failed memory data check sum, or an illegal combination of inputs from the sensors indicating a faulty connection. Whatever the illegal condition, the system should be able to recognize the error, indicate the error to the operator, and take the appropriate action.

The first step is to compile a list of errors and classify them as *soft errors*, *recoverable*, or nonrecoverable *hard errors*. Soft errors include faults that can safely be ignored, or can be handled by clearing the fault and continuing operations. Typically soft faults are user input faults which can be safely either ignored, or handled by reporting a simple error condition. These include minor user input faults, incorrect syntax, or even the entry of out-of-bound values. Recoverable errors are errors in the system due to transitory system faults that, once cleared, will allow the system to continue operation. These include corrupted data memory, control faults that require user intervention to clear, or a lost program counter. Finally, hard errors are those errors classified as a failure in the system hardware requiring diagnostics and repair to clear. These include the detection of an impossible combination of inputs, failure of the program memory checksum, or failure in the operation of a system peripheral.

After the list of errors has been compiled and classified, the criteria for detecting the error should be specified and all acceptable options for responding to the error. As an example, consider a simple lawn sprinkler controller. It is designed to accept data in the form of water time and duration. When the time corresponding to a watering time is equal to the current time, it turns on the sprinkler for the specified duration.

However, what happens if a specified watering time of 25:20 is entered? Or the current time is 24:59? Or the checksum on the time and duration data memory fails a routine check? These are examples of potential faults for a system. Compiling them into a list and classifying them, we get:

List 3.3

Soft Fault

Fault: User enters a start time >23:59.

Test: Determined at input by comparison to 23:59.

Response: Display "bad time" for 5 seconds and clear input.

Recoverable Fault

Fault: Data checksum fails.

Test: Determined by checksum housekeeping function.

Response: Display "MEMORY FAULT" and turn off all sprinklers, clear data memory, and wait for user to reset time and duration values.

Hard Fault

Fault: Clock peripheral reports > 24:59.

Test: Determined at time check by comparison to 23:59.

Response: Display "system failure" and turn off all sprinklers and shut down system.

In each of these possible problems, the system has both a means of detecting the fault, and a way to respond to the fault. If the fault, its detection, or recovery are not listed in the requirements document, then it is up to the designer to find answers to these questions and add them to the document.

Note that some faults should be included as a matter of good programming practice, such as watchdog timer (WDT) fault, brownout reset (BOR) fault, and program/data corruption faults. In most microcontrollers, there will typically be flags to indicate that the last reset was the result of a BOR or WDT. Handling these forms of reset will depend on the specific requirements of the system and suggestions will be made in Chapter 5 on implementation.

Program and data corruption faults are a little different because they rely on software functions to check the CRC or checksum of the data in data memory. While this can be, and typically is, relegated to a housekeeping function for a spot check, it should also be included in any routine that makes changes to the affected data. If it is not included in the modifying functions, the function could make it change, recalculate the checksum and never know that it just covered up a corrupted data value. So it is important to take data corruption seriously and make an effort to provide adequate checking in the design.

For our alarm clock example, the range of faults is fairly limited, but they must still be documented for the next phase of the design.

List 3.4

Soft Fault

Fault: Button pressed is not valid for current mode or command. Press of SLOWSET without FASTSET, ALARMSET, or TIMESET held.

Press of SNOOZE when not in alarm active mode.

Press of any key in power fail mode.

Test: Comparison of decoded button command with legal commands, by mode.

Response: Ignore button press.

Soft Fault

Fault: Button combination is invalid.

Press of SNOOZE with FASTSET, SLOWSET, ALARM-SET, TIMESET.

Press of ALARMSET with TIMESET.

Test: Checked against acceptable combinations in command function.

Response: Ignore button press.

Recoverable Fault

Fault: Alarm time is out of range (Alarm time > 23:59).

Test: Alarm control function test of value before current time comparison.

**List 3.4
(continued)**

Response: If alarm is enabled, sound alarm until ALARMSET button press.

If in any other mode, ignore (fault will be identified when alarm is enabled).

Recoverable Fault

Fault: Power failure.

Test: 5th missing 60-Hz time base pulse.

Response: Goto power fail mode until 5th detected 60-Hz pulse.

Hard Fault

Fault: Watchdog timer timeout, brownout reset.

Test: Hardware supervisor circuits.

Response: System is reset. If BOR, then system held in reset until power is restored.

System will power up in error mode.

With the compilation of the error condition list, this completes the dissection of the requirements document, and all the relevant information required for the design should now be in the design notes file. In addition, all updates to the requirements document should be complete at this point in the design. If it is not, then the designs should make those updates now, before embarking on the system design. This is not just good coding practice—it will also save confusion and disagreement at a later date when the group responsible for testing the design begins comparing the operation of the design against the requirements document. So, fix it now while the change is simple and still fresh in the designer's mind, rather than later when the reasons for the change may have been forgotten.

System-Level Design

At this point, the system level of the design is generated. All the information has been retrieved from the requirements document, and the designer should have a clear picture of how the design must operate. What happens now is the top, or system, level definition of the system.

Tasks will be created and the various functions will be assigned to them. A communications plan will be developed to handle data transfers between the tasks. A system timing analysis will be performed to determine the system timing tick. The system modes and priorities will be analyzed, and a system-level error detection and handling system will be defined. Basically, a complete high-level blue print for the system will be generated, with module specifications for each of the tasks and major systems in the design.

Task Definition

The first step in the system-level design is *task definition*. Task definition is the process of gathering the various software functions from the requirements document dissection together and grouping them into a minimal number of tasks. Each task will be a separate execution module, with its own specific timing, priority, and communications pathways. Because of this, the functions within the module must be compatible, or at least capable of operating without interfering with one another. Now a typical question at this point is "Why a minimal number of tasks—why not create a task for every function?" That would eliminate the need to determine whether or not the various functions are compatible. However, there are two main problems: overhead and synchronization. Overhead is the amount of additional code required to manage a function, the switch statement, the timing handler, and any input/output routines required for communications. Synchronization is the need for some of the software functions to coordinate their function with other functions in the system. Placing compatible functions into a single task accomplishes both goals, the overhead for a group of functions is combined into a single task, and because the functions share a common task, they can coordinate activities without complex handshaking. An example would be combining a cursor function and a display-scanning function into a common task. Putting the two functions together reduces the additional code by half, and it allows the designers to coordinate their activity by combining them into a single execution string. So, there are valid reasons why some of the functions should be combined into a common task.

This is not to say that all software functions should be combined into common tasks. After all, the whole purpose of this design methodology is to generate software that can execute more than one task simultaneously. And there are very good reasons why some software functions are so incompatible that they can't or shouldn't be combined into a common task. Part of task definition is to analyze the various software functions and determine which, if any, functions should be combined.

So, how does a designer decide which functions are compatible and which are not? The simplest method is to start combining similar functions into tasks, and then determine if the combination is compatible. To do this, start by writing the name of each function on a piece of tape. Drafting tape works best because it is designed to be stuck down and taken up repeatedly without much trouble. Next, take a large piece of paper and draw 10–15 large circles on it, each about 5–8 inches in diameter. The placement of the circles is not critical; just distribute them evenly on the paper. Then take the strips of tape with the function names, and place them within the circle on the sheet of paper. Try to group like functions together, and try to limit the number of circles used. Don't worry at this point if some circles have more names inside than others do. We are just trying to generate a preliminary distribution of the functions.

Once all the functions have been distributed into the circles on the paper, take a pencil (not a pen) and name the circles that have pieces of tape in them. Use a name that is generally descriptive of the collection of functions within the circle. For example, if a circle contains several functions associated with interpreting and executing user commands, then COMMAND would be a good label. Try not to be too specific, as the exact mix of functions will most likely change over the course of the analysis for compatibility. And don't be concerned if all the functions are moved out of a specific circle. The names are just for convenience at this point. The final naming and grouping of functions will be decided at the end of the process.

Now that a preliminary grouping is complete, we can begin evaluating the compatibility of the various software functions within each circle.

The first step in the process is to place the strips of tape equidistant around the circumference of the circle. If there is not enough room for the tape to lay along the circle, place it on the circle, extending out radially like a star. Next, draw a line from each function to all of the other functions, and then repeat the process for any functions that are not connected to all the other functions. This web of lines defines all the possible relationships between all the functions in the circle, one line for each relationship.

Now that we know all the different combinations to examine, we need a set of basic criteria on which to base our decisions. The criteria will be based on timing, priorities, and functionality. However, the designer should remember that the criteria are just guidelines, not hard and fast rules. The final choice will come down to a judgement call on the part of the designers as to which functions should be combined. For some functions there will be one criterion that states that two functions should be combined, and another that states they should not. This should not come as a surprise; no single set of rules will apply to 100% of all designs. When this happens, the designer should review the reasons given for compatibility and incompatibility and decide which is more important. For example, two functions could have completely different timing and priorities, which would demand that they couldn't be combined. However, if they are also mutually exclusive in execution (they never execute at the same time), then they could be combined into a common task without conflict. The task will simply have to adjust its timing and priority level based on which function is currently active. It would then be up to the designer to decide whether the combination is worth the trouble, or if one or both of the functions should be shifted to another task.

Note: If two functions are combined against the recommendation of one or more criteria, the designer should note the reason in the design notes and make sure that the verbiage is included in the header comments for the resulting task. This will save any later engineer the trouble of determining why one of the compatibility criteria was disregarded.

If the designer finds a function that is incompatible with most or all of the other functions in a circle, it should be moved to another circle with similar functions, and evaluated there. The new circle should be an existing named task, but if it cannot be placed in an existing circle, it can be placed in a new empty circle as a last resort. Remember, we are trying to minimize the total number of tasks, but if the function is completely incompatible, it needs to have its own task.

There will also be cases in which a function should be separated into its own task for priority reasons, specifically if the task is intermittent in operation. In the next chapter, we will examine a priority handler that can make use of this lone function characteristic to reduce the processing load on the system. Against that possibility, the intermittent task should be labeled and set within its own circle for later evaluation.

Criteria for Compatible Software Functions

The criteria in this section should be used to determine if a pair of software functions should or must be combined into a single task. Any criterion that states two functions *should* be combined is making a recommendation. Any criterion that states two functions *must* be combined is stating that the combination should be required and only overruled in the event of a serious incompatibility. Note that this list should be considered a good starting point for developing a designer's own personal list; it is by no means all-inclusive. Over a designer's career, a personal list of criteria should be compiled and fine-tuned as the complexity of their designs increase. Like a good library of custom functions, the design methodology of a designer should grow and improve with time. Therefore designers should feel free to add or modify these criteria to fit their level of experience and programming style.

- *Software functions that execute sequentially*
  This one is pretty obvious: if two software functions always execute one after the other, then it makes sense to put them in a common task. The state machine that implements the task will just execute the states required for the first function, and then continue on, executing the states of the second function. The only restriction to this criterion is that software functions that

have to execute simultaneously may need to be separated into different tasks. For more, see the next criterion.

- *Software functions that execute synchronously*
  This criterion has a number of restrictions on it. The functions must always execute at the same time, never separately. The functions must also be linear. This means no branches, computed GOTOs, loops, or conditional statements—just a straight linear sequence for both functions. This type of task can also be difficult to implement because the two functions must be interleaved together into a single set of states. As a result, it is only recommended for functions that meet the restrictions exactly. If not, then they must be combined.

- *Software functions that control a common peripheral*
  This criterion has to do with managing control over a peripheral. If two tasks exercise control over a common peripheral, then there is the possibility that they may come into contention. This happens when one task is using the peripheral with a specific configuration, and then the other task inadvertently takes control and changes that configuration without the first task's knowledge. If both functions are placed in a common task, it removes the question of control arbitration entirely because the state machine can typically only execute one function at a time. However, if the two functions are incompatible for other reasons, a good alternative is to generate a third task specifically designed to handle the arbitration between the original functions. This kind of task takes on the role of gatekeeper for the peripheral, granting control to one task and holding the other until the first task completes its operation. The second task is then granted control until its operation is complete. Because the separate peripheral task is the only software in direct control of the peripheral, and all data transfers must go through the peripheral task, contention is avoided and both controlling tasks eventually obtain undisturbed use of the peripheral.

- *Software functions that arbitrate control of common data*
This criterion is very similar to the last criterion concerning peripheral control, with the exception that it deals with control over a commonly controlled data variable. Just as two functions may come into contention over the control of a peripheral, two functions may also come into contention over control of a variable. So, this criterion is designed to simplify the arbitration of control, by recommending the combination of the software functions into a common task. However, as with the peripheral criterion, if the two functions are incompatible for other reasons, then a third arbitrating function may need to be created to handle the actual updates to the variable.

- *Software functions that are mutually exclusive in operation*
Often in a design it may be necessary to force two functions to be mutually exclusive in their operations. The two functions may have opposite functions, such as heating and cooling, or they may control a common resource. In any event, mutually exclusive functions are defined as functions that never execute at the same time, or with any degree of overlap. So, functions that meet this requirement must be combined into a single task. This criterion may sound unimportant; after all, the reduction in overhead from combining functions is not so great that it would warrant the arbitrary combination of functions. However, what combining the functions into a single task will do is guarantee their mutually exclusive operation. This is because the state machine can typically only execute a single function at one time. By combining the two functions into a single task, the two functions are accessed by the same state variable, and it will require a specific transition event to move from one function to the other, guaranteeing the mutually exclusive nature of the functions.

- *Software functions that are extensions of other functions*
This criterion is fairly obvious: if two or more functions are related in function, then they should reside in a common task. A good example of this relationship is the display function in

our alarm clock example. The functions for scanning the LED display and flashing the display in the case of an alarm are related, and the flashing function is really an extension of the scanning function. Both functions deal with the LED display, and the flashing function is really just a timed blanking of the displays, so combining them together into a single function makes sense. They affect a common resource, their operation is related, and their control of the common display peripheral may require arbitration between the functions. So, combining the functions is a must, it will reduce overhead, simplify the arbitration, and places both display related functions into a single object.

- *Software functions with common functionality*
  This criterion has to do with functions that share common aspects with one another—for example, two functions that require a common multistep math sequence, such as a running average. If the functions are placed in a common task, then the math functions can be coded into a common set of states within the task. If the functions are not combined, then the steps for the math function may have to be repeated in both tasks, at the cost of additional program memory. Combining the functions into a common task does save program memory by eliminating the repeated states, but there is a restriction. By placing the two functions into a common task, the two functions are forced to be mutually exclusive in operation. So, if the two functions do not operate in a mutually exclusive fashion, then this criterion does not apply. See the incompatibility criterion following concerning subfunctions.

Criteria for Incompatible Software Functions

The criteria in this section should be used to determine if a pair of software functions should not or must not be combined into a single task. Any criterion that states two functions *shouldn't* be combined is making a recommendation. Any criterion that states two functions *must not* be combined is stating the combination should never be attempted.

Note, as previously, that this list should be considered a good starting point for developing a designer's own personal list and is by no means all-inclusive.

- *Software functions that have asynchronous timing*

    This criterion is pretty obvious. If two functions can execute at any time and with any degree of overlap in execution, then they must not be combined into a single task. Separating the functions gives them the freedom to execute at any time appropriate to their operation without any interference from the other function. And, this is, after all, the reason for designing a multitasking system, so different functions can execute independent of each other's timing.

- *Software functions that execute at different rates*

    This criterion is another obvious restriction, in that it excludes functions that have to operate at different rates. As an example, consider a software serial port operating at 1200 baud and a sound generator operating at 3 kHz. Due to its timing, the software serial port will be required to execute 1200 times a second, and the tone generator function will be required to execute at 6000 a second. While a common state machine could be created to handle the two different functions, the overhead and timing problems make separate tasks a simpler solution. So, separating the two functions is a more efficient solution. However, if the two functions are mutually exclusive, then the complexity in the timing functions is alleviated, and the two functions could be combined. The timing for the task would then depend upon which function is currently operating, with the task itself switching the timing as needed for the two functions.

- *Software functions with different priorities*

    Just as with the previous criterion concerning timing, functions with different priorities should also be separated into different tasks. If two functions with differing priorities were to be combined into a single task, the decision of whether to execute the task or not would have to take into account the current function being performed by the task state machine. It would also require that some of the state transitions within the state machine might have to include additional input from the priority handler. This would unnecessarily complicate both the priority handler and the state machine, and any savings in program memory due to the combined overhead could be consumed in the more complicated coding of state machine and the priority handler. So, while it is recommended that the functions should reside in separate tasks, it is up to the designer to weigh any potential savings against the increased complexity.

■ *Software functions that operate as subfunctions to other tasks*
Just as common routines in a linear program can be written as a single subroutine and called from two or more places in the program, a subroutine task can be used in a similar fashion by other tasks. While the optimal solution for minimal program memory would have been to combine the subfunction and both calling functions into a common task, incompatibilities between the calling functions may not allow that option. Breaking the subroutine function out into a separate task, which can then be called by the calling tasks, may be preferable to duplicating the function in both controlling tasks, even with the added overhead of a separate task. Separating the subfunction into a separate task will also alleviate any problems with arbitrating control of the subfunction.

■ *Software functions that operate intermittently*
One of the priority management systems, described later in this book, makes use of the fact that some tasks only need to be active intermittently. If a function is not needed full time, then from the standpoint of efficient use of processing time, it makes sense to only call the function when it is needed. So part-time functions are good candidates for this type of priority control, provided the function is separated into its own task. Note, this does not preclude the combination of two or more intermittent functions into a common task, provided the functions are either synchronous or mutually exclusive in operation.

One or more additional tasks may also be required to handle error conditions within the system. These tasks typically monitor the error condition of the various other tasks in the system and coordinate the recovery from all errors. For example, if a serial input task detects an error in an incoming packet, an error-handler task may have to perform several different functions to clear the error:

1. Reset the serial input task to clear the error.

2. Notify the sender of the current packet of data that an error has occurred.

3. Reset any tasks that might be in the process of operating on the serial data.

4. Reset any data buffer between the tasks.

In addition, the order of the sequence used to clear the error may be critical as well, so building this functionality into a separate error-handling task gives the system the flexibility to handle the error outside the normal operation of the other tasks, especially if the response to the error requires the cooperation of more than one task. Complex systems may even require multiple error-handling tasks if the potential exists for more than one type of error to occur asynchronously. The designer should review the list of potential errors and list all the required recovery mechanisms. Then group them like the software functions in the previous section and apply the criteria for compatible and incompatible functions. Don't be surprised if the list of tasks grows by two or more tasks by the time the evaluation is complete.

Once all the software functions and error recovery functions have been placed in a circle of compatible functions, a final descriptive name for each task/circle can be decided, and a Task list can be compiled. The list should include the name and descriptions of the individual functions in each task, plus any special reasons for including the functions in the task, or excluding it from another task.

Once the list is complete, it should be included in the design notes for the project. Again, be complete in documenting the task list, and be verbose. When the documentation is complete, it should look something like the following:

List 3.5

```
TASK LIST FOR THE ALARM CLOCK PROJECT
Task1      Display
  a)       Function to scan LED displays
  b)       12 hour display function for time
  c)       24 hour display function for time
  d)       12 hour display function for alarm
  e)       24 hour display function for alarm
  f)       PM indicator display function
  g)       Alarm on indicator display function
  h)       Display flashing function for the alarm
  i)       Display blanking function for operation from
           internal clock time base

Task2      TimeBase
  a)       Time increment function based on 60Hz power
           line time base
  b)       Time increment function based on internal
           clock time base
  c)       60-Hz monitoring function
  d)       60-Hz Fail/Recovery monitoring function

Task3      Buttons
  a)       Control input monitoring function
  b)       Debounce function
  c)       Auto repeat function
  d)       Command Decode function (combined SetAlarm
           and SetTime functions)
  e)       Routine to increment alarm by 1 min
  f)       Routine to increment alarm by 20 min
  g)       Routine to increment Time by 1 min
  h)       Routine to increment Time by 20 min
  i)       Toggle 12/24 hour mode
  j)       Alarm on/off toggling function
  k)       Activate Snooze

Task4      AlarmControl
  a)       An alarm control function
  b)       Snooze function

Task5      AlarmTone
  a)       Generate alarm tone function

Task6      Error Task
```

The decisions that lead to this combination of functions and tasks are listed below:

List 3.6

TASK1 DISPLAY

1. The function which scans the LED displays seems to be the primary function of this task.

2. All of the displays functions use a common peripheral with the LED display scanning function.

3. The 12/24 hour display functions for the alarm and current time drive a common aspect of a peripheral, the numeric LED display.

4. The 12/24 hour display functions for the alarm and current time are mutually exclusive in operation.

TASK2 TIMEBASE

1. The 60-Hz monitoring function seems to be the driving function of this task.

2. Both time base increment functions and the failure/recover monitoring function are extensions of the 60-Hz monitoring function.

3. The 60-Hz time increment function executes sequentially following the 60-Hz monitoring function.

4. The internal clock increment function is mutually exclusive in operation to the 60-Hz increment function, and the control of both functions is via the failure/recover monitoring function.

5. The failure/recover monitoring function is executed sequentially after the 60-Hz monitoring function.

6. Both the 60-Hz time increment function and the internal time base increment function control a common variable, the current time.

→
List 3.6
(continued)

TASK3 BUTTONS

1. The control input monitoring function is seen as the overall function of this task.

2. The debounce function is executed under the control of the control input monitoring function.

3. The auto-repeat function is an extension of the debounce function.

4. The command decode function, a combination of the set alarm and set timer functions, is executed sequentially after the debounce and auto-repeat functions.

5. The four alarm and time increment function perform nearly identical functions on the alarm and current time variables, denoting common functionality.

6. The four alarm and time increment functions mutually exclusive in operation.

7. The four alarm and time increment functions, plus the 12/24 hour toggle function, and the alarm on/off function are executed sequentially following the command decode function.

Note: In this example, it proved to be more efficient not only to combine the alarm and time set functions in a common task, but to also combine the SetTime, and SetAlarm functions into a common function within the task.

TASK4 ALARM CONTROL

1. Both the alarm control and snooze functions control two common peripheral functions, the display and the tone generator function.

2. Both the alarm control and snooze functions have common functionality in the form of the alarm / current time comparison function.

→
**List 3.6
(continued)**

TASK5 ALARMTONE

1. Looking toward the priority control section of the design, the tone generation function is isolated into a separate task due to its intermittent operation.

2. Two functions within the alarm control task control this function, so a separate task will allow arbitration, if needed.

TASK6 ERROR

This task is separate for control of other tasks.

So we have five separate tasks, with one additional task for error handling. All the tasks were generated using the same criteria listed previously, for compatible and incompatible functions. With the compilation of the final task list, this completes the task definition at the system-level design. The final task list, with the rationale behind the decisions, should be copied into the system design notes, and any changes or addendum to the requirements list should be made at this time.

Communications

The next step in the system level of the design is to map out the communications between the various tasks and peripherals in the system. This accomplishes a couple of things for the design: one, it helps provide the designer with a rough estimate on the amount of data memory that the system will require and, two, it defines all of the variables in the system, which is not specific to a task so they can be defined in a common header file. And, three, it provides a quick check for a very troublesome systemic communications problem called *state lock*.

The method employed to generate the communications plan is graphical, just like the method used in the task definition phase of the system-level design. The type of diagram used to map out the communications pathways is called a *data flow diagram*. It consists of a collection of circles 1–2 inch circles, each circle representing a peripheral or task within the system. The circles will be the sources and destinations for information moving around the system. Between the circle are arrows that represent the data pathways along which the information will flow.

The direction of the arrow indicates the direction of the data flow. The resulting diagram should show graphically all the communications between the various tasks within the system. Any significant data storage associated with the various tasks are also noted on the diagram. A variable list and dictionary is then compiled, based on the information in the data flow diagram. The resulting documentation will then form the basis of all system-level variable definitions in the next chapters. So, designers are encouraged to be as accurate as possible in both the diagram and the resulting variable documentation. Note: The usefulness of the data flow diagram does not end once the variable list and dictionary is completed. It also a graphical representation of all system-level data storage that is a convenient reference diagram during the component and implementation phases of the design.

To start the diagram, take large piece of paper and draw a 2–3 inch circle for each of the tasks and peripherals in the system. Try to evenly space the circles on the entire sheet, with as much space between the circles as possible. Note: Don't try to optimize the placement of the circle at this point in the design, as the diagram will be revised at least once during the course of this exercise. Just make sure that there is a circle for each source and destination for data in the system. Then, label each circle with the name of its associated task or peripheral.

For systems that link two or more subsystems by communications pathways, place circles in the diagram for the tasks in both systems. Separate them on the diagram, with a boundary line to show the separation of the two systems, and label the tasks charged with communications between the systems. A short heavy line is used to indicate the system-to-system communications pathway.

Once all the circles have been placed on the diagram, use the communications information from requirements document dissection and the function listing in the task list, to draw arrows between the circles to represent information passed between the various tasks and peripherals. The arrows denote the various task-to-task and task-to-peripheral communication pathways. Start the arrow at the circle representing the task, which contains the sending function, and place the head of the arrow on the circle representing the task, which contains the receiving function. Each of the arrows should then be labeled with a name descriptive of the information being passed along the pathway. See Figure 3.3 for an example of a data flow diagram for our alarm clock project.

Note: The direction of the arrow should indicate the direction of the information flow. Some data pathways may have handshaking flags, which will pass in both directions as part of their communication. However, the direction of the arrow in this diagram is to indicate the direction of the actual communications, so even though handshaking may return, the direction of interest is the direction in which information is actually moving.

For pathways that transfer information from one sending task to multiple receiving tasks, start each pathway arrow at the same point on the sending task's circle to indicate that the same information is being sent to multiple destinations. Then, place the head of each arrow on the circle of each receiving task. Figure 3.3a shows this form of data pathway. It is also acceptable to branch an arrow off from an existing arrow, partway down its length. In fact, a very handy method of showing the distribution of data from one task to multiple other tasks is to create pseudo distribution bus in the diagram, originating at the sending task, with arrows branching off to the receiving tasks as it passes near. Our only purpose here is to clearly indicate that multiple receivers are listening to a common sending task. There are no hard and fast rules to the diagram, and the designer is encouraged to generate whatever form of short hand is convenient.

In the very likely event that the diagram starts to become cluttered and confusing, try overwriting the pathways with different color pens to distinguish one pathway from another in the diagram. Be careful not to overwrite two crossing pathways with the same color as this will only add to the confusion. Also, make sure that pathway arrows only cross at right angles, to further reduce confusion.

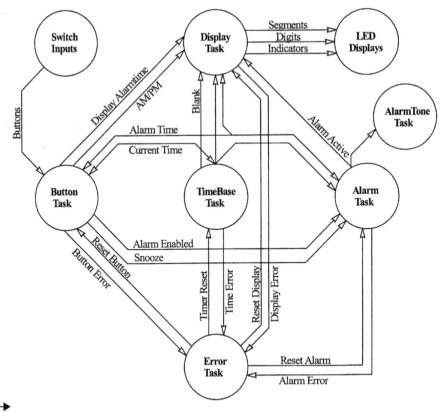

Figure 3.3   *Alarm Clock Data Flow Diagram.*

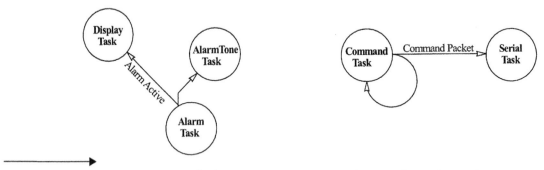

Figure 3.3a   *One Source, Multiple Destinations.*   **Figure 3.3b**   *Storage Loop.*

If the diagram becomes too cluttered or confusing, it is perfectly acceptable to redraw it on a larger piece of paper and relocate the circles that are causing the problem. Remember, I did say that we would be redrawing this diagram at least once, and probably more than once. Plus, after making a few of the pathway connections, the designer will have a better feel for where the task and peripheral circles should be located to simplify the connections. Just remember to follow same procedure and verify that no pathways are inadvertently left off the diagram.

The next step is to label each data pathway with a name and a general description of the data moving along the pathway. If the diagram is sufficiently large, this information can be noted along the length of the data pathway arrow. If, on the other hand, the diagram is too convoluted or cramped, it is also acceptable to legend the arrow with a number and then build a list with the information. Particularly for larger systems, this method is typically easier to manage, and it also lends itself to electronic documentation better than trying to place the text along the arrow in the diagram.

Once all the data pathways between tasks are documented, it is time to add the information related to significant data storage. This information was gathered at the end of the communications section of the requirements document dissection. To show the storage required by the individual tasks, draw an arrow from the task associated with the storage, wrap it around 180 degrees, and place the head on the same task. Then label the loop with a name indicating the nature of the storage. Use the same form of notation used in the last section when describing task-to-task pathways.

In the event that the information is also passed to another task, start the tail of the arrow at the same point on the circle as the arrow leading to the other task, and then loop the arrow around just like the other storage arrows. Label both the loop and the arrow with the same name to show that the information is local storage and a data pathway. Figure 3.3b demonstrates an example of a storage loop.

When the diagram is complete, the designer should go back through the information from the requirements document dissection to verify that all task inputs and outputs have connections to other tasks. The designer should also review the function and task lists to verify that new connections have also been made. Often in the process of task definition, new communications pathways may be created, but through an oversight, the information was not back-annotated to the requirements document. Checking the function and task lists should catch these missed pathways. Note: The designer is strongly discouraged from skipping over this step as it is a valuable check on the design of the tasks as well as the communications layout of the system.

Unconnected pathways can indicate any one of a number of system design problems:

- The inadvertent generation of redundant data.

- Missing data that must be generated.

- An omission in the task list documentation.

- Or, even a failure in the designer's understanding of the operation of the system.

In any event, the problem should be identified and corrected before continuing on with the design and the affected documentation should also be revised to include the corrections. And yes, the function and task lists, *as well as* the requirements document should be updated.

Once all questions have been resolved and the documentation updated, the diagram should be redrawn one last time in a single color of ink with related peripherals and tasks grouped together so that the pathway arrows are reasonably straight and easy to follow. The diagram should also leave plenty of room for the addition of new pathways. And there will be additional data pathways generated as the design evolves. No design methodology, regardless of how methodical, can accurately predict every possible need in advance. A good methodology though, should be sufficiently adaptable to handle new requirements as the project progresses.

Next, make a list of all the data pathways, prioritizing the list by name of the pathway and the name of the sending task. For pathways with multiple destinations or sources, make a single entry in the list, but list all sources and destinations for the pathway. For each pathway, note the type of data to be transferred, whether the storage is static or dynamic, plus the estimated width and storage requirements. This information should have come from the dissection of the requirements document earlier in this chapter. The designers should take their time in the generation of this list, making it as comprehensive as possible, as the list will be the basis for the final variable dictionary and the header file that will declare the variables used for communications. For dynamic variables, make a note of any estimates made concerning input and output data rates as well.

Once the preliminary list is complete, it is time to assign an appropriate data transfer protocol to each pathway. The protocol used, either broadcast, semaphore, or buffer, will depend on the needs of the pathway and the speeds of the sending and receiving tasks. If in doubt about the operation of the protocols, the designer is encouraged to review the protocol definitions in Chapter 2 before continuing with the design.

How do we determine which protocol is the right one for a given data path? Each protocol has specific advantages and limitations. The buffer protocol has the ability to cache data between fast and slow senders and receivers, but has difficulty with more than one receiving task. The semaphore protocol transfers not only information but also event timing information. However, it can introduce state lock problems if a circular link of pathways in generated. And the broadcast protocol is useful for sending data from one or more senders, to one or more receivers, but it does not transfer event timing. The secret is to match the needs of the pathway to the correct protocol.

The best place to start is with the pathways that were identified as needing dynamic. Because this type of storage is variable, it is best implemented with a buffer type of protocol. The buffer handles variable-length storage well, and the circular storage format allows the sending task to start a second message, prior to the receiving task completing the first message. The only exception to this recommendation is for those pathways that use dynamic for the transmission of a single variable, such as a command flag. Leave these pathways unassigned for now.

Once the pathways using dynamic storage are identified, overwrite them with a green pencil or marker to identify them as buffer protocol pathways.

The next group of pathways to identify are those that need to include event-timing information as part of their data transmission. These pathways will typically fall into a couple of categories:

- *Commands*: data that initiate an activity by the system; this is typically a user-initiated command or request from external to the system.

- *Events*: an event within the system requiring a response or action be taken in response to the event. This could be a flag indicating that a critical temperature or time has been reached.

- *Changes*: a notification to the system that some important parameter has changed and the system must respond in some fashion. For example, a notification from one task to another that it has completed a its task and a common resource is now available for use.

The semaphore protocol is typically used for these pathways due to its ability to transmit both data and event timing information. The very nature of handshaking requires that both the sending and receiving tasks must temporarily synchronize their operation to complete the transfer. So, it makes the protocol invaluable for not only making sure the receiving task has current information, but also for making the receiving task aware that the current data has changed. Data pathways using the semaphore protocol should be overwritten using a red pencil or marker in the data flow diagram to identify them as semaphore protocols.

The remaining data pathways can be assigned the broadcast protocol. These pathways should be static, and should not require event timing information as part of the transfer. Pathways with multiple destinations should also use the broadcast protocol, due to the complexity involved in handshaking between multiple a sender and multiple receiving tasks. These will typically be system or task-specific status information within the system. For example, the current time in our alarm clock design should use a broadcast protocol. This is because the various tasks within the system will either not need to know each and every change in the current time. Or the receiving tasks can poll the current time with sufficient speed to see any changes with out the need for an event timing information. Finally, overwrite all the broadcast protocol pathways in the data flow diagram with a blue pencil or marker to identify them.

Once protocols have been assigned and identified by color on the data flow diagram, the diagram should be examined to determine if a potential state lock condition is possible. To find this systemic problem, follow each Semaphore pathway, head to tail, from task to task, to determine whether any combination of pathways will produce a complete loop. If they do, then the system is potentially susceptible to a state lock condition. Be sure to check not only pathways within the design, but also pathways that may travel over a communications link into another system. This is the reason that the data flow diagram of multiple linked systems must be drawn on a common diagram.

In a state lock condition, two cross-coupled tasks have both initiated a semaphore data transfer to the other before recognizing the each other's transfer request. This can be between two adjacent tasks, or it can happen between two tasks that have several intermediate tasks between them. The only requirement is that all pathways that form the circle must be semaphore, as it is the handshaking nature of the semaphore that causes the problem.

Because both tasks in a state lock condition have sent data and are now waiting for the other to acknowledge the transfer, they have become locked, perpetually waiting for the other to respond. But, because they themselves are waiting, the condition cannot be resolved. Once in the state lock condition, the only remedy is to break the protocol for one of the transfers.

There are several methods to recover from state lock; however, the best solution is simply to avoid the condition in the first place. The first step is to recognize the possibility. Graphically representing the communications in the system makes this very easy; any complete loop formed exclusively by semaphore communications has the potential to exhibit state lock. The next step is to simply break the circle by replacing one of the semaphore pathways with either a broadcast or a buffer protocol. Even a buffer protocol with only a two-variable storage capability is sufficient to break the cycle. All that has to happen is that one of the two tasks must have the ability to initiate a transfer and then continue on executing within the task. Eventually, the task will notice the other transfer and complete it, breaking the lock.

If all of the pathways in a circular link must be semaphore due to the nature of the software functions in the tasks, then the designer should back up one step and determine if the specific combination of functions is actually necessary. Often, by simply moving a function from one task to another, one or more of the semaphore pathways will shift to a different task and the circle will be broken. Designers should remember that a design need not be fixed at the end of each step; sometimes a decision early in the design leads to a configuration that simply won't work. When this happens, take the design back a step or two in the methodology and try something different. Because the design notes for the design detail every decision in the process, it is a simple process to back up and take the design in a different direction to avoid a problem.

If the problem can't be avoided, the designer need not despair, there are other solutions for avoiding, recognizing, and recovering from state lock conditions. Unfortunately, they are not as simple as just changing a protocol, and they will require some additional overhead in the design, so the discussion on their operation will be tabled until the component phase of the design. For now, the designer should note the problem on the data flow diagram, so it can be addressed in a later phase of the design.

Once all of the potential state lock conditions have been addressed, the variable list should be updated with the selection of communications protocol. Any pathways that still have the potential for state lock should be identified and highlighted with a note concerning corrective action later in the design. The variable list for our alarm clock example is included following, with its associated data flow diagram (Figure 3.4).

Table 3.3

PRELIMINARY COMMUNICATONS VARIABLE LIST

Variable	Source	Destination	Number & Size	Type	Protocol
• Current_Time	TimeBase Buttons	Display Alarm	6 BCD nibbles	static	Broadcast
• Alarm_time	Alarm	Display Buttons	4 BCD nibbles	static	Broadcast
• Blank	TimeBase	Display	flag	static	Broadcast
• Alarm_enabled	Buttons	Alarm Display	flag	static	Broadcast
• Alarm_active	Alarm	Display Alarm_tone	flag	static	Broadcast
• Snooze	Button	Alarm	flag	static	Semaphore
• AMPM_mode	Button	Display	flag	static	Broadcast
• Display_alarm	Button	Display	flag	static	Broadcast
• Segments	Display	LEDs	7 bit word	static	Broadcast
• Digits	Display	LEDs	6 bit word	static	Broadcast
• Indicators	Display	LEDs	2 flags	static	Broadcast
• Command buttons	Switches	Button	6 flags	static	Broadcast
• Time_error	Timebase	Error	flag	static	Broadcast
• Alarm_error	Alarm	Error	flag	static	Broadcast
• Display_error	Display	Error	flag	static	Broadcast
• Button_error	Button	Error	flag	static	Broadcast
• Reset_time	Error	Timebase	flag	static	Semaphore
• Reset_alarm	Error	Alarm	flag	static	Semaphore
• Reset_button	Error	button	flag	static	Semaphore
• Reset_display	Error	display	flag	static	Semaphore

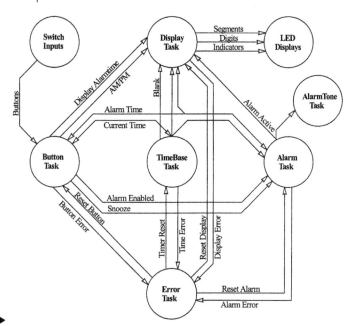

Figure 3.4   *Alarm Clock Data Flow Diagram.*

There are several interesting things to note about the variable list compiled for our alarm clock example. One, all of the variables are static, even though several dynamic variables were identified in the requirements document dissection. This is because the dynamic storage was needed for communications between functions that were later combined into a single task. As a result, the sending and receiving functions are now operating at the same speed and no longer need dynamic storage to communicate. Two, there are no pathways using a buffer protocol in the list; this is because the only multibyte data transfers in the system are the time and alarm time values and they are a parallel transfer. And three, there are only five pathways that use a semaphore protocol. This is because the designer chose to put most of the user's commands in the same task with the button test, debounce and command decoder. As a result, the only communications requiring event-timing information are the snooze command and the error reset flags from the error task.

Timing Analysis

One of the key points in this design methodology is that it must generate real-time programming. So, it follows that the analysis of the system's timing requirements should be part of the systems design. In this section, we will examine the timing requirements of each of the software functions in the various tasks, and from this information, determine a timing system that will meet the systems needs.

The first step is to list all the timing specifications from the requirements document. Note, if the functions grouped into a task have different requirements, then the specifications for each function should be included separately. Now is also a good time to review the reasons for combining the function to verify that they should really be in a common task.

In the example shown following, the timing requirements for our alarm clock design example are listed. Entries for both the event-to-event timing and response timing are included in the time domain. If the timing requirement is listed in the form of a frequency, it should be converted to the time domain at this time for easier comparison with the other timing requirements.

——————————▶

List 3.7

```
Task1    Display
         360Hz +20/-0    2.635 - 2.777mS
         Alarm flash     0-50mS following time update (1Hz)
                         50% duty cycle +/-10%
         Blank           909.9mS to 1111.1mS +/-0 overall
         Sync to Time update
         Response to Blank 8mS maximum


Task2    TimeBase
         1sec +/-0 overall relative to internal or 60Hz
         timebase switchover must occur within 8mS of pres-
         ence or absence of 5th pulse


Task3    Buttons
         Button bounce is 100mS
         Debounce is 50mS
         Response to decoded command 34mS maximum
         Auto Repeat 909.9mS to 1111.1mS +/-0 overall
         Sync to time update 0-50mS following time update


Task4    AlarmControl
         Alarm response to time increment, 100mS maximum
         including tone startup
         Snooze response time 50mS including tone shutoff


Task5    AlarmTone
         Alarm Tone     .454mS min, .5mS typ, .555mS max
         Modulation     454mS min, 500mS typ, 555mS max
                        event to event
                        492mS min, 500mS typ, 510mS max
                        overall
Task6    Error Task
         no timing specified.
```

From this information an overall timing chart for the individual tasks of the system can be compiled. This should list all optimum, minimum, and maximum timing values for both event-to-event and response timing requirements. Any notes concerning exceptions to the timing requirement should also be included.

	Minimum	Optimum	Maximum
Task1			
scan	2.635	2.777	2.777
flash response	0.000	25.000	50.000
flash offtime	450.000	500.000	550.000
blank	909.900	1000.000	1111.100
blank response	0.000	4.000	8.000
Task2			
timebase	1000.000	1000.000	1000.000
switch response	0.000	4.000	8.000
Task3			
bounce	100.000	100.000	100.000
debounce	0.000	25.000	50.000
command	0.000	17.000	34.000
autorepeat	909.900	1000.000	1111.100
aoutr response	0.000	25.000	50.000
Task4			
time response	0.000	50.000	100.000
snooze response	0.000	25.000	50.000
Task5			
tone	0.454	0.500	0.555
var modulation	454.000	500.000	555.000
modulation	492.000	500.000	510.000

Table 3.4

Note: all values in milliseconds

All the information needed to determine the system *tick* is now present. The system tick is the maximum common time increment, which fits the timing requirements of all the tasks in the system. The tick chosen must be the largest increment of time that will be divided into all of the timing requirements an integer number of times. While this sounds simple, it seldom is in practice. Timing requirements are seldom integer multiples of each other, so the only solution is to choose a tick that fits most of the requirements, and fits within the tolerance of all the rest. When a suitable tick is found, it should be noted in large letters at the bottom of the chart. This number is the heartbeat of the system and will be at the very center of all timing decisions from this point on.

The best tick for our alarm clock is 250 microseconds.

Sometimes even the tolerances on the timing specifications will not allow a reasonable size tick that will fit every requirement. When this happens, the designer is left with a limited number of options:

1. The designer can review the timing requirements for the system, looking for values that can be changed without changing the operation of the system. Timing requirements for display scanning, keyboard scanning, tone generation, and others maybe a matter of esthetics rather than an externally imposed requirement. The only real requirement may only be that they have consistent timing. If the timing for one of these functions is the hard to fit value, experiment with the timing requirements for these functions. Often this will suggest other tick increments that may fit within the requirements of all the functions. For example, the timing for the scanning routine in our example is 2.635 ms to 2.777 ms. However, if it were reduced to 2.5 ms for the minimum, then the system Tick could be increased from 250 µS to 500 µS. This still scans the displays at a greater than 60-Hz rate, so no flicker would be introduced.

2. The second option is to consider moving some of the more difficult to accommodate tasks to a timer-based interrupt. The interrupt can be configured to operate at a faster rate that accommodates the difficult tasks, and frees up the balance of the tasks to operate at a different rate. Note: if a task is moved to an interrupt, communications to and from the task will require either a semaphore or buffer protocol. This is because the task will be completely asynchronous to the other tasks, much as the tasks in a preemptive operating system. So, additional handshaking is required to prevent the transmission of partially updated communications variables, in the event that the timer interrupt falls in the middle of a task's update. More information concerning the use of interrupts is available in Chapter 5.

3. The third option is to consider using a tick that is smaller than the smallest task timing increment. Sometimes, using a tick that is 1/2 or 1/3 of the smallest task timing increment will create

integer multiples for hard to accommodate tasks. Note, this option will decrease the time available in each pass of the system and increase the scheduling job for the priority handler, so it is not generally recommended. If fact, the original tick value of 250 μS was obtained using this option. However, shifting the display timing would eliminate the need for a smaller tick, so it was chosen instead.

At this point there should also be a quick mention of the system clock. Once the system tick has been determined, a hardware mechanism within the microcontroller will be needed to measure it accurately. Typically, this job falls to one of the system's hardware timers. The timers in small microcontrollers usually have the option to either run from a dedicated crystal oscillator or from the main microcontroller oscillator. If a dedicated oscillator is available, then the oscillator frequency must be set at a 256 multiple of the desired system tick frequency. In our example, that would be 512 kHz, or 256 times 1/.5 ms. If the system clock is employed, a pre- or postscaler will be needed to allow the system clock to operate in the megahertz range. Assuming a prescaler based on powers of two, that means a 1.024 MHz, 2.048 MHz, 4.096 MHz, 8.192 MHz, or 16.384 MHz oscillator. If none of these options are available, then an interrupt routine can be built around the timer, for the purposes of preloading the timer with a countdown value. This value is chosen so that the timer will overflow at the same rate as the desired tick. Note that an interrupt routine is needed for this job because there will very probably be task combinations that will periodically overrun the system tick. An interrupt routine is the only way to guarantee a consistent time delay between the roll-over and the preload of the timer. For our example, we will use a 4.096-MHz main system clock and a divide-by-8 prescaler to generate the appropriate timer roll-over rate for our system tick, and avoid the interrupt option.

Once a suitable timing tick is chosen, the skip rates for all of the system tasks can be calculated. This value will be used by software timers which will hold off execution of the state machine associated with the task, for X number of cycles. This slows the execution of the state machine, so its operation is within its desired timing. Using the timing information from our alarm clock design, and assuming the modified Task1 scan timing, the following table is constructed.

Table 3.5

	Optimum	Skip Rate	
Task1			
scan	2.500	5	
flash response	25.000	50	(100)
flash offtime	500.000	1000	(1100)
blank	1000.000	2000	(2222)
blank response	4.000	8	(16)
Task2			
timebase	1000.000	2000	
switch response	4.000	8	(16)
Task3			
bounce	100.000	200	
debounce	25.000	50	(100)
command	17.000	34	(68)
autorepeat	1000.000	2000	(2222)
aoutr response	25.000	50	(100)
Task4			
time response	50.000	100	(200)
snooze response	25.000	50	(100)
Task5			
tone	0.500	1	
var modulation	500.000	1000	(1110)
modulation	500.000	1000	(1020)

Note the values in parentheses following the skip rates. These are the skip rates for the maximum times. Assuming that the optimum time is not the maximum, then these values constitute the amount of leeway that is still available in the task's timing. We noted this information for its potential use later in the design, when we define the priority handlers.

Up to this point in the design, we have assumed that the system would use a rigid timing system that regulates the timing of the software loop holding the task state machines. However, there is another option for systems that are not required to comply with specific timing requirements. The option is to run the system without a timing control. By far, the first option using a rigid timing control is the most common.

However, in rare instances, when the timing tolerances are very broad or nonexistent, the second option can be implemented. Now as a designer, you may ask, "What is the advantage to a completely unregulated system and what possible design could possibly operate without some regulation?" The truth is, no system can operate completely without timing regulation, but some systems can operate by only regulating the functions that actually require specific timing. The other tasks in the system are run at the maximum speed of the main system loop.

For example, consider a simple user interface terminal with a display and keyboard. Button presses on the keyboard result in ASCII data being sent to the host system, and data received from the host is scanned onto the display. The only functions in the system that require specific timing are the serial transmit and receive functions interfacing with the host system. The display and keyboard scanning rates only have to comply with a reasonable minimum scanning rate. In this example, the serial input and output tasks are typically regulated by the baud rate of the serial interface. The control, display scanning, and keyboard scanning tasks could then be run at the fastest rate possible given the microcontroller clock frequency. The rate at which these three tasks operate would be variable, based on the execution time of each task on each pass through the system loop. However, as long as the minimum scanning rates are achieved, the system should operate properly.

The advantage to this type of system is that it operates more efficiently and more quickly than regulated systems. There is no dead time at the end of each cycle as the system waits for the next tick; the system just jumps back to the top of the loop and starts into the next task. This saves program memory, complexity, and it means that every available system instruction cycle is used to perform a system function. As a result, the system is very efficient, and will outperform a more rigidly regulated system. The only down side is that the tasks within the loop cannot use the loop timing to regulate their operation. Instead, they must rely on hardware-based timer systems for accurate timing.

The major downside to this system is that it requires a hardware timer for every software-timed function, and only works well for systems with few, if any, routines with strict timing requirements.

Priority Handler

So far in this chapter, we have gathered together the various priority requirements and used them to define the system's modes. This covers the majority of the work at this level of the design. The only additional work is to update the table with the information from the task definition performed earlier in the chapter. Basically, we need to rewrite the priority list and the criteria for mode change list using the task names. We also need to note any functions that should be disabled by a specific system mode.

So, to review the information from the requirements document dissection, we have defined the following list of system modes:

- *Timekeeping mode*: Current time display, alarm is disabled, no commands are in progress, and normal power.

- *Time set mode*: Current time display, alarm is disabled, normal power, and time set commands are in operation.

- *Alarm pending mode*: Current time display, alarm is enabled, normal power, no commands in progress, and alarm is not active.

- *Alarm set mode*: Alarm time display, normal power, alarm set commands are in operation, and alarm is not active.

- *Alarm active mode*: Flashing display of current time, alarmed is enabled, alarm is active, no commands in progress, and normal power.

- *Snooze mode*: Current display time, alarm is enabled, snooze is in progress, and normal power.

- *Power fail mode*: Display is blank, internal time base in operation, alarm is inhibited, and battery supplied power.

Replacing the individual functions with the tasks that now incorporate the functions, we have the following priority list:

Table 3.6

System Mode	High Priority	Med Priority	Low Priority
Timekeeping mode	Time Base Task	Display Task	Button Task Error Task
Time set mode	Button Task	Display Task	Time Base Task Error Task
Alarm pending mode	Time Base Task Alarm Control Task	Display Task	Button Task Error Task
Alarm set mode	Button Task Time Base Task	Display Task	Error Task
Alarm active mode	Time Base Task Alarm Tone Task Alarm Control Task	Display Task	Button Task Error Task
Snooze mode	Time Base Task Alarm Control Task	Display Task	Button Task Error Task
Power fail mode	Time Base Task	Display Task	Error Task
Error mode	Error Task Time Base Task	Display Task	Button Task

There are several interesting things to note about the new priority list. Many of the newly defined tasks include both low- and high-priority functions. This means that some tasks can be classified as either low, mid, or high priority. When compiling the table, always list the task only once, and at its highest priority. When we get to the implementation of the priority handler, we can adjust the task priority based on the value in the state variable, if needed.

Also, note that some of the functions do not change in priority. For example, the display task is always a medium priority. Other tasks do shift in priority based on the system mode; they may appear and disappear, like the alarm tone and alarm control tasks, or they may just move up or down as the button and time base tasks do.

Once the priority list has been updated to reflect the task definition information, we also have to perform a quick sanity check on the criteria for changing the system modes. To be able to change mode, it make sense that the task charged with providing the information that triggers the change must be active before the change can occur. What we want to do at this point is review each criterion, checking that the task providing the trigger for the change is in fact active in the original mode. If not, then the priority list needs to be updated to include the task, typically at a mid or low level of priority. For example, using our alarm clock design example:

Table 3.7

Original mode	Next mode	Trigger event
Powered down	Error	Initial power up
Error	Time set	Press of the TIME SET button
Error	Alarm set	Press of the ALARM SET button
Timekeeping	Time set	Press of the TIME SET button
Timekeeping	Alarm set	Press of the ALARM SET button
Time set	Timekeeping	Release of the TIME SET button
Alarm set	Timekeeping	Release of the ALARM SET button
Timekeeping	Alarm Pending	Alarm Control Switch to enabled
Alarm Pending	Timekeeping	Alarm Control Switch to disabled
Alarm Active	Timekeeping	Alarm Control Switch to disabled
Alarm Pending	Alarm Active	Alarm time = Current time
Alarm Active	Snooze	Snooze Command
Snooze	Alarm Active	Alarm time + snooze time = Current time
{all modes}	Power Fail	5th consecutive missing 60-Hz pulse
Power Fail	Timekeeping	5th consecutive 60-Hz pulse
{all modes}	Error	Error condition

In each of the original modes, the task responsible for providing the trigger, whether it is a button press or missing time base pulses, must be active at some priority level to provide the necessary triggering event. If the task is not active, then the system will hang in the mode with no means to exit. Note that there may be instances in which the response time requirement for a system mode change requires a higher priority for the task providing the mode change trigger. If so, then both system priority and timing requirements may have to shift in order to accommodate a faster response. Make sure to note the reason for the change in priority and timing in the design notes and adjust the priority list accordingly.

Once all the priority information has been cataloged and the necessary task trigger event information verified, copy both the priority list and the list of criteria for making a system mode change into the design notes for the system. Include any information relating the changes made to the design and list any options that were discarded and why they were discarded. Be clear and be verbose; any question you can answer in the text will save you time explaining the choices later when the support group takes over the design.

Error Recovery

So far in our design of the system, we have touched on a few error detection and recovery systems. These include error and default states for the task state machines, a system error task to handle errors that affect more than one task, and a definition of the severity of several system-level failures. In fact, one of the primary software functions in the design of the alarm clock is the automatic switch over to an internal time base if the 60-Hz time base stops; this is also an example of an error detection and recovery system.

What we have to do now is define how these faults will be handled and what tasks will be affected by the recovery systems. In our dissection of the requirements documents, we define soft, recoverable, and hard errors for the system:

List 3.8

Soft Fault

Fault: Button pressed is not valid for current mode or command.

Press of SLOWSET without FASTSET, ALARMSET, or TIMESET held.

Press of SNOOZE when not in alarm active mode.

Press of any key in power fail mode.

Test: Comparison of decoded button command with legal commands, by mode.

Response: Ignore button press.

List 3.8
(continued)

Soft Fault

Fault: Button combination is invalid.

Press of SNOOZE with FASTSET, SLOWSET, ALARM-SET, TIMESET.

Press of ALARMSET with TIMESET.

Test: Checked against acceptable combinations in command function.

Response: Ignore button press.

Recoverable Fault

Fault: Alarm time is out of range (Alarm time > 23:59).

Test: Alarm control function test of value before current time comparison.

Response: If alarm is enabled, sound alarm until ALARMSET button press.

If in any other mode, ignore (fault will be identified when alarm is enabled).

Recoverable Fault

Fault: Power failure.

Test: 5th missing 60-Hz time base pulse.

Response: Goto power fail mode until 5th detected 60-Hz pulse.

Hard Fault

Fault: Watchdog timer timeout, brownout reset.

Test: Hardware supervisor circuits.

Response: System is reset. If BOR, then system held in reset until power is restored.

System will power up in error mode.

We now need to add any new faults that have come to light during the course of the design. These include error conditions within the state machines, or any communications errors between the tasks. We also need to decide on recovery mechanisms, the scope of their control, and whether the recovery system resides in the state machine, or the error task state machine.

Let's start with a few examples. Consider a state variable range fault in the display task state machine. The detection mechanism is a simple range check on the state variables, and the recovery mechanism is to reset the state variable. Because the display task is a control end point, meaning it only accepts control and does not direct action in another task, the scope of control for the recovery mechanism is limited to the task state machine. As a result, it makes sense that the recovery mechanism can be included within the state machine and will not require coordination with recovery mechanisms in other tasks.

A fault in the time base task, however, could have ramifications that extend beyond the task state machine. For example, if the state machine performs a routine check on the current time and determines that the value is out of range, then the recovery mechanism will have to coordinate with other tasks to recover from the fault. If the alarm control task is active, it may need to suspend any currently active alarm condition until after the current time value is reset by the user. The display task will have to display the fact that the current time value is invalid and the user needs to reset the current time. The time base task will have to reset the current time to a default value. And, the system mode will have to change to Error until the user sets a new current time value. All of this activity will require coordination by a central entity in the system, typically a separate error task acting as a watchdog. In fact, the specific value present in the error task state variable can be used as an indicator as to the presence and type of error currently being handled by the system.

To document all this information, we will use the same format as before, classifying the fault as to severity, soft, recoverable, or hard. Name the fault with a label descriptive of the problem and the task generating the fault condition. List the method or methods for detecting the fault, and detail the recovery mechanism used by the system. Remember that each task will have a state machine, and each state machine will have at least one potential error condition, specifically the corruption of its state variable. In addition, there will likely be other potential error conditions, both in the operation of the task and its communications with external and internal data pathways.

Another potential source of errors is from the communications system. Semaphore protocol pathways have the potential to create potential state lock conditions. If the problem cannot be averted by changing one or more of the pathway protocols, then the state lock condition will be an error condition that must be detected and recovered from by the system. Buffers also have the potential to create error conditions, should they fill their buffer space. While these errors are typically considered soft errors because they don't require user intervention, the error-handling system may need to be aware of the problem. Once all the potential system errors have been identified, the severity of the error condition must be determined, a test developed to detect the condition, and a recovery mechanism devised to handle the problem.

This can be particularly problematic for communications errors, specifically potential state lock conditions. This is because both communications in a state lock condition are legitimate data transfers. However, due to the nature of the lock, one of the two pathways will likely have to drop their data, to allow the other communications to continue. So, basically, the error recovery system will have to decide which data pathway to flush and which to allow to continue.

Using our clock design as an example, the following additional error should be added to the system-level design:

List 3.9

Soft Error

Fault: Display task state variable corruption.

Test: Range check on the state variable.

Response: Reset the state variable.

Recoverable Error

Fault: Button task state variable corruption.

Test: Range check on the state variable.

Response: Reset the state variable.

            Cancel any current command semaphores.

            Reset all debounce and autorepeat counter variables.

Recoverable Error

Fault: Time base task state variable corruption.

Test: Range check on the state variable.

Response: Reset the state variable.

            Range check time base timer variables.

            If out of range, then reset and notify error task to clear potential alarm fault.

Recoverable Error

Fault: Alarm control task state variable corruption.

Test: Range check on the state variable.

Response: Reset the state variable.

            If alarm is active, disable then retest for alarm time.

            If alarm enabled or active, range check alarm time.

            If alarm time out of range, then notify error task of fault condition.

List 3.9
(continued)

Soft Error

Fault: Alarm tone task state variable corruption.

Test: Range check on the state variable.

Response: Reset the state variable.

Recoverable Error

Fault: Error task state variable corruption.

Test: Range check on the state variable.

Response: Reset the state variable.

Check status on other system state machines.

If error condition, then set error system mode, set current time to default.

Wait for user control input.

Recoverable Error

Fault: Alarm disabled but also active.

Test: Routine check by error task.

Response: Reset alarm control task state variable.

Recoverable Error

Fault: Snooze active when alarm is disabled.

Test: Routine check by error task.

Response: Reset alarm control task state variable.

Hard Error

Fault: Program memory fails a CRC test.

Test: CRC check on power-up.

Response: System locks, with a blank display.

These additional fault conditions and recovery mechanisms are then added to the design notes. The description of the fault condition should include an appropriate, verbose description of the type of error condition, the error condition itself, the method for detection of the error, and the recovery systems. Include notes on the placement of the new software functions to detect and correct the error condition, plus any options in the design that were discarded and the reasons why.

Notes concerning any additional software functions required to handle the error detection and recovery should also be added to the appropriate task descriptions so they can be included in the state machine design. This includes both errors from the corruption of data variables and the corruption of the state variable for the task state machine.

All notes concerning an Error task or tasks should also be added to the design notes. This includes updates to the task list, the system data flow diagram and variable dictionary, timing calculations, and priority handling information. Remember to review any additions to the communications plan, for potential state lock conditions.

System-Level Design Documentation

At this point, the design should include all of the system-level design information for the design. It may not be final, but it should be as complete as possible. Remember, the next level of the design will use this information as the basis for design, so the information from this level must be as complete as possible.

To recap, the information generated so far includes the following:

- The requirements document: Should be updated with all the current system information, including functions required for operation, communications and storage requirements, timing information, and priority information. It should also include detailed information concerning the user interface and finally, all information available on potential system errors, methods used to identify the error conditions, and methods for recovering from the errors.

- Information retrieved from the requirements document: Should include information concerning the following:

  - *Task Information*: This includes a list of all the functions the design will be required to perform, any information concerning algorithms used by the functions, and a descriptive write-up detailing the general flow of the functions.

- *Communication Information*: This includes all information about the size and type of data, for internal communications between functions, external communications with off-system resources, and any significant temporary storage. Also any information about event timing that is tied to the variables used, as well as the classification of the data storage as either static or dynamic, plus all rate information for dynamic variables. Both peak and average should also be included.

- *Timing Information*: This includes not only the timing requirements for the individual tasks, but also the overall system timing, including both event-to-event and response-time timing. Should also include all timing tolerance information, as well as any exceptions to the timing requirements based on specific system modes.

- *Priority Information*: This includes a detailed description of all system modes and the trigger events that change the system mode. Should also include the overall priorities for the system, changes in function priorities due to changes in the system mode, and the priorities within each task based on current activities.

■ Documentation on the task definition phase of the system-level design: This should include descriptive names for the various new tasks in the system, what software functions have been grouped into the functions, and the reasons for combining or excluding the various software functions. In the event that conflicting criteria recommend both combining and excluding a function, the reasoning behind the designer's decision should also be included. The final documentation should also include the preliminary task list, plus any updates due to changes in subsequent areas of the system-level design.

■ Documentation on the communications plan for the design: This should include all revisions of the system data-flow diagram, the preliminary variable list and all related documentation concerning protocol assignments, memory requirements, and timing information. Special note should be made of any combination of pathways that can result in a state lock condition, and the reasons for not alleviating the problem through the assignment of a different protocol for one of the problem pathways.

- Documentation on the timing analysis for the system: This should include all calculations generated to determine the system tick, including both optimum and worst-case timing requirements. Reasons for the choice of system tick should be included, and any functions that are to be handled through an interrupt-based timing system. For systems with unregulated timing, the reasons for the decision to use an unregulated system should be included, along with the plan for any timing critical functions. Finally, the tick itself should be documented along with the skip timer values for all tasks in the system.

- Documentation on the systems priorities: Include the updated priority list, using the task name generated in the task definition phase of the design. Note any tasks that combine lower priority and higher priority functions, and the new priority assigned to the task. Note all events that trigger a change in system mode and all information generated in the validation of the trigger event information.

- Documentation on the error detection and recovery system in the design: Particularly any new error conditions resulting from the task state machines, potential communications problems, and general data corruption possibilities.

One final note on documentation of the system-level design: in all the design decisions made at this level, some will require back annotation to earlier design notes and even the requirements document for the system. As a designer, please do not leave this to the last moment; there will always be something missed in the rush to release the documentation to the next level of the design. As a general rule, keep a text editor open on the computer desktop to make notes concerning the design. A second instantiation holding the requirements document is also handy. Bookmarks for tagging the main points of the design, such as task definition, communications, priorities, and timing make accessing the documents quick and help to organize the notes. If the notes are made as the information is found, then the information is fresh in the mind of the designer, and the notes will be more complete.

I know this sounds like a broken record, but remember the points made in Chapter 1. Good documentation allows support designers to more readily take up the design with only minimal explanation for the designer. Good documentation also aids designers if they ever have to pick up the design in the future and rework all or part of the design. And, good documentation will help the technical writers in the development of the manuals and troubleshooting guides for the system. So, there are a wealth of reasons for being accurate and verbose in the documentation of the design, both for the designers themselves and for any other engineers that may have to pick up the design in the future.

At this point in the design, it is also a good idea to go back through the design notes and organize the information into four main areas: task, communications, timing, and priorities. The information in the design notes will be the basis for all of the design work in the next chapter, so spending a few hours at this point to clean it up and organize the data will be time well spent. Note—do save the original document under a different name in case information is lost in the translation and clean-up.

We have now completed the system level of the design. In the next chapter, we will take the information gathered and generated at this level and push the design down to the component level. The next level will not involve actual writing of code for the design, but it will specify the actual layout of the program, and the generation of any algorithms not currently designed. Once the design is complete at the component level, then Chapter 5 will move into the actual implementation of the design.

One final note: Throughout the design methodology presented in this book, we will be using either the C programming language or a pseudo C-like language for defining the algorithms to be used. While the methodology is equally applicable to both assembly and higher-level languages, we will be using C or pseudo-C, as it represents the design at a higher, less complex level. This helps us see the forest for the trees, as it were—basically allowing the reader to concentrate on the big picture of the design without obscuring the message with the more complex description in assembly.

4

Component-Level Design

In this chapter, we continue the design process, translating the system-level design from the last chapter into the individual software components that will make up the final system. While we will not begin the actual implementation of the software until the next chapter, we will be designing the state machines, timing controls, and priority handler, as well as defining the variables used for communications. When we are finished, we will have a collection of module specifications, one for each block in the system.

Task State Machines

Once again we start with the tasks. Our job at the component level of design is to determine the type of state machine, what states will be needed, what the various conditions are that will change the state, and what communications that state machine will need to operate in the final system.

From Chapter 2, we know that there are three types of state machine: *data indexed, execution indexed,* and *hybrid.* While the execution indexed will typically be the most common, we will start with the data indexed for simplicity. Once we are comfortable with it, we will move on to the execution indexed and the hybrid.

Data-indexed state machines execute the same block of code each time they are called, and it is the data operated on by the block of code that changes from call to call. This means that our state variable in a data-indexed state machine is responsible for indexing the data to be operated on. This typically implies that our data will be held in an array data structure. In fact, if the processing of the data requires constants that must also be indexed, then it follows that the constants must be held in an array as well. Because variable and constant arrays use a linear addressing system, our states must be a linear collection of values as well. Typically, this means two to N states, starting at zero, and our state variable will be an unsigned CHAR, integer or long depending on the number of states required.

One of the simple things about a data-indexed state machine is that the number of states is relatively simple to determine. If a system will be operating on 15 values, then there will be 15 states. If the system operates on 200 values, then we will need 200 states. So, typically, the number of data values to be handled automatically determines the number of states and the size of the state variable. Defining the states is then just a simple matter of labeling the state and building any constant arrays that may be required.

So, what kinds of tasks lend themselves to a data-indexed state machine format? Tasks that handle more than one piece of data, tasks that continuously repeat the same task, and tasks that complete their function every time they are executed. Typically these types of tasks tend to be scanning functions, such as Display routines that scan data onto a multiplexed display such as LEDs or a CRT. Or they could be functions that poll inputs, such as a keyboard routine or an analog-to-digital converter routine that monitors multiple signals, or even some math routines, such as a DSP filter that multiplies a group of samples by a group of coefficients to obtain a new result for each new sample. All of these tasks perform the same function each time they are called, whether it is output a digit on a display, poll a push button, or calculate a value. They operate continuously, keeping up the refresh on the display, scanning for new key presses, or supplying a continuous stream of new output values. And they all operate on changing data, such as different digits, different push buttons, or different samples, each time the function is called.

One example is the LED display-scanning Task in our alarm clock example. Either the current time or alarm time is displayed on the six digits of numeric displays. There are six digits to be scanned for both of the current time display modes, and four digits to be scanned in the alarm time display modes. Because the four-digit display is a subset of the six-digit display, we can define the 6 states and only use the first four for the alarm time. The preliminary list of states would be as follows:

Table 4.1

STATE	DIGIT FUNCTION
0	Display tens of hours
1	Display ones of hours
2	Display tens of minutes
3	Display ones of minutes
4	Display tens of seconds
5	Display ones of seconds

When displaying the current time, the state machine will cycle through all six states; when displaying the alarm time, the state machine need only cycle through the first four states.

OK, we have determined what states we need, so what next? Well, as we noted previously, for some modes of the display, it will scan four displays, and for others, it will display all six. And wasn't there a flash and a blank function as well? That would indicate that we may need additional states for some modes and fewer states for other modes. However, to maintain the same perceived intensity, the percentage of time that a digit is lit will have to remain the same. So, we will have to scan through the same number of states for each of the different modes.

Let's start with the current time display. Our current list has six states for six digits. If we can set up the other modes so they also step through six states, then the time each digit is lit will remain the same and the intensity won't change. If we add two blank states that don't light a digit but just take up a cycle in the state machine, then the four-digit mode for alarm time will have the same digit on time as the six-digit display of the current time. So, let's add two blank states in 6 and 7, and define the state transitions based on the flag Alarm_Enable. To completely blank the display, we can then jump to the blank states and stay there until battery-powered operation ends. The result is the following state list:

→

Algorithm 4.1

STATE	DIGIT FUNCTION	Condition	If true	If false
0	Display tens of hours	always	1	
1	Display ones of hours	always	2	
2	Display tens of minutes	always	3	
3	Display ones of minutes	alarm mode	6	4
4	Display tens of seconds	always	5	
5	Display ones of seconds	always	1	
6	Blank display	always	7	
7	Blank display	blank	6	1

If the display is showing alarm time, then the sequence is 0, 1, 2, 3, 6, 7, 0. If the display is showing time, then the sequence is 0, 1, 2, 3, 4, 5, 0. If a blank condition exists, then both sequences go to 6/7 and stay there until the condition clears. Both time and alarm display sequences have six states, and alarm time display leaves the tens and ones of seconds blank.

At this point, someone is probably asking, why go to all this trouble? Just disable the displays during states 4 and 5 if the display is showing alarm time. And if the display is blanked during battery operation, just blank all the digits and save the two extra states. Well, yes, that will work. It means adding in a conditional statement that tests for states greater than 3, and blanks the display if alarm time is active. It also means the conditional statement will have to blank the display if the blank signal is true. In fact, the resulting conditional statement would probably be smaller than the additional code to implement the state transitions.

However, it also means that any other state machine, or the priority handler, will also have to use a copy of that conditional to determine if the display is doing something that is high priority, or just wasting time in a blank. Creating the two new blank states allows every other task in the system to know exactly what the priority of the current activity in the display task is, just by looking at its state variable. So, yes, the other method is smaller in the display task, but it also makes determining what the display task is doing more complex. It is also makes the code more cryptic, while a blank state is pretty obvious. In addition, using two identical conditional statements in two different places in the software is an accident waiting to happen. If someone in the future modifies the conditional in the display task, there is no guarantee that they will know to change the conditional other places in the project. Now other tasks and the priority handler are making erroneous priority decisions about what the display task is doing. Using a simple blank state predigests the conditional statement and publishes a clear flag of the result to any other entity in the system that is watching the display task's operation.

OK, we have states and state transitions, so what else do we need? Any algorithms used by the state machine should be documented, as well as any assumptions made in the design. For instance, the algorithm for converting 24-hour time to 12-hour AM/PM time, and whether the current time and alarm time will be held in a 12- or 24-hour format. All inputs and outputs to the state machine should also be documented at this time. At the end of this phase of the design, the design notes for the project should contain the following notes on the Display state machine task:

→

Algorithm 4.2

```
DISPLAY STATE MACHINE TYPE:      DATA INDEXED
```

STATE	DIGIT FUNCTION	Condition	If true	If false
0	Display tens of hours	always	1	
1	Display ones of hours	always	2	
2	Display tens of minutes	always	3	
3	Display ones of minutes	alarm mode	6	4
4	Display tens of seconds	always	5	
5	Display ones of seconds	blank	7	1
6	Blank display	always	7	
7	Blank display	blank	6	1

```
ALGORITHM FOR CONVERTING 24-HOUR TO AM PM
    K is a temporary variable
    digit0 is the tens of hours digit
    digit1 is the ones of hours digit

    K = (digit0 * 10) + digit1     // convert digits to 0-23 value

                                   // test for time of 13:00 - 23:59
                                   // in AMPM mode, displaying hours

    If (state = 0) and (AMPM_mode = true) and (K >= 13)
    {
         digit0 = (K - 12) / 10   // subtract 12 and take tens digit
         digit1 = (K - 12) - 10   // subtract 12 and take ones digit
    }

STATE MACHINE INPUTS:
         Three flags: alarm_enable, blank, AMPM_mode
              All three flags are positive true logic

         Two arrays: Time_data[6]* and Alarm_data[6]*
              *Note, data is in 24:00 hour format for

STATE MACHINE OUTPUTS:
         One state variable: Display_state

         Two I/O ports:          Segments(7) and Digit_drivers(6)

         Two LED indicators: PM and ALARM_ON
              Indicators are positive true logic
```

Note: One of the interesting characteristics of the C programming language is that, using dynamic variable allocation and data pointers, it is possible to create a linked list of data that does not require an index value to access the data. Using these constructs it is certainly possible to create a data-indexed state machine in which there are no defined states or a specific state variable. The system just links sequentially through the list using pointers. While the ability to dynamically allocate data is very powerful, most small microcontrollers do not have the resources to maintain a variable heap, and the design would be quite cryptic without extensive documentation, so this technique may be of only limited value in most applications. However, in larger systems this can be a powerful method for reducing the amount of data memory required for the system, particularly if the system is processing large quantities of data.

OK, data-indexed state machines work well for scanned and polled functions, but what about functions that execute different code in every state? To build a state machine that can handle this kind of function, we need to turn to the next form of state machine, the *execution-indexed state machine*.

In an execution-indexed state machine, the overall sequence of instructions that make up a task are broken into individual smaller blocks. These blocks become the states of the state machine. A state variable is then used to specify which block is executed each time the state machine is called. Conditional statements, added to each block, manipulate the state variable so that the original flow of the overall sequence of instructions is recreated when the state machine is called repeatedly. The challenge in designing an execution-indexed state machine is breaking up the overall sequence of instruction that make up the functionality of the task.

So, before we can start the design of the execution-indexed state machine, we must understand how the task operates. We need to understand how the functions themselves operate, and how they operate together to form the whole task.

Information on the operation of the software functions making up the task was gathered in our dissection of the requirements document in the last chapter. Information on how the functions operate together should have come from the description of the overall system operation, which should also be present in the requirements document. Together, they should give the designer a big-picture view of the task's operation.

To illustrate the process, consider the Buttons task from our alarm clock example:

List 4.1

```
Task3      Buttons
           a) Control input monitoring function
           b) Debounce function
           c) Auto repeat function
           d) Command Decode function (combined SetAlarm
              and SetTime functions)
           e) Routine to increment alarm by 1 min
           f) Routine to increment alarm by 20 min
           g) Routine to increment Time by 1 min
           h) Routine to increment Time by 20 min
           i) Toggle 12/24 hour mode
           j) Alarm on/off toggling function
           k) Initiate Snooze
```

From our understanding of how the user interface works, and our understanding of each of the software functions in the task, we know:

1. The control and input monitoring function first detects the button press.

2. The debounce function determines when the button has stopped bouncing. This prevents the system from trying to execute a command on every contact bounce.

3. The command decode function determines which command to execute based on the button pressed, or even if the button press is a valid command,

4. The appropriate command routine is executed.

5. If the command supports auto-repeat, the command is executed again at the repeat interval until the button is released.

Rewriting the previous description using a pseudocode format, we have the following algorithm, which outlines the task's execution.

Algorithm 4.3

```
Start
  Wait for a button press
  Wait for the button to stop bouncing
Repeat
  Decode the function of the button
  If button press is invalid then goto Start, Else decode the button
  If (increment alarm by 1)        then alarm = alarm + 1
  If (increment alarm by 10)       then alarm = alarm + 10
  If (increment time by 1)         then time  = time + 1
  If (increment time by 10)        then time  = time + 10
  If (toggle 12/24)                then toggle AMPM_mode flag, goto
                                   Release
  If (alarm on)                    then alarm_enable = true, goto
                                   Start
  If (alarm off)                   then alarm_enable = false, goto
                                   Start
  If (snooze)                      then toggle snooze, goto Release
  Delay
  If (button is still held down) then goto Repeat

                                   Else goto Start
Release
  Wait for button release
  Goto Start
```

Two notes of explanation about the algorithm are needed. One, if a command is not followed by a GOTO, it is assumed that it will fall through the command decoder, to the Delay and then the IF statement that checks to see if "button is still held down." Two, commands that do not have auto-repeat capability either go to the start of the algorithm or go to Release, where the state machine holds until the button is released. The wait for the release of the button prevents the inadvertent repeat of command.

We can now use the algorithm as a basis for the development of the task's state machine. Note that the algorithm that is generated at this point and the next few steps in the design process will largely fix how the state machine will implement the operation of the functions, so the designer is encouraged to take the time needed and do a thoughtful design. It is also possible that the grouping of software functions within the task cannot be worked into a reasonable algorithm, even if the functions did agree with all the task definition criteria from the last chapter. If this happens, revisit the decisions in the task-definition phase of the design and see if another grouping might be more efficient. There is no law that says that the group of functions within a task is fixed once the task definition is complete. In fact, part of the reason for doing a top-down design is to find these kinds of problems before the design progresses to thousands of lines of code.

The next design challenge is to break up the flow of the algorithm into logical blocks, for the states of the state machine. This tells us how many states we need and how the execution will flow through the states to perform the operation of the state machine. With time, a designer will cultivate the ability to look at an algorithm and see where to break up a task. Until then, the following list of general rules provides a good guideline for determining how to break up the task:

1. Any place in the task where execution stops pending an external event, such as the reception of a command or a signal from another task, should be a state change. This allows the system to poll for the condition until true, then move on by moving to the next state.

2. Any place in the function where execution stops waiting for a time delay, such as the delay between bits in a software serial output function, should be a state change. This allows the use of a delay state in the state machine to handle timing. When the timer times out, it just moves on to the next state.

3. Any place that the function will return to when executing a loop or a jump should mark the start of a state. This is necessary for the state machine to start execution at the loop-back point in the task.

4. Any time a function reaches a point where the execution path splits to two or more directions should be the start of a new state for each alternative path.

5. Anywhere a linear segment of code is too large to execute within the system timing tick can be broken into two or more states.

6. In rules 1 and 2, it was stated that a wait or delay should be immediately followed by a change of state. If the next action following the wait or delay is a change of state either always, or on a condition, the state change may follow the command changing state.

Continuing with our example of the button task, the task can be broken into the following states, based on the previous guidelines:

Algorithm 4.4

```
        (rule 3)
Start
   Wait for a button press
        (rule 1)
   Wait for the button to stop bouncing
        (rule 1 & 3)
Repeat
   Decode the function of the button
   If button press is invalid then goto Start, Else decode the button
        (rule 4)
   If (increment alarm by 1)      then alarm = alarm + 1
        (rule 4)
   If (increment alarm by 10)     then alarm = alarm + 10
        (rule 4)
   If (increment time by 1)       then time  = time + 1
        (rule 4)
   If (increment time by 10)      then time  = time + 10
        (rule 4)
   If (toggle 12/24)              then toggle AMPM_mode flag, goto Release
        (rule 4)
   If (alarm on)                  then alarm_enable = true, goto Start
        (rule 4)
   If (alarm off)                 then alarm_enable = false, goto Start
        (rule 4)
   If (snooze)                    then initiate snooze, goto Release
        (rule 4)
   Delay
   {no state change, per rule 6}
   If (button is still held down) then goto Repeat
                                  Else goto Start
        (rule 4)
Release
   Wait for button release
   {no state change, per rule 6}
   Goto Start
        (rule 3)
```

A quick count shows 13 states generated by splits in the execution path, waiting for external events, time delays, and looping. The next step is to give each state a name that is descriptive of the actions performed in the state.

Again, using the Button task example, the following list of preliminary state names was generated:

Algorithm 4.5

```
Preliminary state names for Button task
1.  Wait_4button       Idle state, waiting for a button press
2.  Wait_4bounce       Wait state, waiting for the contacts to stop
                       bouncing
3.  Decode             The button is combined with other buttons and
                       decoded
4.  Alarm_plus1        Command: Increment alarm time by 1 minute
5.  Alarm_plus10       Command: Increment alarm time by 10 minutes
6.  Time_plus1         Command: Increment current time by 1 minute
7.  Time_plus10        Command: Increment current time by 10 minutes
8.  Toggle_AMPM        Command: Toggle AM/PM versus military time
9.  Alarm_on           Command: Disable alarm
10. Alarm_off          Command: Enable alarm
11. Initiate_snooze    Command: Snooze alarm
12. Repeat_delay       Wait state for autorepeat of increment commands
13. Button_release     End state for button release
```

In addition to the listed states, a minimum of two additional states should included: default and error. The purpose of the default state is to catch the error condition in which the state variable for the state machine has been corrupted. The cause could be static, EMI, or a low battery; whatever the cause, including a default state provides the state machine with a safeguard mechanism to handle the error and creates a place to put code for resetting the state variable. The related error state provides a place to put additional error-handling functions. The state may only contain an instruction to reset the state variable, or it may be a group of states that coordinate the reset of several state machines and the clearing of several variables. Regardless of the complexity of the system, an error state provides the state machine with a place to put error-handling functions defined in the requirements document.

Note: Error conditions within the Buttons task are limited to either a corrupted state variable or illegal button press combinations. Corruption of the state variable can be handled by simply resetting the state variable in the default state. Illegal button press combinations are just ignored, as defined in the user interface section of the requirements document, so no action is presently required in the error state. However, rather than delete the state, it should be retained for the sake of completeness. At some time in the future, different responses to illegal button press combinations may be required, and the error state will be needed. Having the state present and decoded gives designers making that future change a place to put the new code. And having the state now doesn't cost that much in program memory.

Now that the blocks have had states assigned to them and the states have been named, the next step is to define the state transitions and the conditions that cause them. The transitions are implemented by modifying the contents of the state variable, so that the next time the state machine is called, a new state will be selected and executed. Using this method, all of the traditional conditional and looping constructs can be implemented. For more on this subject, refer to the state machine section of Chapter 2.

Adding the state transition information to our list of states, we have the following:

Algorithm 4.6

Current State	Condition	Next State if true	Next state if false
Wait_4button	Button pressed	Wait_4bounce	Wait_4button
Wait_4bounce	100-msec delay	Decode	Wait_4bounce
Decode	Alarm_set & Slow_set	Alarm_plus1	
Decode	Alarm_set & Fast_set	Alarm_plus10	
Decode	Time_set & Fast_set	Time_plus1	
Decode	Time_set & Slow_set	Time_plus10	
Decode	Fast_set & Slow_set	Toggle_AMPM	
Decode	Alarm_switch_on	Alarm_on	
Decode	Alarm_switch_off	Alarm_off	
Decode	Alarm_enabled & Alarm_active	Initiate_snooze	Button_Release
Alarm_plus1	always	Repeat_delay	
Alarm_plus10	always	Repeat_delay	
Time_plus1	always	Repeat_delay	
Time_plus10	always	Repeat_delay	
Toggle_AMPM	always	Button_Release	
Alarm_on	always	Wait_4bounce	
Alarm_off	always	Wait_4bounce	
Initiate_snooze	always	Button_Release	
Repeat_delay	1 second delay & Button is held	Decode	Wait_4button
Button_Release	Button is released	Wait_4button	Button_Release
Error	Reset from Error task	Wait_4button	Error
Default	always	Error	

The final step is to assign actions to the states and document the inputs and outputs of the state machine. The actions come from our original algorithm for the task and can be documented in text or in the form of an algorithm. The inputs and outputs will be a list of the data pathways into and out of the task. Using our button example, the following is an example of the actions and input/output documentation:

Table 4.2

State	Action	Input	Output
Wait_4button	Test for button press	Button	none
Wait_4bounce	Delay and test	Button	none
Decode	decode command from button	none	none
Alarm_plus1	increment alarm time	Alarm_time	Alarm_time
Alarm_plus10	increment alarm time by 10	Alarm_time	Alarm_time
Time_plus1	increment time	Alarm_time	Alarm_time
Time_plus10	increment time by 10	Alarm_time	Alarm_time
Toggle_AMPM	Toggle AMPM_flag	AMPM_flag	AMPM_flag
Alarm_on	Set Alarm_enable flag	none	Alarm_enable
Alarm_off	Clear Alarm_enable flag	none	Alarm_enable
Initiate_snooze	Test for conditions and Set snooze flag	Alarm_enable Alarm_active	Snooze
Repeat_delay	delay 1second & test button	button	none
Button_release	test for button release	button	none
Error	Notify error task & Reset state machine	Reset	Button_error
Default	set statevariable to Error	none	none

The list of states and the table of state transitions comprises the documentation required for an execution-indexed state machine. From this information, we will produce the state machine in the next chapter that implements the button task. There is a strong temptation to just skip ahead to the actual implementation of the state machine at this time. The designer is strongly cautioned against this; as the other state machines in the system are designed, there will be trade-offs made that will affect this design. Functions may move from one task to another, and the communications pathways may change as well. It is much more efficient to wait and have a complete definition for the system, rather than jump ahead now and have to rewrite the task later when the design of another task necessitates changes.

The final form of state machine is the hybrid design. It combines the data-indexing capabilities of our first state machine with the variable execution of the second. It should not come as a surprise to find that the design of a hybrid state machine is a combination of the design methods for both the execution and data-indexed state machines.

Typically, a hybrid design grows out of an execution-indexed design as part of an effort to make the original design more efficient. So, it makes sense to start the design exactly as we did for the solely execution-indexed state machine.

We start by gaining an understanding of how the functions within the state machine and the overall task operate. From this, we build an algorithm for the state machine. To illustrate the design, let's take a software serial port transmit task as an example. In this task, the state machine will have to:

Algorithm 4.7

1. Wait in an idle state, pending detection of a character to transmit.
2. Retrieve the character to be transmitted.
3. Start the transmission by sending a Start bit.
4. Send each bit of the character in turn.
5. Send a Parity bit.
6. Send a Stop bit, and return to its idle state.

The algorithm for this task is also relatively simple:

Algorithm 4.8

```
Idle
    Wait for a Character to send
    Retrieve the character
    Send a zero as a start bit
    Wait 1 bit time
    Send bit 0 of the character
    Wait 1 bit time
    Send bit 1 of the character
    Wait 1 bit time
    Send bit 2 of the character
    Wait 1 bit time
    Send bit 3 of the character
    Wait 1 bit time
    Send bit 4 of the character
    Wait 1 bit time
    Send bit 5 of the character
    Wait 1 bit time
    Send bit 6 of the character
    Wait 1 bit time
    Send bit 7 of the character
    Wait 1 bit time
    Send a parity bit based on the character value
    Wait 1 bit time
    Send a one as a stop bit
    Wait 1 bit time
    Goto Idle
```

In examining the algorithm, it is readily apparent that repeating the "send bit x of the character," followed by "Wait 1 bit time," eight times will be very inefficient, especially considering each bit would probably be assigned its own state. So, at this point in the design, we should have come to the obvious conclusion that we need a better way. Fortunately, a hybrid design is the better way, and it will be a much more efficient implementation for this task.

To design a hybrid state machine, we will continue as before with the design of a standard execution-indexed state machine. The only exception is that the algorithm will be modified to use data indexing for the transmission of the bits. The following shows the modified algorithm:

Algorithm 4.9

```
Idle
   Wait for a Character to send
   Retrieve the character
   Set bitcounter = 8
   Send a zero as a start bit
   Wait 1 bit time

Loop
   Send lsb of the character
   Decrement bitcounter
   Shift character left 1 bit
   Wait 1 bit time
   If (bitcounter>0) goto Loop

   Send a parity bit based on the character value
   Wait 1 bit time
   Send a one as a stop bit
   Wait 1 bit time
   Goto Idle
```

The new algorithm has a number of changes in its design. First of all, the eight data bits are now transmitted by the data-indexed section of the design starting at Loop. Further, a new variable, bitcounter, is used to keep track of which bit is being sent. This makes bitcounter the state variable for the data-indexed portion of the design, even though the variable does not directly index access to the data. Once bitcounter reaches zero, the state machine returns to execution-indexed operation, and the parity and stop bits are sent.

If we take this algorithm and apply the same rules for segmenting the task into states that we used in purely execution-indexed designs, we end up with the following:

Algorithm 4.10

```
                (rule 3)
Idle
    Wait for a Character to send
            (rule 1)
    Retrieve the character
    Set bitcounter = 8
    Send a zero as a start bit
    Wait 1 bit time
            (rule 2)
Loop
    Send lsb of the character
    Decrement bitcounter
    Shift character left 1 bit
    Wait 1 bit time
    If (bitcounter>0) goto Loop
            (rule 6)

    Send a parity bit based on the character value
    Wait 1 bit time
            (rule 2)
    Send a one as a stop bit
    Wait 1 bit time
    Goto Idle
            (rule 6)
```

This gives us six states, as opposed to the 12 or more states that would have been required in the original algorithm. Assigning names, and including a default and error state, we get the following list of states for the hybrid design:

List 4.2

```
Preliminary state names for Button task
    1. Idle         (wait for a character)
    2. Start        (send start bit)
    3. Data_bit     (data indexed section)
    4. Parity       (send parity bit)
    5. Stop         (send stop bit)
    6. Error
    7. Default
```

Adding the state transition information to our list of states, we have the following:

Algorithm 4.11

Current State	Condition	Next State (if true)	Next state (if false)
Idle	Data ready to be sent	START	Idle
Start	always	Data_bit	
Data_bit	bitcounter = 0	Parity	Data_bit
Parity	always	Stop	
Stop	always	Idle	
Error	Reset from error task	Idle	Error
Default	always	Error	

Performing the same design functions for the data-indexed portion of the design, we obtain the following states for data-indexed state variable:

List 4.3

STATE	DIGIT FUNCTION
1.	Transmit bit 0
2.	Transmit bit 1
3.	Transmit bit 2
4.	Transmit bit 3
5.	Transmit bit 4
6.	Transmit bit 5
7.	Transmit bit 6
8.	Transmit bit 7

and the list of state transitions for the data-indexed state variable:

Algorithm 4.12

STATE	FUNCTION	Condition	If true
1.	Send bit 0	always	2.
2.	Send bit 1	always	3.
3.	Send bit 2	always	4.
4.	Send bit 3	always	5.
5.	Send bit 4	always	6.
6.	Send bit 5	always	7.
7.	Send bit 6	always	8.
8.	Send bit 7		

The final step is to assign actions to the states, both data- and execution-indexed, and document the inputs and outputs of the state machine. As with the execution-indexed example, the actions come from our original algorithm for the task and can be documented in text or in the form of an algorithm. The inputs and outputs will be a list of the data pathways into and out of the task. Using our serial port example, the following is an example of the actions and input/output documentation:

→

Algorithm 4.13

State	Action	Input	Output
Idle	Test for new character	Ready_flag	none
Start	Send start bit	none	TX_PIN
Data_bit(1)	Send bit 0	Char_in	TX_PIN
Data_bit(2)	Send bit 1	Char_in	TX_PIN
Data_bit(3)	Send bit 2	Char_in	TX_PIN
Data_bit(4)	Send bit 3	Char_in	TX_PIN
Data_bit(5)	Send bit 4	Char_in	TX_PIN
Data_bit(6)	Send bit 5	Char_in	TX_PIN
Data_bit(7)	Send bit 6	Char_in	TX_PIN
Data_bit(8)	Send bit 7	Char_in	TX_PIN
Parity	Calculate and send parity	Char_in	TX_PIN
Stop	Send Stop bit	none	TX_PIN
Error	Notify error task & Reset state machine	Reset	PORT_error
Default	set statevariable to Error	none	none

The documentation for all three types of state machine should be included in the design notes for the design, and should include the same information:

1. A list of states, including a default and any necessary error states.

2. A list of all state transitions and the conditions that cause them.

3. A list of all actions performed in each state.

4. A list of all input and output pathways.

One final note on state machine design: just as no two artists are likely to paint a scene in exactly the same way, no two designers will design a state machine in exactly the same way. The design will be influenced by the designer's experience and coding style. And, as I mentioned previously, the criteria for making the state breaks in the design will become individual to the designer doing the work. As long as the design works and performs the functions included within the task, then the design is good. However, this should not be taken as a license to build obfuscated code. Remember, our purpose here is to design a project that can be easily understood by others, so it can be supported by individuals other than the original designer.

Communications

In the last chapter, we defined all of the data pathways within the system and any significant data storage associated with the individual tasks. Our purpose in this chapter is to define the individual variables of the various pathways and make any final decisions concerning the operation of the protocols used for each pathway.

Let's start with some general guidelines concerning the naming of variables. Variable names must be descriptive. Naming a generic timer variable `B232` may have been convenient when the code was written, but when trying to support the design, it is less than useless because it might lead the support engineer to the mistaken belief that it is actually a data variable for the B channel of an RS-232 serial interface. Using the name `B_Timer` is more descriptive, less confusing, and only takes three more characters. So, be descriptive, be verbose, and don't scrimp on the characters. Disc space is cheaper than a support engineer's time to reverse-engineer a unhelpful variable name.

Next, when generating variables that work together, consider giving all the variables a common prefix. For example, consider a circular buffer with an input and output pointer variable. Naming the buffer space `Serial_in_buff` is descriptive of both the function and the task that uses the buffer. Naming the input and output pointers `Serial_in_input` and `Serial_in_output` is also descriptive of the function and task using the variable, but also indicates that they are associated with the `Serial_in_buff` variable and are likely part of the pathway's communications protocol.

A descriptive postfix is also a good habit to cultivate. If all input and output pointers for buffer protocols also use `_input` and `_output`, then support engineers that follow will have a simple convention that tells them a great deal about the function of the variable, just by looking at the variable name. The flip side of this coin is that, once you establish a convention, stick with it. Changing the convention in the middle of a design can be more confusing than having no convention at all.

Finally, make an entry in the system design notes, that clearly spells out what your conventions are and how they were applied. This simple piece of reference data will earn you the thanks and admiration of every support engineer that ever has to touch your code. Note: you might want to surround it with asterisks with a bold title, so it will be easier to find. And, as always, be verbose. If you developed a handy convention, the support engineers should recognize your ingenuity and continue the use of your convention throughout the support of the project.

Another area that benefits from a good naming convention are constant numeric and logical values. Most beginning programmers tend to put the value in the equation or the assignment statement. However, if the value is instead replaced with a descriptive label, it is easier to read and understand. For example, the equation A=B*3 could refer to any number of possible calculations, but with the equation A=B*PI there is very little doubt concerning what the constant is and how it is being used.

There is also another very good reason for replacing numeric constants with labels—it makes changing the constants both easier and less error-prone. If a constant is used multiple places in a design, then changing that constant becomes a search-and-replace nightmare through multiple files. However, if the value is assigned to a label, then only the entry making the assignment need actually be changed. The compiler or assembler will do the actual work, guaranteeing that the substitution is made correctly in each and every instance the value is used.

Still another reason for replacing numeric constants with labels is to extend the scope of their use. Often when performing complex computations within a task, there may be a need to combine two or more constants into a single value to simplify the math. If a numeric constant is used, then the origins of the constant will be lost in the simplification. However, using a label to represent the new constant, and defining the new constant based on the original constants, not only documents the origins of the new constant, it also guarantees any changes to the original constants will be included in the calculation of the new constant as well. For example, simplifying 2*3.14159 into 6.28318 will simplify any math by pre-multiplying the two constant values. However, defining TWOPI = 2 * PI, and using the label TWOPI in any subsequent equation, accomplishes the same goal, and allows any updates of PI to flow down through all the equations that use the value.

As indicated previously, note all labels for constants in the design notes file on the design. You may have noticed that I seem to be harping on the notion of making notes in the design notes file for the design. Well, I have been, and there are several good reasons for it:

1. More documentation can only help in the creation of the design. The days when a designer could keep the complete picture of the design in their head is long gone.

2. Documentation helps the designer get back up to speed on a design, should there be a need to fix a bug or add a feature.

3. Documentation also helps the support engineer get up to speed on the design quickly. This limits the number of interrupting phone calls during the next design.

4. Documentation also facilitates the reuse of the code in the next design. And, yes, reusing variable definitions and protocols saves time, just as reusing a state machine or subroutine saves time.

5. Finally, and best of all, documentation in the design notes file is a ready source of copy and paste comments for the header and source files of the design, when it comes time to comment the code.

So, we have naming conventions for our variable storage, and labels for our constants. What else needs an alias? Well, one last place that a good naming convention is handy is the naming of peripheral control registers and input/output pins. For example, if the port pin used as the transmit output of a software-based serial port is labeled with the name SERIAL_TX instead of PORTD.5, then all that is needed to reuse the serial port routine in a new project is to define SERIAL_TX with the new port pin in the new design.

This practice has the somewhat cryptic name of *hardware abstraction*. Basically, it involves giving any hardware-specific value a generic name. This hides, or abstracts, the specifics of the hardware, and leaves the designer with a generic and very portable routine that can be used over and over. It also has the side benefit of making the code much easier to read and understand because the function of the pin is now defined clearly. For information on how to label specific bits within a register or I/O port with names, consult the section on STRUCTUREs in Chapter 2.

One final note on good practices and general operating procedures: during the course of this design we will be creating separate tasks designed to communicate and work together. This causes a problem: while the code for each task, its constants, and even its internal variables can be grouped together into a task-specific header and source file, the communications variables have to cross the task boundaries and tie the various tasks together. So, where do the variable definitions for the communications variables go? We can't scatter them through the task files, and picking one task and lumping them into its files is not a solution either.

The best solution is to create a single set of master source and header files. The master source file will call all of the initialization routines for each of the tasks and contain the main system look which calls all the individual tasks. The master header file contains all the communications variable definitions, all the hardware abstraction definitions, and the labels for any system-wide constants. This places all the global information in one central location and it keeps each individual task file more generic, so it can be cleaned up for inclusion in the developer's code library.

At this point, create a master header file for the design. This will give us a place to define our variable, a place to label our constants, and also to define hardware abstraction labels.

Now that we have some standard operating procedures for the communications system in place, it is time to determine what elements are needed in each protocol and in each pathway, and determine the variables we will need, the algorithms we will use, and the interface functions that will be needed.

As *broadcast* is the simplest protocol, let's start with it. A pathway using a broadcast protocol is defined to be either a single variable, or a single variable with a secondary flag, which is used to determine the validity of the data in the variable. So, any pathway using the broadcast protocol will need an appropriate variable and, potentially, a secondary flag.

In the master header file, a separate section should be generated for each broadcast data pathway, and a header comment generated. The header comment should include all the information from the variable dictionary generated in Chapter 3, including:

1. The type of data, CHARs, INTs, FLOATs.

2. The size of the data.

3. A list of all source and destination tasks that send or receive data through the pathway.

4. A range of acceptable values for the data.

5. Any information concerning the rate of new data.

A definition for the variable can then be generated using an appropriate name, with any appropriate pre-and post-fixes to define its function. If a secondary data valid flag is needed, it should also be defined with the same prefix and an appropriate postfix to define its function. A notation should also be made in the header comments section defining which states denote valid and invalid data.

The next pathway protocol to tackle is the *semaphore*. A pathway using a semaphore protocol is defined as either one or two flags used in a handshaking system with an optional data variable. This means we will need to define one or two flag variables, and a possible data variable.

The first step is to determine what form of handshaking system is needed. For this we have two options: a two-way handshaking system or a four-way system. Two-way systems are just simple set and acknowledge systems where the sender sets a flag indicating an event, and the receiver accepts the information and clears the flag to acknowledge the transfer.

Four-way systems expand the basic two-way system to include a secondary layer of send and acknowledge. The sender sets its flag signaling an event and the receiver sets its flag to acknowledge the event. The receiver then processes the event, and clears its flag to indicate it has completed processing the information. The sender then clears its flag to acknowledge the receiver has completed its work.

The form of handshaking required will depend on the use that the receiver has for the data, and whether the sender needs to know that the receiver has completed its operation. Typically, a two-way system is sufficient for a transfer as the sender is usually only interested in sending data. However, if the transfer of information is bidirectional—specifically, if the sender expects to receive data back from the receiver—then a four-way system is needed. The bidirectional transfer could be handled by two semaphore protocol pathways, but remember that cross-linking two tasks with semaphore protocols can result in a state lock condition if the two state machines get out of synchronization. Using a four-way system accomplishes the same thing as cross-linking two semaphore pathways, but avoids the state lock condition, because the second semaphore is tied to the first as part of the protocol and the second transfer can only be initiated in response to the original request from the sender.

For example, if task B is charged with accepting raw commands from task A, decoding the raw command, and then passing the decoded information back to task A, it follows that two handshaking events are required, one to transfer the raw data from A to B, and a second to pass the decoded data back from B to A. However, with two separate semaphores, this opens up the system to a state lock because a simple two-way handshaking system releases task A, once task B has acknowledged reception of the data. A four-way system does not release A until after B has both accepted *and returned* the data, thus avoiding the state lock condition.

Moreover, the use of two flags also provides a simple method for determining a transfer fault condition. For example, after task B has completed decoding the command, it attempts to return its decoded data to A. But A has already ended the transfer by clearing its flag. Then

B knows that the transfer has been aborted by A and it can safely discard the data without any further direction from A. It will not be stuck waiting for an acknowledgment from A because it knows A has already gone onto other business and lost interest in the returned data.

So, if four-way handshaking semaphore systems get around the problem of state lock, why not just define all semaphores as four-way systems? The reason is that four-way systems only work if the two transfers are tied together in the same data pathway, making them essentially a single transfer. If we tried to tie two unrelated transfers together, then the only way the receiver could ever send data to the transmitter is when the transmitter specifically asked for it. And, that eliminates all event information from the data the receiver was trying to send. It would be no different than using a broadcast protocol to transfer the data from the receiver to the transmitter because the timing is still driven by the transmitter and not the event. And, making the sender wait for the receiver when it is not interested in the receiver's status wastes the sender's time, so four-way systems should only be used when needed.

After determining the type of handshaking, the definition of the variables becomes very similar to the procedure used with the broadcast protocol. A new section is added to the master header file for the semaphore protocol pathway, and the appropriate information is noted in the section's header comments. One or two flag variables are defined, with appropriate names, prefixes, and postfixes. And the logic of the flag(s) is noted in the section's comments. If a data variable is included in the pathway, it is also defined with an appropriate name, common prefix, and descriptive postfix. And information concerning its data type, width, and acceptable range of values is noted in the section's comments.

For both the two-way and four-way systems, four functions should also be defined for use with the variables. These functions will handle the actual set, clear, and test of the two flags involved in the transfer. Comments showing the prototypes and algorithms for these functions should be included in the master header file, in the section associated with the semaphore variables. When we get to the next chapter, these functions will be generated and held in a source file associated with the master header file. The documentation is included here as an explanation of how the variables will be used, and to note that the actual routines reside in the associated source file.

For a two-way handshaking system, the sender needs only a set function to set the flag and a test function to determine if the flag has been cleared by the receiver. The receiver has a corresponding clear function and its test function checks for the initial set of the flag. Both the set and clear functions should return an error in the event they are asked to set an already-set flag, or clear an already-cleared flag. This is to flag the sending and receiving tasks that a handshaking fault has occurred.

For a four-way handshaking system, things get a little more complicated. Both tasks now have set/clear functions for their flags and test functions for their partner's flag. In addition, the sender's set/clear function is also subject to some special conditions.

The sender can only set the flag if the receiver's flag is cleared, and can clear the flag at any time, but must return an error if the receiver's flag is still set. The interlock on setting the flag prevents the sender from over-running the receiver, and the error condition in clearing the flag confirms to the sender that it did abort the transfer. The sender's test function returns both the current state of the receiver's flag and the sender's flag, so the current state of the semaphore is completely defined. This helps the sending task to determine what the receiver is doing, as well as what the receiver thinks the sender is doing.

The receiver also has a set/clear function; the difference is that the receiver can only set its flag if the sending flag is set, and clear the flag only if the sending flag is clear. Any other action results in the return of an error. This prevents the receiver from inadvertently creating a transfer fault.

Both tasks also have test functions for monitoring the state of the other task's flags.

The first question is usually, "Why all this overhead for a simple set of flags? Why can't I just set, clear, and test the bits directly in the state machine code?" There are two reasons. One: making them separate functions means the code inside the routines can be defined by a single macro, and that prevents copy and paste errors. It also means any problems will only have to be fixed once in the source macro, not repeatedly in each section of the code. Two: it provides a simple mechanism for connecting test drivers to the state machine tasks for testing. By renaming one, or at most two, source macros, all of the semaphore connections to a task's state machine can be redirected to testing software, without touching the code in the state machine.

Now, some may question the value of point two. I would point out that, when a supposedly tested and working subroutine suddenly stops working, it is typically due to some minor change made when the test hooks were removed from the code. Using a simple name substitution to replace one working macro with another will either cause a blowup at compile time due to a typing error, or it will work. The evils of copy and paste should not be underestimated!

One final aspect of semaphores to discuss is how to deal with potential state lock conditions. As we discussed in the last chapter, there will be designs that simply can't avoid conditions leading to state lock. And if we can't avoid a configuration that has the potential for state lock, then we will have to have some system for dealing with it. There are two basic methods: we can attempt to predict the condition and move to avoid it, or we can detect its occurrence and recover from it. Both methods have an upside and a downside.

Let's start with trying to prevent state lock from occurring. In our design system, we use state machines to implement the various tasks in the system, and use the state variables associated with the state machines to hold the task's context while other tasks are running. So, it follows that any task in the system can determine the current activity of any other task in the system, by simply examining the other task's state variable.

Therefore, to prevent state lock, all a sending task need do is examine the value in the receiving task's state variable to determine if that task is currently involved in a semaphore transfer. If the receiving task is busy with that transfer, the sending task must defer its transmission until the receiving task is in a state conducive to receiving its information.

For example, task A is preparing to send data to task B. Task A should then test the state variable of task B to see if B is already trying to send data to A. If it is, then task A will have to complete the transfer from B before it can attempt to transfer data to B.

The upside to this system is that it prevents the occurrence of state lock by deferring the second transfer until the first transfer is complete. The downside is that the logic for handling the handshaking just became significantly more complicated. Using this system, the routines in both tasks will have to be expanded to:

1. Test for every wait state in the receiving task state machine associated with a semaphore transfer.

2. If it detects a wait state, the sending task will have to put its current transfer on hold.

3. Save its current context.

4. Jump to a state capable of receiving the transfer.

5. Then, once the transfer is complete,

6. Retrieve the saved context.

7. Return to the sending state and test once again.

8. Once it completes its transfer, it will then have to retrieve the received data.

9. Then respond appropriately.

As you can see, this method can become complicated and cumbersome very quickly. Also, it still raises the question of which of the two tasks involved has the higher priority, which determines which task should defer to the other.

The second option is to detect the state lock condition and try to recover from it. This method changes state lock from a condition that we are trying to avoid, to an error condition requiring recovery. And, it means that the recovery will, by design, disrupt the operation of both state machines. Basically, we are designing our system to classify state lock as an error condition and then handle it as either a hard or soft error.

There are two relatively simple methods for detecting a state lock condition: one, a communications timeout timer; and two, a function in our system that looks for fatal combinations of state variable values.

Of the options, the timeout timer is perhaps the easiest to implement. It involves adding a timer function to the state decoding logic of both tasks. Every time there is a state change, the timer is preset to its timeout value. If the state does not change from one call to the next, the timer is decremented. If the timer ever reaches zero, the current state variable value is saved in a temporary variable and the state is redirected to the error state associated with state lock. Then, the next call to the task will execute the recovery routine and resolve the conflict.

This assumes that the designer knows the maximum possible timeout for each pathway using a semaphore protocol. It also assumes that the task can wait until the timeout is reached without causing unrecoverable damage to other tasks in the system.

Determining the timeout period is relatively easy if the operations of both tasks are well defined and their timing is constant. The designer simply has to count the maximum number of calls to the receiving task between states in which it tests for transfers from the sending task. The value is then scaled by the ratio of the skip timer values associated with the sending and receiving tasks. For example, task A has a skip timer reload value of 10, task B has a skip timer reload value of 5. Task B has a worst-case time of four calls between states in which it can monitor transfer requests from task A. This means that the timeout timer for task A must be 8, or 4 * (10 / 5). Task A is called twice as often as task B, so a wait of 4 in task B results in a wait of 8 in task A.

Determining the timeout period is not so easy if the operations of both tasks are not as predictable. The timeout may be dependent upon other conditions that affect either or both of the tasks involved. Plus, state lock conditions that pass through one or more secondary tasks in a loop add the timing uncertainty of those tasks as well. While this dependence can be predicted with sufficient time and paper, the simpler solution is often to just test the tasks using inputs that simulate a worst-case timing condition.

Once the timeout has been determined, the next step in the process is determining which transfer is more important, and which can be sacrificed to recover from the problem. Typically this involves testing the state variables of both tasks and making a determination as to which task has the higher priority state. But be careful; the decision should also factor in which transfer can be safely killed without causing other conflicts in the system. Once a set of rules has been defined, the error state can then either kill its own transfer by setting its state variable to a state that can receive the other transfer, or kill the other task's transfer by setting its state variable to a receptive state, and just reloading its state variable with the value in the temporary holding variable.

One important thing to note with this system; only one of the tasks should have a timeout and error recovery function. If both tasks have timeout systems, then there is the potential for the two tasks to try and reset each other and cause yet another conflict. But what if a task has more than one potential partner that can cause state lock? Or there are more than two tasks with a potential state lock problem? In this case, the simplest system is often to define an error task, whose job it is to monitor the operation of all the other tasks in the system. The error task with then be the sole judge and jury for any problems and hand down one solution for all parties involved.

The second recovery option involves adding a monitoring routine to check for potentially fatal combinations of state variable values for all combinations of tasks that have the potential for state lock conditions. To accomplish this task, the function will need to regularly access all of the state variables associated with the at-risk tasks, and determine if a state locked combination has been created. This means the monitoring function will need access to all of the state variables, all of the skip timers, and a database of problem combinations, referenced by task and state. If it detects a combination that indicates state lock, the monitoring routine would then determines which transfer is less important and load the state variable of the appropriate task with a state value corresponding to a receptive state for the task.

As this system has many of the same complications associated with the first task, all of the same problems expressed previously are also present here. How will the monitoring routine determine which transfer is more important, what if more than two tasks are involved in the loop, and what happens if routines for two different tasks conflict on the resolution? In addition, this method will require an extensive database to determine which combinations are a problem. This is complicated by the fact that there may be intermediate tasks that may or may not be contributing to the problem by their current states.

So, while adding a recovery mechanism may sound simple, the implementation of a detection and recovery mechanism is seldom simple. That is why the original recommendation of changing one or more of the pathway protocols was stressed so stridently. However, if there is no possible way to avoid the configuration, select a method for detection and error recovery and make the appropriate additions to the task list and the communications plan. Also, add a very verbose entry to the design notes concerning why the potential state lock configuration could not be avoided, along with a clear description of how the detection method will work, how the recovery system operates, and the criteria it will use to determine which transfer can be safely killed.

The master and task header files can then be updated appropriately with definitions for any variables, constants, and functions. Remember to include all the associated information in the header comments for the variables. And, once again, be verbose in your description of the variables and their use.

That covers broadcast and semaphore, but what about buffers? Well, like the semaphore, we have some decisions to make concerning how we will implement the system.

Remember back in Chapter 2, when we were first introduced to buffers, we discovered that there are three conditions for a buffer that are important to us as designers. Those conditions were: when is the buffer empty, when is it full, and when is it not empty. Determining these conditions will depend on the convention we adopt for the input and output pointers.

The choice boils down to whether we want to increment the pointers before we use them or after we use them, and whether we treat them differently. The reason we examined all of those combinations was to determine whether one was significantly faster than the other to determine, and, if a specific combination was faster, was it faster for the faster task, or the slower task.

Reviewing the information in Chapter 2:

Pointer definitions	Comparisons	Meaning
Storage > last element stored	IF (Storage == Retrieval)	then buffer is empty
Retrieval > last element retrieved	IF (Storage+1 == Retrieval)	then buffer is full
	IF (Storage <> Retrieval)	then data present
Storage > last element stored	IF (Storage+1 == Retrieval)	then buffer is empty
Retrieval > next element retrieved	IF (Storage == Retrieval)	then buffer is full
	IF (Storage+1 <> Retrieval)	then data present
Storage > next element stored	IF (Storage == Retrieval+1)	then buffer is empty
Retrieval > last element retrieved	IF (Storage == Retrieval)	then buffer is full
	IF (Storage <> Retrieval+1)	then data present
Storage > next element stored	IF (Storage == Retrieval)	then buffer is empty
Retrieval > next element retrieved	IF (Storage+1 == Retrieval)	then buffer is full
	IF (Storage <> Retrieval)	then data present

It is given that the sending task is only interested in whether the buffer is full or not, and the receiving task is the one concerned with whether there is data present in the buffer or not. Then a faster sending task would prefer the second and third option because the buffer-full condition can be determined by a simple compare, while a faster receiving task would prefer the first or fourth option for the same reason. Choosing a pointer convention is therefore a simple matter of reviewing the input and output rates specified for the data pathway and selecting the appropriate convention.

Once the pointer convention has been chosen, an estimate for the size of the buffer is needed. This comes from the information garnered from the dissection of the requirements. Remember that we compared the peak and average rates and made an estimate of the buffer size required. Now don't panic, we can only make an estimate at this point, and nothing is carved in stone. We will discuss additional techniques in Chapter 5 for testing that we have the optimum size buffer, but for now, we just need an estimate.

Given this information, we can make the appropriate additions to the master header file. A new section needs to be added with all the appropriate background information on the data in the pathway, type, size, name, and so on. To this we will add buffer size, pointer conventions, and prototypes for routines for adding and retrieving data from the buffer, as well as testing functions for determining if the buffer is full, empty, or has data available. Remember to use a common prefix for all variable names, and descriptive postfixes to denote the variable's function.

Again, we are using prototypes for all the reasons put forth in the previous section. The only difference is that each instantiation of the buffer routines will have a separate constant to denote the size of the buffer. In fact, another advantage of the prototype and macro system for defining buffers is that, once all four conventions have been developed, they can be reused every time a buffer protocol is needed in a design. This alone is worth the trouble of defining separate routines in that I only had to fight through the design of the comparison routines once for each type, and then I never had to suffer through the frustration again.

Once all the information has been added to the master header file, and all of the variables, constants, and peripherals have been named and defined, we have completed the definition of the communications system at this level. The only thing remaining is to implement the actual routines for accessing the variables. We will do that in the next level of the design. In fact, it will be one of the first things we will do in the next level of design, as the communications system is the hook that we will use to drive the task state machines during their development.

At this point, we should also create a header file for each of the tasks in the system. In these header files will go the definitions for the state variable of the associated task, and any other variables specific to the task's operation. Of particular interest at this point of the design are any variables for the additional significant data storage that were specified in the communications plan in the last chapter.

To define the variables to handle this storage, we need to know a few things about how the variables will be used. Specifically, are the variables static or dynamic? Are the variables accessed by other tasks in the system? What type and size are the variables? And, will pointer variables be needed to access the data? Based on these answers, we can determine the number, type, and width of the variables to be defined.

Static variables are relatively simple and should be defined in the task header file first. Start by adding a new section to the task header file, and then create the definitions for the variables. Strive to group related variables together, and label them with an appropriate comment denoting their shared function.

In the event that the variables are used together as part of a more complex data structure or protocol, name the variables with a prefix that identifies the task, a name descriptive of the common function, and a postfix that is descriptive of the individual variables function within the group. This makes it very easy to determine a variable's function with just a glance at the name, especially if a naming convention is used that employs common postfixes for common functions.

In the event that the variable stands alone in the system, name it with the same prefix as the other variables in the task, to identify the task as its owner. Then give it a name that is descriptive of its function within the task. If the variable is used as a generic holding variable, resist the urge to name it hold1 or hold2. The name is descriptive of the variables use, but it gives no information concerning what it might be holding at any given moment. The better solution is to give it a name that describes the function, or functions, within the task that will be using it. For example, a generic holding variable used by a function that converts ASCII values to hex could be called CMDTASK_ASCII2HEX_INTVAL. This identifies the task that owns the variable, identifies the function that uses the variable, and describes its function as an intermediate value variable. Remember, be descriptive and BE VERBOSE.

One final note, when defining the state variable for the task, include constant defines that give names to the specific state values in the state machine. This will make the SWITCH statement that will decode the state variable, and any state transitions, much easier to understand when the state machine is written. It will also make adding a new state to an existing state machine much easier, as the only updates required will be in the constant defines in the header file. Personally, I think this also makes the code look much more professional, and it certainly helps in getting back up to speed on a state machine, when I have to come back to it after an extended period of time.

Dynamic variables present more of a challenge to define because their storage requirements are not constant. So, just like the storage requirements for a buffer protocol pathway, we will have to make a few decisions about how the storage will be used before we can define it in the task header file.

The first step is to define how the information will be accessed. Typically dynamic storage will use data pointers for access, so a description of how the pointers work and their number will be needed. Next, we will need an estimate for the amount of storage needed for the raw mass of information. Both pieces of information should be readily available from the design of the task that will manage the data storage. If not, then a good estimate can be generated based on the peak and average rates at which data enters and leaves the storage. For a more detailed explanation of the estimating process, refer to the section in Chapter 3 that discusses the dissection of the requirements document for storage requirements.

Once the pointers and the amount of memory required for the storage has been determined, the variables can be defined in the header file for the task. As with the static variables, a descriptive naming convention should be used, and the variables associated with the storage block should be defined with the definition, or block reservation, for the main storage area. Remember to use common names, with descriptive suffixes to define each variable's function, and use a prefix that identifies the task that has ownership of the variables.

Because the variables are dynamic in nature, the comments for the storage block should also include information on inflow and outflow rates, the operation of the pointers, and any other information concerning the access of the data. It is also a very good idea to use functions to access the data within the data block. This gives the designer the flexibility to place the information, either in general data storage or nonvolatile storage, simply by calling a different macro in the function definitions. Another good reason for this system is that the access and test routines for the storage will probably look very much like the access and test routines used for a buffer protocol, so the designer can save some work by reusing the existing macros.

System Timing

In the previous chapter, we defined a system tick. This tick set the execution time for each pass through the system loop, and determined values for the various task skip timers to be used by the system. What we will do in this chapter is define how the timing system will ultimately operate.

To start, let's examine the tick in light of the system clock to determine how many execution cycles are available. To do this, we multiply the tick (in seconds) by the MIPs of the system (in instructions per second). The result will be the number of instructions that can be executed each system tick.

For typical designs, this number should be greater than 100–200 for projects in assembly language, and 300–500 for projects written in a high-level language. Our alarm clock example assumes a system speed of 1 MIP, and our calculated tick is 250 microseconds. So, we have 250 instructions per tick, generally a little short for a high-level language, but typically more than adequate for an assembly language project. Note that the ranges of 100–200 and 300–500 assume only a moderately complex design. If the work performed in the tasks is more complex, then the values may need to be increased.

If the values for a design are less than the recommended ranges, we have a couple of options:

1. The processing speed of the microcontroller can be increased by using a faster system clock. This is relatively simple, but there is an upper limit to this approach due to the electrical limitations of the microcontroller.

2. If the fast tick was driven by one or two fast tasks in the design, we can drive the fast tasks from a timer-based interrupt, as outlined in the previous chapter. We can then recalculate a newer, slower tick based on the remaining, slower timing requirements.

3. And finally, we can allow select states within task state machines to deliberately overrun the system tick. We are essentially allowing these states two ticks to execute. However, this can be a dangerous proposition, in that the long state must trigger a special operation in the system timer to adjust the skip timers appropriately and the priority handler must keep the second tick free of other tasks.

After we have settled on a final system tick and determined that we have sufficient execution time, the next task is to set up a hardware timer to measure off the tick. Depending on the specific hardware of the microcontroller, the hardware timer used can be either 8- or 16-bit, with optional pre- and postscaler functions. For our purposes, we will have to find a combination that can count the requisite number of instruction cycles.

Now, the question at this point is typically "What if the number of instruction cycles per tick is not a convenient power of 2? The timer will not automatically roll over at the right time and our system tick will be off." Yes, this is true, but don't worry, we have several options to compensate.

1. We can adjust the system clock so that the tick is a power of two, and the rollover is once again automatic.

2. We can use a timer that has an automatic reload function. This automatically preloads the timer with a constant value each time it rolls over, creating a divide-by-N counter.

3. We can build a timer interrupt service routine, driven by the rollover interrupt, to preload the timer manually.

Of the three options, 1 and 2 are the most accurate as they are handled automatically in hardware. Option 3 is typically the most used, but it can suffer from accuracy problems due to variations in the interrupt response timing.

Once the method for timing the tick is determined, note the information in the design notes files. And don't forget to let the hardware designer know about any changes you have made in the system clock frequency requirements.

The next step is to determine the placement of the skip timer functions for the various tasks in the system. The two choices are to either put the skip timer functions together in a common timer function, or put the skip timers into the individual state machines. Both options have advantages and disadvantages in the final design of the system.

If the skip timers are gathered together into a single function, then individual GO flags will be required to communicate between the timer function and the actual state machine routines. These GO flags can be convenient, because the priority handler can make use of them to defer execution of a given task, by simply clearing the flag temporarily. The skip timer for the task should have been automatically reloaded by the timer function when it reached zero, so clearing the flag will not have a lasting effect on the task timing—it will only defer the current execution.

A common timing routine also makes it much easier to coordinate the timeout of the skip timers. One of the priority systems we will explore later in this chapter offsets the initial skip timer values so that the timers will never time out together. This limits the execution load for each pass through the system loop, and requires little or no additional overhead to accomplish. However, if the timers are scattered throughout the various task state machines, then coordinating the initial values for such a system is more problematic.

Using a common timing function also makes the individual state machine more generic, in that the timing is regulated externally. As a result, reusing the state machine in the future only requires that the new system generate a GO flag at the appropriate rate to guarantee proper operation. If the skip timer had been buried in the state machine itself, then reusing the task would require edits to the module to accommodate a potentially different system tick.

One final advantage of a common timer function is the ability to generate longer delay through the nesting of two or more skip timers within a prescaler timer. This reduces the overhead in that both timers can be smaller variables, and the additional decrement time for one of the skip timers in eliminated. For example:

Algorithm 4.14

```
if (--timer_prescaler == 0)
    timer_prescaler = prescaler_value
    if (--cmd_skiptimer == 0)
            cmd_skiptimer = cmd_skip_value
            cmd_task_go = true
    if (--key_skiptimer == 0)
            key_skiptimer = key_skip_value
            key_task_go = true
```

Using this system, the code to decrement and test the `cmd_skip-timer` and `key_skiptimer` variables is only executed when the `timer_prescaler` variable reaches zero. While this may not seem like a dramatic savings, it does save one byte of data storage and eliminates multiple instruction cycles from all but an occasional pass through the system loop.

The downside to using a central timing system is that it requires the additional communication pathways, with their attendant overhead and the possibility of potential state lock problems, as the new GO variables typically use a semaphore protocol.

Placing the timers within the various task state machines, instead of within a common timer function, also has distinct advantages in that it allows each task the option to evaluate its need to execute on every pass through the system, essentially giving the tasks the option to disregard the skip timer, or modify its skip rate to accommodate the needs of the task.

This can be particularly valuable if the task is attempting to synchronize its execution to an external trigger. On each pass through the system loop, the task can test for the trigger event and, when it occurs, the task need only reload its skip timer with an appropriate value and execute the appropriate state. If the timers were in a common timer function, this activity would require the task to either reset the counter long distance, or use a handshaking flag to trigger the action in the timer function.

Self control of its own skip timer also allows the task to use a variable skip rate based on its current activities. Because the task itself is responsible for reloading the timer, two or more different reload values can be used. For instance, two values, such as 23 and 24, can be alternated as reload value for the skip timer, to produce a net skip rate of 23.5. Or, the task can load the skip timer with a much smaller value to speed up execution of a given collection of states, creating in essence a turbo mode for certain states within the task. Or, the reload value can be adjusted dynamically on each pass to maintain synchronization with sequential external events.

Self control also has a downside in that each state machine will execute at least some code on each pass through the system. This overhead will tend to eat away at the execution cycles available in each pass, reducing the number of cycles available for actually accomplishing useful work in the system. It also makes the job of the priority handler more complicated in that it must now keep track of the timing for any task in which it defers execution.

Of the two systems, a central timing function is typically the least complicated and most efficient, for both timing and priority control. And, most, if not all, of the desirable features of the self-control timing system can be implemented in a central timing system with a little work and a few broadcast protocol variables and flags.

For our clock design example, we determined that a system clock rate of 1 MIP required that our time roll over at 250. However, if we push the system clock rate to 1.024 MIP, then the roll over happens at 256, and we avoid the requirement for preloading the system. So, the decision is made to run at the slightly higher rate, the hardware engineer is notified, and a note is added to the design notes to remind us to set up the 8-bit hardware without a pre- or postscaler. Because the tick is still 250 microseconds, no additional modifications are needed for the skip timer values.

With the system clock issue settled, we can now move on to designing the system timer function. The first step is to review the skip timer information generated at the system level of the design:

Table 4.3

	Optimum	Skip Rate
Task1 (LED)		
scan	2.500	5
flash response	25.000	50 (100)
flash offtime	500.000	1000 (1100)
blank	1000.000	2000 (2222)
blank response	4.000	8 (16)
Task2 (TIME)		
timebase	1000.000	2000
switch response	4.000	8 (16)
Task3 (CMD)		
bounce	100.000	200
debounce	25.000	50 (100)
command	17.000	34 (68)
autorepeat	1000.000	2000 (2222)
aoutr response	25.000	50 (100)
Task4 (ALARM)		
time response	50.000	100 (200)
snooze response	25.000	50 (100)
Task5 (TONE)		
tone	0.500	1
var modulation	500.000	1000 (1110)
modulation	500.000	1000 (1020)

Taking each task in turn, we can now begin the design of timer functions for each task. We start with the basic timing information for the task and a quick review of how the timing information is organized:

Notes
```
Task1 (LED)
      scan                      5
      flash response       50 ( 100)
      flash offtime      1000 (1100)
      blank              2000 (2222)
      blank response        8 (  16)


LED Display task notes:

Scan rate for the task is 360Hz +20/-0 (2.635 - 2.777mS)
The scan rate if for one digit to the next digit update
(not time between same digit updates)

Alarm flash    0-50mS following time update
Alarm flash is ½ second off, ½ second on +/-10%

Blank time    909.9mS to 1111.1mS +/-0 overall
(basically, if blank, then blank for full second)

Blank response within 8mS after time update, maximum
Blank is synchronized to time update
```

Next, we separate the event-to-event timing requirements from the response time requirement. Continuing our example with the clock:

Notes
```
Task1 (LED)
Event-event
      scan                      5
      flash offtime      1000 (1100)
      blank              2000 (2222)

Response
      flash response       50 ( 100) after time update
      blank response        8 (  16) after time update
```

One important point to note about both response times is that the minimum can be zero; only the maximum is specified. So, it will typically be more convenient for the design to just use the event to trigger the start of the function, rather than create a skip timer for it.

The only caveat is that the task must recognize the event within the specified response times. The way we check this is to compare the response time skip timer values to the fastest task skip timer value. In this example, the scan skip timer is fastest at 5, and the response values are 8 and 50. So, as long as the LED task state machine can recognize a blank event in every possible state (8/5), and a flash event within every 10 states (50/5), then the response times will be within the specification.

If the task state machine cannot recognize an event within the specified time, then there are a couple of options open to us:

1. The skip rate of the task state machine could be reduced to increase the number of LED task calls within the response time. In this example, reducing the LED scan task skip rate to 1 would mean the task would have 8 ticks (8/1) in which to respond to a blank event.

2. We can go back to the writers of the requirements document and ask if the response time actually has to be that fast. It could be that a slower response is acceptable, in which case the task state machine would have more time to respond to the event.

3. The timer can use its access to the state variable to force the state machine into a state that will recognize the event.

In this specific instance, the task is implemented using a data-indexed state machine. Because data-indexed state machines execute the same code each time they are called, we need only add a statement to test for the events and blank the display if needed.

But, wait a minute. What if the blank condition occurs 3 to 4 cycles prior to the task skip timer reaching zero? If the state machine requires one state to recognize the event, and then blanks the display on the next state, those 3–4 cycles, plus the 5 between calls to the task, could push the blanking of the LEDs past the 8 millisecond response time. How do we meet the response time, if the display scan rate is too slow?

Well, we either speed up the rate at which the state machine is called and recalculate the skip timer value, or we modify our scan state machine to use two skip timers and add logic to preset the next state to a blank state. Our original task skip timer will still regulate how often the state machine executes a LED scanning state. And, the new skip timer will regulate a small routine in front of the state decoder which handles recognition of the events. For example:

Algorithm 4.15

```
Void  LED_Scan_task()
{
    if (LED_Scan_task_test_go)
    {
        LED_Scan_task_go = false;
        If (LED_blank) LED_Scan_state_variable = 6
        //blank_state
    }
    if (LED_Scan_go)
    {
        LED_Scan_go = false;

        {DATA INDEXED LED SCANNING STATE MACHINE}

    }
}
```

The new skip timer flag, `LED_Scan_task_test_go` will be driven by a skip timer with a two-tick timeout, causing the task to check for blank conditions on every other tick. If a blank event is detected, the state variable is then preset to the blank state, and the next scheduled output from the state machine turns off the displays. Because the display is now turned off in the next call to the state machine, rather than in two calls to the state machine, the response time is now less than the 5 tick time out of the task skip timer. The second skip timer flag, `LED_Scan_go` operates normally, and triggers the execution of the next state at the normal operating rate of the task. Using this system, the task state machine can now respond to a blank event within five ticks which meets the blank timing requirement of eight ticks.

Once we are satisfied that the system can meet the timing requirements, we can design a timer system algorithm. Using the LED scan task example, we end up with something like the following:

Algorithm 4.16

```
Task1 (LED)
    If (--LED_scan_skiptimer == 0)
            LED_scan_skiptimer = 5
            LED_go   = true

    If (--LED_test_skiptimer == 0)
            LED_test_skiptimer = 2
            LED_test = true

    If (time_update)
            If (ALARM_flash)
                    LED_flashtimer = 1000
            If (TIMEBASE_blank)
                    LED_blanktimer = 2000
            Time_update = false

    if (LED_flashtimer > 0)
            LED_flashtimer-
            TIMER_blank = true
    else
            TIMER_flash = false

    If (LED_blanktimer > 0)
            LED_blanktimer-
            LED_blank = true
    else
            TIMER_blank = false

    LED_blank = TIMER_flash or TIMER_blank
```

Examining the routine, we see that the first IF statement handles the normal five tick skip timer for scanning the display. The skip timer is predecremented and tested for zero. If zero, then the task GO flag is set and the skip timer is reloaded. The next IF statement is our new test skip timer for the state machine; it times out every other pass through the loop and it triggers the test function appended to the task state machine. When it times out, the displays are not scanned, but a test for a blank condition is evaluated and the next state is diverted to a blank state if needed.

The third IF statement is our test for the `time_update` signal. If set, then we have to evaluate the state of both the blank and flash flags from the timebase and alarm tasks. If either condition is true, then their timeout timers are set.

The fourth and fifth IF statements are designed to blank the display in the event that the timeout timers, for either a flash or blank condition, are greater than zero, indicating that a timed blank of the display is in progress. This allows the system to turn off the display for a fixed period of time and then re-enable the display if the condition does not persist. For a blank condition, the timeout is chosen to be 1 second, this forces the display to remain blank until the next time_update. If the blank is not set at the next time update, the timer will timeout and the display will return. For the flash function, the timeout is set for ½ second. Even though the flash condition may persist, the short timeout allows the display to restart at the midpoint of each second. The result is a ½ on, ½ off flash at a 1 Hz rate.

The final statement is just the binary or-ing of the two flags together into a single blank flag for the state machine. Note: while this system will work correctly, we can save some overhead by making one small change to the algorithm. We know when a blank condition becomes valid, because we test for the condition in the timer, so do we really need a second skip timer to force the state machine to a blank state. We could just force the condition in the timer as shown below:

Algorithm 4.17

```
LED_blank = TIMER_flash or TIMER_blank
If (LED_blank) LED_Scan_state_variable = 6     //blank_state
LED_blank = false
```

While this option certainly seems simpler, it is a poor design practice for several reasons:

1. Removing the blanking logic from the LED task hides the operation of the blanking logic in a non-standard location.

2. It complicates the debugging process because the LED scanning task cannot be tested independent of the timing system.

3. The LED scanning task is no longer a reusable module.

4. And, any changes to the blanking design will now require the modification of two modules, instead of one. And anyone making the change must know about the split functionality to be able to do the job.

Remember, our purpose here is to make modular, easy to develop, easy to test, easy to support designs.

OK, so allowing the timer to preset the state variable is not a good idea. Then how does a task state machine make changes in the skip rate of a skip timer, if it is not allowed to reload the timer? And how do we synchronize the execution of the task to an external event? The answer is, we let the timer do the work.

If the reload value of a skip timer needs to change, then we pass a simple flag to the timer function and it reloads the skip timer with the appropriate value. For example:

Algorithm 4.18

```
If (--LED_scan_skiptimer == 0)
        LED_scan_skiptimer = LED_scan_value[rate_index]
        LED_go = true
```

Now each time the skip timer reaches zero, it will be reloaded from the `LED_scan_value` array which holds all the potential skip timer values that may be needed. The control variable `rate_index` is just a value supplied by the task to specify which value it needs. The control is simple, the coding is clean and descriptive of the function and, if necessary, the array could be replaced with a holding variable, set by the task, if the number of potential values becomes too large to manage with an array.

Coding to allow a skip timer to synchronize to an external event is also simple. The skip timer is set to a skip value that is always longer than the worst-case time between events, and the event itself is used as a replacement for the timeout of the timer. For example:

Algorithm 4.19

```
If (--LED_scan_skiptimer == 0) or (external event)
        LED_scan_skiptimer = 100
        LED_go = true
```

The reason we leave the skip timer in the system is to guarantee that the task will be called even if the external event fails to occur.

In fact, a system like this will be used with the 60-Hz time base function in our alarm clock to provide time_events, even if the 60-Hz signal disappears. We simply set the skip timer to a period slightly longer than the 60-Hz event, and if the skip timer times out, we know that one 60-Hz signal is missing. When the system has missed four more, it will then reset the skip timer for an exact 60-Hz rate and use the skip timer timeout to generate time_events in place of the external 60-Hz signal.

OK, what next? Simple—we repeat the same design process for each of the other tasks in the system. When they are all complete, we gather up the design information with the hardware timer configuration information from the first part of this section, and put it into the design notes for the system. We then gather up all the GO flags, temporary flags, and skip timer variables we generated and define them in the master header file for the system. The flags go in the master header file because they are an extension of the communications pathways for the system. The temporary flags and skip timers go in the master header file because the timer function will be housed in the main system source file along with the main system loop and priority manager.

Note: It is a good practice to also note the new GO flags on the data flow diagram for the system and label them appropriately for future reference. The naming convention for the GO flags should also follow the same rules used for naming pathway variables.

Priority Handler

Now that the components of the timer system have been designed, we can turn to the companion function of the timers, the *priority handler*. The priority handler, as we discussed in Chapter 2, works with the timer system to determine which tasks get execution time. However, while the timer system determined when the task was called, the purpose of the priority handler is to determine if the task should be called. This may not sound like much of a distinction but, as we will see shortly, it is definitely different in the implementation.

In the previous chapter, we gleaned information concerning system modes and priorities from our requirements document. We then organized it by task, so we know which tasks should have priority, given a specific system condition or mode. The challenge at this phase of the design is to find a priority handler, or combination of handlers, that can shift execution time appropriately, all while minimizing its impact on the system, in the form of lost execution time and program memory usage.

Let's start by defining how a priority handler works in a real-time system. In any system that has to respond and operate according to a specific timing requirement, the software functions are typically designed to operate at their fastest execution time. So, building a priority handler that adds execution time to a function that is already operating at its correct operating rate will cause timing problems with the function because it will be executing faster than it was originally designed. Therefore, the purpose of a priority handler in a real-time system is not to add execution time, but rather to make sure the function has its allotted time, at the time it needs it. We do this by denying time to other lower-priority functions that would conflict with the high-priority routine when it needs to run.

Our purpose is to make sure that high-priority routines have execution time, when they need the execution time. We can do this in a number of ways. We can defer the lower-priority function's execution until after the higher-priority function has completed its task. Or, we can disable the lower-priority task to ensure that it cannot conflict with the execution of the higher-priority task. Or, we can arrange the timing of the two tasks, so that they will never conflict for execution time. The priority handlers that will be discussed fall into one of these three categories.

The first such system we shall examine falls into the third category—specifically, systems that arrange the timing of tasks so that they never conflict. The system is referred to as a *passive priority handler*. It operates by manipulating the initial values in the skip timers used by the various tasks in the system. The idea is to create a situation in which none, or at least most, of the timers do not time out on the same pass through the system loop.

The advantage to the system is that it requires no system resources to implement. The initial values loaded into the skip timers are offset from the values used to reload the timers. After the initial timeout, the actual reload values are used from that point on. The result is that the timers are offset or, in a sense, out of phase with one another, and remain offset throughout the continued execution of the system. Once offset, there is no code required to maintain the offset, and no variables required to track the tasks, save the skip timers themselves.

The downside of the system is that it is not adaptive to changes in the system's mode. It only maintains the time separation of the tasks; it cannot defer the execution of a task to make room for another. While this would seem to exclude this system from the job of a priority handler, it should be pointed out that it does guarantee that the tasks will have clear time to operate during the execution of the system. And, its simplicity does make it very attractive as a priority-handling system.

OK, so how is this system designed? The first things required are the skip timer values for all the tasks that will be managed by the priority handler. These values are examined to find the largest common integer value that will divide into each of the values. For example, the following are the skip timer values for a selected group of tasks from our alarm clock design:

List 4.4

```
Task                    Skip timer value
Display Task                   5
Time Base Task              2000
Alarm Control Task           100

Largest common value           5
```

The value of 5 is the largest integer factor that divides into each of the skip timer values. So, if the skip timer initial values are offset by 1 from each other, and the offset is never greater than 5, then the timers will never time out together on the same pass through the system loop. One possible configuration is shown below.

List 4.5

```
Task             Initial Skip timer value   Reload value
Display Task                5                      5
Alarm Control Task        101                    100
Time Base Task           2002                   2000
```

In the fifth pass through the system loop, the Display task will time out and be reloaded with the value 5. On pass 101, the Alarm control task will time out, and be reloaded with the value of 100. On pass 100, the Display task skip timer will have timed out, and will again on the 105th pass. But, because the Alarm Control task is offset, it will always timeout on the pass immediately following a Display task timeout, never on the same pass. In a similar manner, the Display task will timeout on the 2000th pass through the system loop, the Alarm control task on the 2001st pass, and the Time Base task on pass 2002.

As you can see, this is a simple system that uses no resources beyond those already committed to the skip timers, and it takes no additional execution overhead to maintain. However, there are a few conditions required for the system to work, one: the skip timers must have a minimum common factor to make the offset work, and two: the skip timer values for the tasks must be greater than 1.

There are also two other conditions that can cause problems, and they must also be taken into account in the design. First of all, if a task uses its skip timer to regulate the rate at which it executes states, then the system operates normally. However, if the skip timer is used to regulate only an initial state transition, then the passive system must be modified to account for the additional states that are executed following the initial state transition. For example, if the Alarm Control task used its skip timer as a gating function on the initial state transition of a three state sequence, then the Alarm Control task would execute on the 2001st, 2002nd, and 2003rd pass through the system loop. The Alarm Control task's execution on the 2002nd pass would therefore cause a collision with the Time Base task executing on the same pass.

However, as long as the initial offset of the Time Base Task skip timer accounts for the additional passes of execution, then the system would still be able to operate. When designing with tasks that use their skip timer timeouts as a state transition gating function, rather than a gate function for the entire state machine, it is important that the offset be sufficient to accommodate the worst-case number of states in a sequence. Again, using the previous example, the design would look like the following:

Algorithm 4.20

Task	Initial Skip timer value	Reload value
Display Task	5	5
Alarm Control Task (3 states)	101 (102, 103)	100
Time Base Task	2004	2000

The sequence of tasks would be the display task on pass 2000, the Alarm control task on pass 2001 through 2003, the Time Base task on pass 2004 and, finally, the Display task once again on 2005.

The other condition that can cause problems with a passive priority handler is the occasional execution of other tasks, which do not have skip timer values that fall on even multiples of the largest integer factor. The execution of these other tasks will therefore routinely coincide with the execution of some or all of the states in the tasks that use the priority handler.

While juggling the offset values solved our previous problem, this problem is going to require a little more design effort. To solve this problem, we will have to do a timing study on all of the tasks in the system, building up a table of execution times for each state of each task. We can then identify those combinations of states and tasks that will take longer to execute than the available execution time in the system tick. We can then take the states in the tasks that cause a problem and break them into two or more states, reducing their execution time. The result is a collection of states in the handler-control tasks and coinciding states in the nonhandler-controlled tasks which can have coincident execution, without overrunning the system tick.

For example, consider the previous example, combined with the execution of the Command task, which has a skip timer reload value of 34. 34 does not share the common integer factor of 5 with the other skip timer values in the Display, Alarm Control, and Time Base tasks. As a result, we can expect the Command task to execute coincident with all three of the priority handler controlled tasks during the course of the system's execution. Looking at a hypothetical list of states and execution times, shown below, and assuming 145 instruction cycles available per system tick, we can expect to overrun the system timing tick whenever the time required for a command state, added to a Display, Time Base, or Alarm Control state, exceeds 145 total cycles.

Table 4.4

Task		Cycles
Display		85
Time Base	state 1	15
	state 2	40
	state 3	70
Alarm Control	state 1	20
	state 2	50
	state 3	75
	state 4	60
	state 5	95
Command	state 1	12
	state 2	60
	state 3	48
	state 4	65

In this example, an overrun occurs whenever the following combinations of states occur:

Algorithm 4.21

```
Command   state 2   60   Display, Alarm Control(state 5)
          state 4   65   Display, Alarm Control(state 5)
```

To correct this problem, we have three possible solutions. One, state 2 and 4 in the command task can be broken into two or more smaller states with execution times less than 50 instruction cycles. This will guarantee that the execution times for these states cannot combine with the other task state machines and overrun the system timing. Two, we can use some of the timing leeway for the Command task, and change its skip timer reload value to a multiple of 5, such as 35. This would allow us to force the command task to always execute coincident with the Time Base task, which did not have a timing conflict with the command task. This solves the problem, without requiring modifications to the task state machine designs. And, three, we could allow the system to overrun the timing tick. This will cause some variance in the timing of inputs, and outputs, but the worst-case delay would be 15 instruction cycles, approximately 10.4%. The choice of solutions would depend on the timing requirements of the system and the difficulty in breaking the appropriate task states into smaller states.

Even with the difficulties in designing the system, the passive priority handler has several points in its favor: minimal design difficulty, no impact on system resources, and no ongoing drain on the system performance. The downside is that it cannot adjust to changing system requirements, and tasks outside the system may cause additional design time.

Concerning documentation, the design notes should be updated with information concerning the calculation of the largest common factor and the initial skip timer values. Additional notes concerning the evaluation of other tasks in the system and their impact on the processor workload should be included, plus any information concerning modifications to the tasks or the possibility of overrunning the system tick. All notes should include a clear and verbose explanation of the decisions involved with any design changes.

The next priority handler to be examined is the *time-remaining* system. The time-remaining system is designed to get the most execution accomplished within a fixed time frame. In the case of our design methodology, the idea is to get the greatest number of tasks executed within a system's timing tick. To accomplish this task, the priority handler requires two pieces of information—the amount of time that a task will require to execute its current state and the time remaining in the system timing tick.

The time remaining is reasonably simple to obtain; it is just a matter of reading the current value of the hardware timer, which controls the system tick. Knowing the period of the timer and the current value, the handler can then determine the number of instruction cycles left in the tick. This represents the amount of time remaining, and therefore the amount of time available for the execution of a task's current state. The next step is to find a task whose current state can execute within the remaining time and call the task's state machine.

The advantage to this system is that it tries to optimize the execution throughput of the microcontroller, basically fitting together segments of execution with the objective of keeping the microcontroller busy 100% of the time. While 100% utilization of the microcontroller is not practical, it will give the designer the maximum processing power available, given the microcontroller and its clock frequency.

The downside of this system is that it requires an extensive knowledge of the execution times for every state in every task state machine. Further, any future modifications to any of the state machines not only requires that the information be renewed, it also means that the resulting system will change the way and order in which tasks will be executed. After all, changing the number of cycles required to execute a task will affect the amount of time remaining after the task, which will subsequently change the number of potential states and tasks that will fit in the time remaining.

So, the first step in the design process is to build an execution timing database for all of the states, in all of the task state machines. Next, the latency times for the timing system and the priority handler have to be measured. Once this is complete, the execution database and system offset times can be built.

In operation, the priority handler will first read the current value of the system timer used to regulate the system tick. The next step is to subtract the offset value, representing the latency times for the timer and priority handler, from the time remaining. Then the resulting value is compared against the execution times for any tasks requesting execution. The highest priority task with a state that will execute within the remaining time is then executed, and its request for execution time is reset. Once the task finishes executing its current state, the handler once again checks the time remaining to determine if there is time remaining for another task to execute.

There are three aspects to this system that a designer should question: one, how can a task maintain constant timing, if it cannot be guaranteed execution time in a specific tick? Two, does the system give a preference for the best fit in the time remaining, or on the basis of priority? And, three, how does the system respond to changes in the system mode? One: fixed timing can only be guaranteed by using a buffered input/output system that is tied to the main system timer. Two: the tasks are tested in the order they are encoded into the design of the priority handler, so tasks that are tested earlier in the tick have higher priority than tasks that are tested later in the list. As a result, order of testing translates directly to priority, however, if a higher priority task will not fit into the time remaining, it will be bypassed for a lower priority task that does fit in the time remaining. And, three: like the passive priority handler, there is no mechanism for changing the priorities of the system based on the system mode. However, combining this system with one of the later priority handlers does give the system that capability.

One other question that should come up: doesn't the testing in the priority handler also decrease the time remaining in the tick? The answer is yes, it does, and, yes, it will affect the calculation of time remaining for each subsequent task that is tested. However, after each test, the remaining time can either be retrieved again from the system timer, or be offset by the test time through a simple subtraction from the test value. This will compensate for the time required to perform the last test, and keep the time-remaining value current for each new test.

While this system does get the optimum execution throughput out of the system, in many applications, the additional design and test overhead, plus the execution time required to determine which task should execute is often such a drain on the throughput that a point of diminishing returns is reached. When this happens, the priority handler is consuming more execution time than it saves and the system has no value. So, the designer is encouraged to carefully consider the time and resources required using this method of priority handler before investing large amounts of time in its design. Remember, a priority handler's job is getting the most from the available resources, not necessarily getting every last instruction cycle of throughput out of the microcontroller.

As an example, consider a system including three tasks, A, B, and C. Each of these tasks has between one and four states, with execution times represented in instruction cycles. Further, assume the timing for the system is regulated by a hardware countdown timer, Timer0. An application algorithm of the time remaining system would look like the following:

Algorithm 4.22

```
Database[3][4] = {execution times for states, by task}
While(1)
   Switch (index)
      case 0:  if Timer0 > Database[0][task0_statevariable]
                  task0()
      case 1:  if Timer0 > Database[1][task1_statevariable]
                  task1()
      case 2:  if Timer0 > Database[2][task2_statevariable]
                  task2()
   System_timer()
```

The database is indexed by both task number and state number, and contains the time to execute every state in every task. The SWITCH statement then searches through the three different tasks, looking for a state execution time that is less than the time remaining in the system tick. If it finds one, it calls the appropriate state machine and the state is executed and the next task is tested for the time remaining after the called task. If not, then the case statement falls through without executing the state machine and tests the next task in the list. When the time remaining is so small that no task will fit, the SWITCH statement will fall through to the end and the loop will wait out the end of the time in the timer function and then start the loop over again.

One method for simplifying the system is to combine the passive system with the time-remaining system. In this hybrid, the passive system manages the execution of the high-priority tasks in the system, and the time-remaining system attempts to fit in lower-priority tasks in the time left over. This eliminates the impact of shifting execution patterns from the high-priority tasks, as well as guaranteeing them execution at specific times. And, it still attempts to get the maximum throughput out of the system by filling in the extra blocks of time with lower priority functions. The following algorithm shows how this would be accomplished:

Algorithm 4.23

```
Database[3][4] = {execution times for states, by task}
While(1)
   Hi_prioritytask_A()
   Hi_prioritytask_B()
   Switch (index)
      case 0:  if Timer0 > Database[0][task0_statevariable]
                  lo_priority_task0()
      case 1:  if Timer0 > Database[1][task1_statevariable]
                  lo_priority_task1()
      case 2:  if Timer0 > Database[2][task2_statevariable]
                  lo_priority_task2()
   System_timer()
```

A variation on this system is to use some other form of priority handler on the high and middle priority tasks, and use the time-remaining system to fit in so-called housekeeping functions. A housekeeping function is a task or software function with no definitive timing requirements—for example, a function to periodically check the battery voltage could be considered a housekeeping function, in that it has no specific time that it must be performed. As a result, the time-remaining system can fit it into the tick whenever there is sufficient excess execution time to accommodate it. The execution time is not guaranteed, but a good probability exists that it will be executed at some time when the right combination of higher-priority tasks leaves a window of execution time. The following is one example of an algorithm that would implement this type of system:

Algorithm 4.24

```
While(1)
    Hi_prioritytask_A()
    Hi_prioritytask_B()
    Hi_prioritytask_C()
    if Timer0 > Min_housekeeping
         housekeeping()
    System_timer()
```

Of course, the probability can be based on an analysis of the execution times for the various states in the various tasks and the skip timer values for each of the tasks, though typically the easier solution is just to implement the system and then build in a software counter to count the number of calls to the housekeeping function while the system is tested. If the function is not called sufficiently often, the initial values used to load the skip timers for the other task can be juggled in an attempt to create more frequent open slots for the housekeeping task to execute.

For most of the priority handlers discussed in this section, a numerical spreadsheet, with the ability to graph its results, is often very helpful in trying different combinations of tasks, and in the search for patterns of dead time for the execution of infrequent tasks.

A priority handler that does respond to changes in the system mode, is the *variable-order* system. In the variable-order system, the number and order of task state machines called is dependent upon a variable driven by the system mode. When the mode changes, this system uses the variable to select a different calling order to change the priorities and availability of task state machines. This allows the system to create a custom calling list for each of the system modes and eliminate any tasks that are either not used or mutually exclusive to tasks that are needed in the current system mode.

The advantage to this system is that the tasks that are active in a given mode are only those tasks actually needed for operation. Other tasks are essentially removed from the system and do not constitute a drain on the systems resources. In addition, combining this system with another system, such as time remaining, allows the system to change the order of the tasks tested in time remaining, which in turn changes the priorities of the tasks.

The only information required to implement this type of system is the system modes and the tasks that are required for each mode. The rearrangement of the system is then handled through a SWITCH statement driven by the mode variable. The only difficult part of the system is generating a function that quantifies the system mode into a simple integer value. The following is an example of how this system could be applied to our alarm clock design example:

Algorithm 4.25

```
While(1)
    switch (mode)
        case Timekeeping:                    TimeBase_task()
                                             Display_task()
                                             Button_task()
                                             Error_Task()
                                             break

        case TimeSet:                        Button_task()
                                             Display_task()
                                             TimeBase_task()
                                             Error_Task()
                                             break

        case AlarmPending, SnoozeMode:       TimeBase_task()
                                             AlarmControl_task()
                                             Display_task()
                                             Button_task()
                                             Error_Task()
                                             break

        case AlarmSet:                       Button_task()
                                             TimeBase_task()
                                             Display_task()
                                             Error_Task()
                                             break

        case AlarmActive:                    TimeBase_task()
                                             AlarmTone_task()
                                             AlarmControl_task()
                                             Display_task()
                                             Button_task()
                                             Error_Task()
                                             break

        case PowerFail:                      TimeBase_task()
                                             Display_task()
                                             Error_Task()
                                             break

        case ErrorMode:                      Error_Task()
                                             Display_task()
                                             Button_task()
                                             Break
```

Note that the list of tasks follows exactly the priority list generated in the last chapter. The only addition is the SWITCH statement and the use of a switch variable mode. While this may look long and complex, it is actually very simple and surprisingly compact when compiled. The only additional code needed is the logic to load the mode variable with the appropriate value corresponding to the system mode.

One cautionary note on the generation of the value in the mode variable: if the value is generated either wholly, or in part, by the tasks themselves, then the designer must make sure that the tasks are present in the calling list for each system mode. If not, then it is possible to get the system into a mode, but not back out again, because the logic for determining the mode change has been disabled by the priority handler. So, now is a good time to evaluate which tasks contribute information concerning each to the mode changes, and the triggers that generate the change. While different tasks may contribute to a mode change, there must be at least one task active that can cause the system to exit any given mode.

Two related priority-handling systems are the *excuse-me* and *excuse-you* systems. Both systems use knowledge of the system mode and the state of other tasks in the system to decide whether to defer execution if the demands on the system are heavy. The difference is whether the task making the decision decides to defer its own execution, the excuse-me version, or force the deferment of another task, the excuse-you version.

While the systems evaluated so far work on a system-wide scope, these two systems are tailored more toward a task-by-task priority control. They typically handle priority management on a more one-on-one format, releasing the resources of a specific task in favor of another task. As a result, the tasks in the system are typically related to each other in function. For example, Task A handles serial transmission of data over a serial port, Task B handles serial reception of data. In an excuse-me scenario, Task A would check on the status of Task B before initiating a serial transmission. If Task B is busy receiving data, then A excuses itself out of the system until B has completed its task. This is predicated on the premise that the priority of A is low until it begins transmission, and then its priority increases. So, if it defers the initiation of a transmission, it is holding itself at a lower priority until system resources are freed up.

An excuse-you scenario would involve the receiving task B forcing the transmitting task A to hold in its low-priority state until B has completed its job. Then task A would be released by B and allowed to continue with its transmission.

While these two systems sound very similar, there are some important differences. In the excuse-me system, only the task deferring its own execution is held off. In the excuse-you system, more than one task could be held in a low-priority state. Also, the excuse-me system bases its decision to defer on its knowledge of what it is about to do, and what the other task is doing. The excuse-you system makes the assumption that the deferred task *might* make a state change that will affect its status, and the deciding task is preventing the other task from changing priority. So, you might consider the excuse-me system as the polite, politically correct system, and the excuse-you as the rude, domineering system.

Both systems have their place in a design; it will just depend on which tasks have their priority driven by external events, and which have the option to defer their shift in priority. The information to base these decisions on was retrieved from the requirements document, and decided at the system level of the design—specifically, when state changes within the task state machine caused a change in the task's priority within the system and the relative priority of tasks based on the mode of the system.

To implement either system, excuse me or excuse you, the task making the decision will need to consider the general mode of the system. This implies that a variable, or collection of variables, is available with which to determine the system mode. The status of the other task involved also needs to be known; typically this is determined by interpreting the value in the state variable for the other task. Based on these two pieces of information, a decision is made to defer execution, and the appropriate task is forced to defer a change in its state.

As an example, consider the serial input and output tasks discussed earlier. The following examples show how the transmit task can be forced to defer a state change using first the excuse-me system, and then the excuse-you system.

→

Algorithm 4.26

EXCUSE ME

```
Transmit()
{
    Switch(trans_statvar)
    {
        Case IDLE:  If (receive_statevar == idle) & (data_available)
                        trans_statvar = send
                    break
```

EXCUSE YOU

```
Receive()
{
    Switch(recvr_statvar)
    {
        Case IDLE:  if (rcvr_inbuff_full)
                        Tx_defer = true
                        Data_in = rcvr_inbuff
```

```
Transmit()
{
    Switch(trans_statvar)
    {
        Case IDLE:  if (Tx_defer == false) & (data_available)
                        trans_statvar = send
                    break
```

The excuse-me system just requires a change to the state machine that is making the decision to defer its own state change. No modification is required in the state machine that is benefiting from the decision to defer. The excuse-you system requires modifications to both state machines. The state machine that makes the decision to force the other state machine to defer needs the additional logic to make the decision, and the state machine being forced to defer needs logic to prevent it from making the state change.

One thing to remember—when forcing the state machine to defer a change in state, the logic to make the change must occur within the state change logic in the state machine. Using global access to another state machine's state variable, for the purpose of forcing it to defer a change, is a bad idea and poor programming practice for several reasons. One, if a task forces another state machine to change, or not change, its state, then the logic is hidden within the design of a seemingly unrelated task. It makes the design harder to debug, it is harder to document, it limits the portability of the code, and it will be that much harder to support. Adding the conditional statement in the state machine document which is deferring the change in state shows the connection between the state machines, and it shows the reason for deferring the change.

As always, all of the decisions and design information should be noted in the design notes for the design. And once again, be clear and verbose; every comment and note you add to the design notes file will save you phone calls later from the support group.

The last priority handler system we will examine is the *parent/child* system. In this system, one or more parent tasks are assigned the responsibility for the management of a child task. The parents determine when and why the child task is executed and what priority the child task will have in the system. When the functionality of the child task is required, then the parent of the child enables the task and supplies it with any pertinent information it requires. The child then executes its function and notifies the parent when it has completed its work. The parent can then either provide the child with additional work or disable the child, removing its overhead from the system.

Part of the value of the parent/child system is that the parent is assumed to release its execution time requirements during the course of the child's operation. In this way, the parent releases its priority in the system to the child, without requiring additional execution time resources for another task. Basically, the parent loans the child its execution time while the child is performing a task for the parent.

The usual question, is why not just add the child's code to the parent and forget about the additional overhead? The reason has to do with decisions we made in the task definition section of the last chapter. Remember that there are certain functions, such as control of a common peripheral, that require some form of arbitration to prevent contention between two control tasks. A child task is a very simple method for providing that arbitration. If a control task is currently using the resources of the child task, it will have to enable the child task to manage the control. If a second control task wants to use the resources, it will be alerted that the resource is already in use because the child task is enabled. When the child completes the work given to it by the parent, it will be disabled. This will notify the second control task that the resources are now available, and it can lock up the child task by enabling it, until such time as the child task has completed its work.

So, by wrapping the common peripheral with a simple child task, we can arbitrate control of the peripheral by simply enabling and disabling the child task. It does require the parent task to check the status of the child task's enable, but this is a lot simpler than trying to determine whether another task is currently involved in a peripheral control operation or not. The ability to arbitrate is not solely reserved for control of peripherals; the same system can also be used to regulate access and control of data variables, preventing different parent tasks from corrupting a variable by attempting to write to the variable at the same time.

The implementation of a child task is fairly simple. The child task state machine is modified to include a conditional statement which either decodes the task's state variable or not, depending on the state of an enable bit. The parent task then need only enable the bit and the child task state machine will start decoding and executing states. When either the parent or the child clears the enable bit, then the next call to the state machine will result in a return, with decoding or executing a state.

As an example, consider the Alarm_control and Alarm_tone tasks in our alarm clock design example. The Alarm_tone is only needed when the current time has reached the alarm time, assuming that the alarm function is enabled at the time. Then, and only then, the alarm_tone task is enabled to operate. During the operation of the alarm tone, the execution time requirements of the Alarm_control task are almost nonexistent, as its only job is to monitor for an alarm off or snooze command. The following algorithms show how the Alarm_control task could exert its control over the alarm_tone task.

Algorithm 4.27

```
Alarm_tone()
{
    if (alarm_tone_enable == true)
            if (tone_modulation == true) alarm_tone_
            state = ! alarm_tone_state
            else alarm_tone_state = false
            speaker_pin = alarm_tone_state
    else
            speaker_pin = 0
}
```

The control of the Alarm_tone state machine is implemented with a simple conditional statement at the top of the data-indexed state machine. If the enable bit is set, then the state variable toggles between one and zero, assuming the modulation time bit is set. The state is then output to the speaker to generate the tone. If the bit is cleared, then the speaker output is driven low and the state machine takes no further action.

Another method is to tie the enable bit into the skip timers. If the enable bit is cleared, then the skip timer is not decremented, the timer never times out, and the task is never called. When the bit is set, the skip timer behaves normally, and the task is called with the proper timing. This has a downside that the child task cannot be included in a passive priority handler system because the timing for the task is not predictable.

One of the good things about a parent/child priority handler is that the child task need not have an idle task. If the child task automatically disables itself when it completes its work, then an idle state is not needed, and the additional state decoding can be avoided. This requires either the parent task to preset the state variable before it enables the child, or the child will have to leave the correct starting value in the state variable, when it disables itself.

Concerning the documentation of a parent/child system, adequate notes concerning the relationship between the two tasks should be included in the design notes for the system. The enable bit should also be included in the communications documentation for the system because it is specific to neither the parent nor the child, falling instead into the realm of intertask communications. And, finally, any notes concerning the default state of the child task state variable should also be included in the system.

This concludes the examination of the individual priority handler systems. However, a typical system will not employ just one system; often two or more of the systems are combined to create a custom priority handler for the final design. Combination of the time-remaining system and the variable-order system are particularly useful in that the order of tasks in a time-remaining system dictates the priority of the tasks being controlled. Using variable order with time remaining allows the system to reorder the tasks based on the system mode. Other combinations of excuse me and you, with parent/child, can allow the system to create a priority handler that does not rely on a centralized priority handler, but rather disperses the load out to the individual tasks in the system.

There is no statement, expressed or implied, that these systems are the only system appropriate for embedded control designs. In fact, designers are encouraged to develop their own priority-handling systems, either based on these examples or taken from their own imagination. System requirements for specific markets and based on individual coding styles will tend to promote certain types of priority handling over others. Designers should be creative and develop systems that work for their markets and products. These examples are just that—examples designed to show what is possible, what controls are available, and ways in which the controls can be used to manage shifting priorities in a design.

Error Recovery System

At this level of the design, we now need to define the recovery mechanisms for the system. Specifically, what is done when the error is detected, and what actions, if any, the user will have to take to correct the problem.

In the last chapter, we separated the various failures into three classifications: soft errors, recoverable errors, and hard errors. Soft errors were handled within the normal operation of the software; they typically deal with the user interface, syntax errors, input sequence errors, or out-of-range values. Recoverable errors are more serious, usually involving some kind of transient failure in the hardware or software. Once the condition causing the failure is cleared, the system can recover and continue to operate. Recoverable errors may also require intervention by the user to clear the problem. Hard errors are the most serious; they typically involve a more permanent failure in the system, and no intervention by an error recovery system or the user can clear the problem. These errors are usually permanent, barring repair of the system.

Our task in this phase of the design is to define the systems that will detect the errors, classify the severity of the error, and design recovery or management systems for handling the errors. Because the variety of possible errors, and the wide variety of possible recovery systems, is dependent upon the type of system being designed, it is probably best to demonstrate the process through an example. We will work through the error detection and recovery system needed for our alarm clock example. To begin the work, we need to revisit the errors that were defined for the system in the last chapter. Starting with the soft failures, we have the following:

List 4.6

Soft Error

Fault: Button pressed is not valid for current mode or command.

Button combination is invalid.

Test: Comparison of decoded button command with legal commands, by mode.

Response: Ignore button press.

Soft Error

Fault: Display task state variable corruption.

Test: Range check on the state variable.

Response: Reset the state variable.

Soft Error

Fault: Alarm tone task state variable corruption.

Test: Range check on the state variable.

Response: Reset the state variable.

In the first error, the test is already performed in the button task, and the response is to simply ignore the button, so no special test or recovery mechanism is required. However, it is a good idea to review the design for the button task, just to make sure that illegal button combinations were not taken into account in the state machine design.

The second and third soft errors deal with corruption of a state variable. As far as task state machines are considered, the display and alarm tone state machines are the least important. They generate no control or status signals used by the other tasks in the system, and their only purpose is as a user display function. So, if their state variables were to become corrupted, we can just reset either state variable, safe in the knowledge that the variable's temporary corruption has not disrupted any of the other tasks in the system.

To create a detection and recovery system for this fault, we need only assign the default value to the variable, if the state machine ever calls the default state of the state machine. If the default state is called, it is because the value in the state variable does not correspond to a valid state value. The recovery code in the default state then just resets the state variable to one of the blank states for the display task, just in case the display was being blanked, or the zero state for the alarm tone state machine. Once the state variable is reset, the error condition is resolved. As far as our actions in this phase of the design, we need only add appropriate notes to the design notes for the display and alarm tone tasks. Because none of the actions required to clear the errors require user intervention, none of the errors will force an error mode for the system. The error conditions will just be cleared and the system will be allowed to continue.

Moving on to recoverable errors, we get into a little more complex problem. Now the errors become more severe, and there is the potential that the user will be involved in the process of clearing the error. The list of recoverable errors from the last chapter appears following.

List 4.7

1. **Recoverable Error**

   Fault: Alarm time is out of range (Alarm time > 23:59).

   Test: Alarm control runction test of value before current time comparison.

   Response: If alarm is enabled, sound alarm until ALARMSET button press.

   If in any other mode, ignore (fault will be identified when alarm is enabled).

2. **Recoverable Error**

   Fault: Alarm disabled but also active.

   Test: Routine check by error task.

   Response: Reset alarm control task state variable.

3. **Recoverable Error**

   Fault: Snooze active when alarm is disabled.

   Test: Routine check by error task.

   Response: Reset alarm control task state variable.

4. **Recoverable Error**

   Fault: Alarm control task state variable corruption.

   Test: Range check on the state variable.

   Response: Reset the state variable.

   If alarm is active, disable then retest for alarm time.

   If alarm enabled or active, range check alarm time.

   If alarm time out of range, then notify error task of fault condition.

5. **Recoverable Error**

   Fault: Button task state variable corruption.

   Test: Range check on the state variable.

   Response: Reset the state variable.

   Cancel any current command semaphores.

   Reset all debounce and autorepeat counter variables.

List 4.7
(continued)

6. **Recoverable Error**

Fault: Time-base task state variable corruption.

Test: Range check on the state variable.

Response: Reset the state variable.

            Range check time base timer variables.

            If out of range, then reset and notify error task to clear potential alarm fault.

7. **Recoverable Error**

Fault: Error task state variable corruption.

Test: Range check on the state variable.

Response: Reset the state variable.

            Check status on other system state machines.

            If error condition, then set error system mode, set current time to default.

            Wait for user control input.

8. **Recoverable Error**

Fault: Power failure.

Test: Fifth missing 60-Hz time base pulse.

Response: Goto power fail mode until fifth detected 60-Hz pulse.

The various errors can be broken into three main areas. Areas 1–3 deal with corrupted data/control variables in the alarm task, 4–7 deal with corrupted state variables, and 8 deals with a system power failure. Of the different errors, number 8 is the easiest to deal with because the system is already designed to handle it. In fact, it is the main reason for a separate time-base task in the system, so we can ignore it and move on to the other eight errors.

Errors 1–3 handle errors in variables used by the alarm task. Error 1 indicates corruption of the alarm time, which will require user intervention to reset the value; 2 indicates that the alarm state machine has failed to notice a change in system mode—specifically, the task is active when the control input from the button task indicates it should be inactive; and 3 indicates that the snooze mode is active when the alarm is disabled.

Let's start with errors 2 and 3. Both are detected during a normal check by the error task, and both require a reset of the alarm control state variable as a corrective action. To build in the necessary mechanism to detect and correct the error, we need to add two states to the error task state machine. One that tests for both conditions, alarm or snooze active, while the alarm is disabled, and the second to reset the state variable for the alarm control task. If the first state detects either condition, it will then jump to the second state to reset the state variable. Note that this also means that the first state must be in a loop within the state machine, so it can routinely make tests for the conditions.

One side note on the error task: so far we have not made much mention of the error task, or how it operates. That is because, until now, we have not had much in the way of information about its intended purpose. However, in this section on error recovery, we will be defining the error task's operation, as it will be one of the primary systems handling general error detection and recovery for our design. At the end of this chapter, after we have defined all the error detection and recovery systems for the design, we will have all the necessary information to perform a general state machine design on the error task. At that point we will perform the component-level design of the error task, using the same methods employed in the design of all the other tasks in the system.

Error 1 is a little more serious, in that it requires intervention by the user to clear the problem. It is a corruption of the alarm time, detected by the alarm-control task as part of its alarm mode operation. The system's response to the error is to continuously sound the alarm while the alarm is enabled. If the user disables the alarm, or presses the alarm set button to set the alarm, then the alarm will quiet for as long as the button is held or the alarm is disabled. If the button is released, or the alarm re-enabled with a corrupted value in the alarm-time variable, the alarm tone will start again.

To detect the condition, the state in the alarm task that checks for alarm time = current time, must be modified to include code to check the range of the values in the alarm-time variable. If the variable is out of range, then the alarm is activated just as if the current time had reached the alarm time.

Recovering from error 1 is also somewhat more complicated. There needs to be a pathway established between the button task and the alarm-control task to carry the current state of the alarm set button. This is so the alarm tone can be disabled when the alarm set button is pressed. The fast and slow alarm set commands also have to be modified; they have to first verify the alarm time is within a valid range and, if not, reset the alarm time to a default value prior to incrementing the variable.

All the changes to the alarm-control and buttons tasks should be noted in the design notes for the system and in the individual sections relating to each task. The additional data pathway should also be added to the communications plan, the data flow diagram, and the header files generated earlier in this chapter. A write-up of the error recovery system should also be added to the design notes in the sections dealing with the button task, the alarm-control task, communications, and error detection/recovery.

The next group of errors, errors 4 through 8, deals with the corruption of the various state variables used by the task state machines. Detection is typically accomplished through the default state of the various state machine state decoders. If the state is invalid, then the state decoder will jump to the default state, and code in the default state is responsible for effecting the error recovery. The only problem is that the corruption of some of the state machines may affect other state machines in the system, so the errors move from the classification of *soft errors* to the classification of *recoverable errors*. As *recoverable errors*, their recovery mechanism requires coordination through the error task.

While the error is detected in the default state of the state machine, the actual recovery mechanism resides in the error task state machine. The reason to put the recovery into the error task is because the error task state machine is independent of the problem. It can reset any combination of task state variables, in any order, something that a recovery routine in a default state cannot accomplish because resetting its state machine stops the recovery.

To pass the notification of the failure, we will need data pathways for each of the task default states, to the error task state machine. The error task also needs to know the current state of all the state machines, so additional pathways will be required to carry this information. And, finally, the error task will need a mechanism for resetting the state variables of each of the other tasks in the system.

All of the monitoring can be accomplished through additional pathway links between the tasks and the error task. Because the function of the pathways is to allow the error task to monitor the other task's real-time operation, the best protocol for the pathways is broadcast. It will not require the monitored task to handshake and the error task can choose to ignore the data if no error is currently being handled.

The control is a somewhat more complex problem. The tasks being reset by the error task may be in either a valid state, or in the default state when the error task attempts to reset. As a result, tasks being reset may not be able to respond to a reset command through the logic in the individual task states, so the control will have to be added through the command decoder logic for the state machines. Basically, we will be adding a semaphore pathway into each of the tasks. This semaphore is read by the state decoding logic each time the state machine is called, and if set, it resets the state variable. The state decoder then resets the semaphore to acknowledge the reset has occurred.

With both monitoring and control capability, the error task is then set up to monitor the error flags from each of the tasks. The monitoring function is implemented as a loop and when a specific error is detected, the loop then branches out to the specific sequence of states that will reset the appropriate state machines, in the appropriate order.

The last recovery mechanism to define is for recovering from a corruption of the error task state variable. Here, no monitoring system is needed, as the error task will know that its own state variable is corrupted when the state decoder decodes the default state. The error task will then have to do a quick sanity check on the various tasks in the system to determine whether any of the other tasks needs to be reset. Since the sanity check is the normal operation of the error task, all that really needs to happen is that the state variable for the error task be reset so the task can return to polling for errors. Additional sanity checks can be included in the sequence, prior to the reset of the state variable, such as a CRC check on program memory, a range check on any important variables, and/or verification of specific output controls.

With the last part of the design, the error task is finally defined. A state machine design for the error task can now be completed using the design techniques shown at the beginning of the chapter. As with the other system designs, the various states will be defined, and the triggering events that cause a state change. Individual actions are then defined for each of the states and the input and output pathways are cataloged.

Appropriate changes and additions are then made to the communications plan, to accommodate the new monitoring and control functions added to the task's list of responsibilities. The timing chosen for the error task should also be reviewed in light of the new responsibilities the task will have. Finally, the priority list should be reviewed to determine whether or not the error task will be active at all times to handle any errors the system might encounter.

Once the design is complete, the appropriate notes are added to the design notes for the system, the error task, the system communications plan, and the documentation on the priority-handling systems.

The last class of errors to be handled are hard errors. These errors are so severe that the system must be either reset through a power down or by repair of the system. In either event, the configuration of the system will be lost, and the user will be required to completely restart and reconfigure the software. For our design example, we have three hard errors:

List 4.8 →

Hard Error

Fault: Watchdog timer timeout.

Test: Hardware supervisor circuits.

Response: System is reset.

           System will power up in error mode.

Hard Error

Fault: Brownout reset.

Test: Hardware supervisor circuits.

Response: System is reset, and held in reset until power is restored.

           System will power up in error mode.

**List 4.8
(continued)**

Hard Error

Fault: Program memory fails a CRC test.

Test: CRC check on power up.

Response: System locks, with a blank display.

The first two errors are driven by hardware supervisory circuits internal to the design of the microcontroller, or attached externally to the reset line of the microcontroller. Both generate either a system reset or an interrupt. The system software then has to detect the reset or interrupt from these sources and leave the system in the error mode on power up. Detection of an internal watchdog or brownout is usually done through the testing of specific status bits in the microcontroller. For information on which bits and how the source is determined, the designer should refer to the documentation on the device, and any applicable applications notes generated by the manufacturer.

For external sources, some kind of hardware method will be needed that allows the microcontroller to determine the source of the reset.

There is also one reset that is missing from the list, that is the initial power-on reset. This is the first reset for the system following power-up, and like a watchdog or brownout reset, it should also bring the system up in the error mode. This is because on the first power-up, the system will not know what the current time is and, without that knowledge, both the time display and alarm functions are useless. So, putting the system into the error mode is a reasonable solution as well.

This means that all potential sources of reset have the same response, so we can lump them all together and just put the system into the error mode in the event of a system reset. What this means for the design is that all we will have to do to respond to a reset is to preset the mode variable in the Init_var() routine to the code corresponding to the error mode.

In the current design, the response to a watchdog timeout is that the system is reset. This is based on an assumption in the requirements document that a watchdog timer timeout is the direct result of a corruption of the program counter, and any corruption of the program counter introduces the possibility of corrupted data. So, resetting the system to a default condition that forces the user to reconfigure the clock is the only safe course. A reasonable assumption for the alarm clock design, but what about an automated control system for elevators, or an engine controller? A forced restart from zero could actually damage the engine if the controller resets while it is still running.

Another possible response to a watchdog timeout might be to run a routine that shuts the engine down safely. This solves the problem of how to restart the system, but the optimum choice would be to recover and continue to manage the engine. While this scenario may seem unlikely, there are aspects of a state machine-based multitasking system that could make it possible.

Let's assume for now that the system maintains redundant copies of the data, and that the data can be validated with a CRC. With two copies of the data, the design should be able to find one copy of clean data. If it can't, then the system can always shut down using the previous option. However, if the system has clean data, then the only problem is restarting the state machines.

If the state variables were stored with the rest of the data, then they should be valid. Examining the skip timers can tell the system which task was running during the last tick. So, the system should be able to restart, just where it left off. All the reset routine need do is copy the good data into the corrupted data space, CRC the results, set the goflag for any task that has a skip timer equal to its reload value, and jump to the top of the loop. For most systems this should restart the system at the start of the last tick prior to the failure, and the system will never know the difference.

For even greater reliability, additional steps can be taken to help ensure the correct restart of the system:

1. Set the watchdog timer timeout to a period slightly longer than the system tick. This will limit the amount of damage a corrupted program counter can do prior to the time out.

2. There should be only *ONE* clear watchdog command, and it should be at the top of the main system loop. Never put the clear watchdog instruction in the interrupt service routine.

3. Keep one, or preferably two redundant copies of the data, and only copy the new data into the old data at the end of the tick. This should give one copy a decent chance of surviving the corrupted program counter.

4. Fill all unused program memory locations with a GOTO that will direct the microcontroller to the reset routine.

5. If possible, put a write-protect circuit on the data memory that holds the redundant copy of the system variables. The write protect should use an unlock sequence, and it should automatically relock after a fixed number of instruction cycles.

That pretty much cover the error-detection and recovery mechanisms for the system. The component level of the design should now be complete.

Before moving on to implementation, let's take a few moments and review the documentation that should have been generated in this phase of the design.

From the state machine portion of the design, there should be a complete design package for each of the task state machines.

For a data-indexed design, there should be a list of states. Naming the states is optional, as the primary use of the state variable is to index the array of data acted upon by the state machine. There should be a list of the state transitions and the events that trigger the change in state. Any important algorithms should be noted and commented with sufficient detail to explain their operation. And, all the state machines' inputs and outputs should be noted, as well as any additions to the design for handling error detection and recovery should have been added. The following is the updated documentation for the data-indexed display task.

→

Notes

```
DISPLAY STATE MACHINE TYPE:          DATA INDEXED
```

STATE	DIGIT FUNCTION	Condition	If true	If false
0	Display tens of hours	always	1	
1	Display ones of hours	always	2	
2	Display tens of minutes	always	3	
3	Display ones of minutes	alarm mode	6	4
4	Display tens of seconds	always	5	
5	Display ones of seconds	blank	7	1
6	Blank display always	7		
7	Blank display blank	6	1	

```
ALGORITHM FOR CONVERTING 24HOUR TO AMPM
    K is a temporary variable
    digit0 is the tens of hours digit
    digit1 is the ones of hours digit

    K = (digit0 * 10) + digit1        // convert digits to 0-23 value

                                      // test for time of 13:00 - 23:59
                                      // in AMPM mode, displaying hours

    If (state = 0) and (AMPM_mode = true) and (K >= 13)
    {
            digit0 = (K - 12) / 10    // subtract 12 and take tens digit
            digit1 = (K - 12) - 10    // subtract 12 and take ones digit
    }
```

```
STATE MACHINE INPUTS:
        Three flags: alarm_enable, blank, AMPM_mode
                All three flags are positive true logic

        Two arrays: Time_data[6]* and Alarm_data[6]*
                *Note, data is in 24:00 hour format for
```

```
STATE MACHINE OUTPUTS:
        One state variable: Display_state

        Two I/O ports:      Segments(7) and Digit_drivers(6)

        Two LED indicators: PM and ALARM_ON
                Indicators are positive true logic
```

```
ERROR DETECTION AND RECOVERY:
        If the statevariable is greater than 7, it should be reset to 6.
        No additional action required.
```

For execution-indexed state machines, the documentation should include a list of states, with descriptive names for each state. It should include a list of all the state transitions and the events or conditions that trigger the change in state. It should also include a complete list of all the functions that are executed in each state with a clear description of any important algorithms. And, finally, a list of the inputs and outputs for the system should be compiled. If any updates were made to the design as part of the priority or error sections, they should also be included.

Notes

LIST OF STATE NAMES FOR THE BUTTON TASK

```
1.  Wait_4button      Idle state, waiting for a button press
2.  Wait_4bounce      Wait state, waiting for the contacts to stop bouncing
3.  Decode            The button is combined with other buttons and decoded
4.  Alarm_plus1       Command: Increment alarm time by 1 minute
5.  Alarm_plus10      Command: Increment alarm time by 10 minutes
6.  Time_plus1        Command: Increment current time by 1 minute
7.  Time_plus10       Command: Increment current time by 10 minutes
8.  Toggle_AMPM       Command: Toggle AM/PM versus military time
9.  Alarm_on          Command: Disable alarm
10. Alarm_off         Command: Enable alarm
11. Initiate_snooze   Command: Snooze alarm
12. Repeat_delay      Wait state for autorepeat of increment commands
13. Button_release    End state for button release
14. Error             Error recovery state
15. Default           All other state variable values decode to here
```

Current State	Condition	Next State if true	Next state if false
Wait_4button	Button pressed	Wait_4bounce	Wait_4button
Wait_4bounce	100msec delay	Decode	Wait_4bounce
Decode	Alarm_set & Slow_set	Alarm_plus1	
Decode	Alarm_set & Fast_set	Alarm_plus10	
Decode	Time_set & Fast_set	Time_plus1	
Decode	Time_set & Slow_set	Time_plus10	
Decode	Fast_set & Slow_set	Toggle_AMPM	
Decode	Alarm_switch_on	Alarm_on	
Decode	Alarm_switch_off	Alarm_off	
Decode	Alarm_enabled & Alarm_active	Initiate_snooze	Button_Release
Alarm_plus1	always	Repeat_delay	
Alarm_plus10	always	Repeat_delay	
Time_plus1	always	Repeat_delay	
Time_plus10	always	Repeat_delay	
Toggle_AMPM	always	Button_Release	
Alarm_on	always	Wait_4bounce	
Alarm_off	always	Wait_4bounce	
Initiate_snooze	always	Button_Release	
Repeat_delay	1 second delay & Button is held	Decode	Wait_4button
Button_Release	Button is released	Wait_4button	Button_Release
Error	Reset from Error task	Wait_4button	Error
Default	always	Error	

State	Action	Input	Output
Wait_4button	Test for button press	Button	none
Wait_4bounce	Delay and test	Button	none
Decode	decode command from button	none	none
Alarm_plus1	increment alarm time	Alarm_time	Alarm_time
Alarm_plus10	increment alarm time by 10	Alarm_time	Alarm_time
Time_plus1	increment time	Alarm_time	Alarm_time
Time_plus10	increment time by 10	Alarm_time	Alarm_time
Toggle_AMPM	Toggle AMPM_flag	AMPM_flag	AMPM_flag
Alarm_on	Set Alarm_enable flag	none	Alarm_enable
Alarm_off	Clear Alarm_enable flag	none	Alarm_enable
Initiate_snooze	Test for conditions and Set snooze flag	Alarm_enable Alarm_active	Snooze
Repeat_delay	delay 1second & test button	button	none
Button_release	test for button release	button	none
Error	Notify error task & Reset state machine	Reset	Button_error
Default	set statevariable to Error	none	none

Hybrid state machines' documentation will consist of a combination of both the data and execution-indexed state machine documentation. There should be two state lists, one for the data-indexed half of the design, and a second for the execution-indexed half. There should also be an indication of which execution-indexed state holds the data-indexed code. Both lists of state transitions should be included, with a description of how the data-indexed state variable triggers a change in the execution-indexed state variable. There should be one list of state actions, and one list of inputs and outputs for the hybrid.

Documentation for the communications system should include a main system header file, with variable declarations for all of the task-to-task communication pathways. Constant definitions and labels for the system peripherals should also be included in the header file.

The header file should also be linked to an include file that will eventually contain all the access and test routines for the various protocols used with the pathways. For now, the file should contain descriptions of the functions.

Any pathways that could potentially create a state lock condition should be identified and flagged for additional error detection and recovery code. Methods for detection and recovery should be described, and any additions to the task state machine required to correct the problems should be clearly described, and the appropriate documentation updated.

There should also be a clear and verbose description of a naming convention for naming variables. It should identify the pathway with a prefix and a postfix to identify the variable's function. Including a variation on the naming convention for naming access and test routines is not a bad idea either.

The next piece of documentation concerns the timing system. It should describe the general design of the timer, and the hardware system, if any, that regulates it. The description should include any constant values required for configuring the hardware and the description of the algorithm used to determine the timer roll-over.

If a timer interrupt is to be used, either to reload the hardware timer for shortened timeout, or as a high-speed timing driver, the interrupt service routine should be described in reasonable detail, including any additional configuration constants or interrupt enable flags that must be configured. Due to the asynchronous nature of interrupts, any communications variables should use either a semaphore or buffer protocol and be defined in the system communications plan. All the variables and protocols required for communications pathways must be defined and added to the communications documentation listed previously.

Algorithms for all the skip timer routines should be defined in detail, and all constants, variables, and new communications pathways defined and documented both in the communications plan and the main system header and include files.

A clear description of what happens when the skip timer times out should also be defined, specifically if the time-out regulates the state-by-state timing or if the time-out gates an initial state transition, which is followed by execution on each following tick.

Any notes concerning the main system clock frequency should be included in the design notes, along with calculations concerning the number of instruction cycles per tick and any mechanisms for shortening the timer roll-over using interrupts.

All priority-handling routines should be defined clearly, noting which tasks they affect/control and which tasks control, or share control of another task's priority. All timer calculations, decisions, and reasons for those decisions should also be noted.

If a priority handler makes use of information from another task's state variable, then the communications plan must be updated to show the transfer of information. Any new control variables should also be included in the plan, and the appropriate variables generated and documented in the main system header and include files.

Note that the system can use more than one priority-handling system, so the documentation should also contain any notes concerning the expected interaction between the two or more priority handlers.

All error detection and recovery systems should be clearly defined in the design notes for the project. This includes the operation of the error task, which should have documentation comparable to the documentation of the task state machines. All communications and control variables should be documented clearly in the main system header and include files, as should the timing and skip timer reload values for the error task timing. Any change or updates to the system task should also be complete, with a description of why the change was made and how the changes work with the error detection and recovery system.

Whew, that is a lot of information compiled in one place! And the detail of the information is formidable. Designers should not be surprised when the design notes file and the preliminary header and include files are large. In point of fact, we *want* them to be large—the larger the better. Remember that these files are the blueprint for every line of code that will be written for the final system. If done right, the answer to every question in the design should be present in the design notes.

This does not mean that any unanswered question is a failure in the design. It just means that we have one more question to answer next time. Like every other design, this is an experience-building exercise. We learn something from every system we design. I personally look at some of my early design work and wonder how it ever did what it was supposed to. Designers should not be discouraged if an answer is missing here and there.

While we are on the subject, designers should not consider this design methodology the "be all, end all" of design. As I mentioned earlier, every designer sees a problem a little differently. We all have different experiences that we draw from, so it should come as no surprise that there is no single best way to design a system. There is only the method that works best for the individual designer.

The readers of this book are encouraged to take what works for them, incorporate it into their coding and design style, and leave the rest. Don't force your design style to comply with the system—it will lead to frustration and problems. As I learned in writing this book, you have to speak or design with your own voice; anything else is a waste of time and energy.

With that said, it is now time to move on to the implementation phase of the design. That's right, after 288 pages, we will finally start writing code! The difference is, we now know what to write.

Implementation and Testing

In this chapter, we conclude the design process, translating the component-level design from the last chapter into the actual software that will make up the final system. This chapter will cover not only the writing of the software but also individual module tests and integration testing of the complete system. When we are finished, we will have a complete, tested software solution for the design specified in the requirements document.

Before diving into the generation of the code, we should stop and take a minute to talk about the workspace that the software will be developed in. This workspace should be organized in such a way as to help in the development process. It should organize the work and allow separate development areas for the creation of the system's individual components.

All too often in a design project, little if any thought is given to the organization of the development workspace. This typically leads to confusion over the progress of the project, and leads to mistakes that result in lost time and wasted effort. A well-organized workspace helps the designer track the progress of the project by organizing the work along the same lines as the project's design. It should compartmentalize the work in the same way the design has been broken down into individual components. This allows the reuse of testing software on a variety of objects, and separates the different elements of the design, preventing interaction between the elements until it is time to integrate the project.

So, what kind of project workspace works best for the design methodology we have been discussing? The first step is to organize a series of folders, each corresponding to the separate components designed in the last chapter. Separate folders should be generated for each of the task state machines, plus a separate folder for the timing control system, the priority handlers, and the communications variables with their accessing routines. Within each of these folders, another subfolder should also be created to hold development archives for each component. This is important to prevent clutter in the main folder over the course of the component development.

Once the file structure has been generated, the current version of the development tools should be loaded, using the installation instructions that came with the tools package. Note any anomalies during the course of the install, and work with the customer service group attached to the tools supplier to insure that the package is installed correctly and is operating properly before moving on to development.

In addition to the development software, some form of archiving software should also be installed on the system. This can be a full back-up system, generating automatic daily back-ups of the development environment, or just a simple compression package for the manual creation of an archive. The archives purpose is twofold: one, it provides a path back from failed development dead ends, and two, it maintains a recovery path in the event of a catastrophic system failure.

In light of the second reason given for the need of an archive, it is also considered a very good idea to routinely copy archive files onto a separate media for storage, possibly even offsite storage, for protection from everything from fire to accidental erasure. I know that many programmers consider back-ups and archiving to be a waste of time. I also admit that I have even succumbed to this faulty line of reasoning on occasion. However, I can also admit that the practice has bitten me on more than one occasion. Not having a development archive to fall back on has cost me both time and money, recreating software that was already done and working.

The next step is to create software projects for each of the folders, using the software development system that will be used to write the system. The projects should include paths leading the development system back to common include and header files for the communications system, plus any common include files for peripherals ports. Templates for the source files should also be generated. These template files should include common include file commands, and stock header comments at the top of the file identifying the development project and the function of the software contained in each file. A start data and provisions for listing a revision history are also a good idea.

Note: The current version of the development software should be frozen for the duration of the project. If a significant problem is encountered with the development tools during the course of the project, then the new version can be installed. However, all testing performed prior to the change must be repeated to guarantee that no new problems have been generated by the change to the new version of software.

Copies of the design notes should also be linked into the project for quick access using the development editor used with the project. The design notes should not be copied into all of the folders, but rather should reside in a single location, with each development folder accessing it through a path definition in the system. All too often, multiple copies of a document will slowly grow apart, causing confusion of errors. Using a single copy prevents this problem.

Once the directory structure and the development tools have been configured, the next step is to create the source and header files for each of the component modules in the design. The names for the files should be descriptive and be readily recognizable as being linked to the specific task that they contain. Most common operating systems support the concept of long file names, so there should be no reason to limit the length of the name, or resort to cryptic naming conventions to make the name fit in an arbitrary length.

The development workspace is now set up and ready to start development of the system. However, there is one last step that must be completed before we begin writing code for the system. That step is to familiarize yourself with the development tools.

The best way to do this with any system is to perform an audit of the development system. A typical Integrated Development Environment, or IDE, is composed of three parts: the system editor, the assembler or compiler, and a simulator or emulator interface. Each of these components aids in the development of new software, and the ability to use them to their fullest potential is important if the software is to be developed with the minimum work required.

Starting with the editor for the system, the designer should become familiar with the editing and search functions available in the system. These will aid in the generation of the source files for the project. Of particular usefulness will be the SEARCH functions that allow the user to quickly scan through the listing for a specific section of the design. Often a similar structure called a BOOKMARK is also useful in this task. Whether SEARCH or a BOOKMARK is used, an understanding of how to configure and use the commands is necessary to be able to quickly search through a source file for an important scrap of information.

A good method for becoming familiar with the editor's features and functions is to use the editor during the course of the system and component levels of the design for generating and editing the design notes for the system. The effort to organize the design notes at the end of the last chapter is also a valuable exercise for the designers to familiarize themselves with the syntax of the editing and search commands of the IDE editor. By the end of the familiarization process, the designer should know most of the common commands by memory and have a quick reference guide readily available. I personally like to make a copy of the guide and tack it on the wall as a poster.

The next item to become familiar with is the simulator or emulator for the system. Both the simulator and emulator are valuable tools for testing and debugging the design during the course of the project. The simulator allows a low-cost alternative by building a virtual microcontroller in the development system computer, while the emulator performs a similar function within the target hardware. Both typically include the ability to RESET, RUN, STOP, and STEP the development hardware for the purpose of watching the flow of the program. Specialized viewing windows are typically included in the system to allow the designer to watch specific data memory locations and peripheral control registers.

Specialized testing and halt functions, referred to as *break points*, allow the designer to stop execution at specific points in the code for evaluation of the systems operation. When combined with a monitoring system referred to as a *trace buffer*, the designer cannot only stop at any location in the program, but can also view the flow of the execution prior to the stop. Together, these functions form a minimal set of features and functions for most simulation and emulation systems. A designer's ability to make use of these features and functions quickly and effectively is important if the designer is to build and test the system efficiently.

A simulator is similar to an emulator in that it has most of the same commands and abilities, the main difference is the ability of an emulator to test the software using the external circuitry of the final design. This generally involves a plug-in system from the emulator, which samples the incoming data from the circuit and drives the outputs generated by the software. The simulator, on the other hand, will make up for its inability to connect to real hardware by its ability to simulate external hardware through a stimulus and monitoring system. This system creates virtual peripherals to nonexistent external systems which can be programmable through configuration menus or even a scripting language.

If the design work is to be done using an emulator, then the designer needs to become familiar with any limitations inherent in the system, such as a memory limitation on the trace buffer, and the maximum number of break points available in the system. The designer must also become fluent in the configuration and use of the emulator as part of the test and debugging process. Often, programmers learn just the basic commands of the emulator and then rely on conventional tricks of the trade to debug. While this practice is quick and relies on well-known techniques, designers owe it to themselves and the company that paid for the development to get the most value possible from the tools. Anything less is a waste of good hardware and valuable development time.

For low-cost development, and even initial development in a system that will use an emulator, the simulator is a valuable development tool. Often the level of control possible using the virtual microcontroller within the development computer is greater than even those abilities in an emulator. The design sacrifices the ability to debug in the final system hardware, and the simulation will typically not be at the same speed as an emulator. However, the control and access of a simulator can significantly reduce the testing and debugging time of software modules. So, the designer is encouraged to learn the simulation system, even if an emulator is to be used as the final system development tool.

Another value of the simulator is the ability to debug code that might cause system damage, if it were to fail in the final hardware. For example, a control system driving an H-bridge motor drive must never turn on both transistors in the same leg of the driver. To do so would effectively short out the power supply of the driver. Initially testing the routine in the simulator allows the routine to fail without incurring the damage possible in the actual circuit. So, there will be times in the development cycle where the use of a simulator will have advantages over even development with an emulator.

A valuable feature of some emulator/simulator systems is the ability to link break points in the system to program labels within the software. This allows the designer to make semipermanent break points in the design that will retain their location in the listing even through multiple edits and recompile/assembly of the source file have been made. This eliminates the need for the designer to reset the break points after every edit and recompile/assembly cycle in the development. There may also be the ability to time break point functions to changes in data memory, allowing the designer to determine which routines are attempting to set or access a specific data memory location. This data memory break point system can be VERY valuable when it comes time to start integration of the modules into a complete whole, as the typical error found at integration is the unintended corruption of one task's variable by another task.

One final value of the use of a simulator for testing is the ability of the simulator to use either macros or a scripting language to provide a specific sequence of trigger inputs to the system as part of the testing process. Because the timing and sequence is generated in software, the testing sequence can be repeated infinitely and varied by even the smallest detail, making it a valuable automated testing system. Simulator systems also typically have the ability to log output data from some peripherals in the system. This provides a ready-made conduit for test data out of the system. This test data can then be used to compare the operation of the software system from run to run over the course of the development process, allowing the designer to gauge and document the development and debugging process.

A scaled-down version of the emulator, often referred to as a debugger, may also be available. This development tool typically has many of the same abilities as the emulator in regard to sampling and driving the inputs and outputs of the target hardware. However, debuggers tend to be limited in their ability to trace the execution of the software, or support multiple break points. Some are even limited in their ability to operate in real time, making some of the systems only marginally better than full software base simulation. However, the budget for the system may not be sufficient to cover the cost of an emulator, so the debugger may be the only realistic alternative for in-circuit testing. If the debugger is to be used, then the designer must be aware of the difference in operation and the potential limitations to the development process.

The final piece of the IDE that designers need to familiarize themselves with is the compiler or assembler to be used in the system. An assembler is reasonably simple, and only requires the designer to become familiar with the variety of directives in the system and their syntax. Compilers, on the other hand, are more complex and many have the ability to perform optimization of the final object file generated by the system. These tools will require the developer not only to learn the commands and syntax for the tool, but also to learn how to write code so that the compiler will generate the most efficient code possible at its output.

One of the many variables in embedded control design is driven by differences in the architecture of the microcontroller. Some microcontrollers have features that augment their ability to perform math quickly, others have features suited to bit manipulation, and still others have features better suited to digital signal processing. The choice of the microcontroller for the system must take into account these features and the need for these abilities in the system design. The choice of micro-controller will also affect how the compiler will attempt to implement the various features of a level language, and the designer must be aware of how their writing style will either help or hinder the process.

To gain this awareness of the compiler and microcontroller interaction, multiple pieces of test software, written in a variety of programming styles, must be compiled using the various optimization options within the compiler. The various outputs from the test can then be compared to determine which writing style will be most efficient. A typical collection of C commands for use in auditing a compiler is displayed below.

Code Snippet 5.1
```
For (index=0; index<100; index++);
For (index=100; index>0; index--);
```

Code Snippet 5.2
```
Index++;
Index+=1;
Index=Index+1;
```

Code Snippet 5.3
```
If ((A&B)==1);
C=A&B; If (C==1);
```

Code Snippet 5.4
```
While(1);
For(;;);
```

Code Snippet 5.5
```
Int A;
Float B,C;
C=3.14;
B=2160;
A=B*C
```

Code Snippet 5.6
```
Int A,B,C;
C=314;
B=2160;
A=(B*C)/100;
```

While this list is not by any means exhaustive, it does give the reader an idea of the type of writing style that might affect the output of the compiler. The first pair of commands are intended to test for the compiler's ability to take advantage of any decrement and branch if zero type commands in the microcontroller. The second set of commands tests the compiler's ability to optimize math operations and use any increment instructions resident in the microcontroller. The third set tests for the compiler's ability to recognize an infinite loop, and the final set determines the default math format that the compiler selects for every-day math operations. Given the wide variety of compilers available, and the equally wide range of features and optimization capabilities, it is suggested that designers develop a selection of coding examples for the purpose of auditing any compiler they might be asked to use in development. A good set of examples is very valuable to a designer, particularly if the commands and data structures in the example are typical of the commands used in their designs.

Another area to explore in a compiler is the set of nonstandard compiler features. Most, if not all, compilers try to conform to one of a couple different ANSI standards that specify the minimum set of commands and data structures required to handle the C programming language. However, there may also be features and functions that go beyond the ANSI specification, typically taking advantage of some feature in the microcontroller. As a general rule, these features should only be used after careful consideration. The reason for this caution is that any modules developed that use these features may not be compatible with other compilers, and that incompatibility may render the module useless in other development environments. So, just because a compiler has an interesting feature does not mean that it should be used indiscriminately through a development project.

It does mean that the feature should be evaluated as to its usefulness in the design. If the feature is valuable, then it may be worth the effort to create a function, using ANSI compliant commands, that will emulate the feature so it can be migrated to other platforms.

Finally, remember to try the examples with different levels of optimization. Particular attention should be paid to the size of the object code and the execution speed. Generating a matrix showing the changes in output based on coding style and optimization level allows the designer to pick and choose their writing style, dependent upon the desired result, either speed, size, or both.

Once the development system has been configured and the designer is comfortable with its operation and command set, it is time to begin the implementation of the design built through the last two chapters. The logical starting place is the *main system loop* that will eventually hold all the tasks, timing functions, and priority handlers. While we will not be tying all the functions together at once, the loop does provide a good framework in which to do the development and testing of the individual components of the design.

The loop follows a simple format in the primary source file of the project, an initialization routine followed by an infinite loop which will contain the task state machines, timing system, and the priority handler(s). The following is an example in C:

Code Snippet 5.7

```
Void Init_variables()
{
    Init_display_task();
    Init_button_task();
    Init_alarmcontrol_task();
    Init_alarmtone_task();
    Init_timebase_task();
    Init_error_task();
    Init_timers()
    Return;
}
Void Main()
{
    Init_variables();
    Init_peripherals();
    While(1)
    {
        Get_inputs();
        Priority_handler();
        Timer();
        Put_outputs();
    }
}
```

This basic format contains all the systems for the design, and it initializes all variables and peripherals. It then gets the input information for the system to evaluate, calls the priority handler to determine which tasks should be run on this specific pass through the loop, updates all the skip timers and regulates the loop timing, and then drives the outputs from the system before jumping back to the top and the loop and starting over.

While this loop has calls for all of the functions in the loop, initially the routines that are called will typically only contain a return statement. These call/return routines, or stubs, in the system are just placeholders at this point in the implementation. As we move further into the design, we will replace these stubs with working routines to implement the system, or with test routines for exercising other sections of the design. However, for now they simply are there to remind us that a function is needed.

The first piece of the design to place in the main loop is the *timing control* system. We start with the timing, because it is reasonably simple to implement and easy to test. It is also repetitive, so we can easily measure the timing of the system, skip timers, and various timer timeouts using an oscilloscope.

To provide the necessary outputs for measurement, combine the various timeout flags and skip timer flags into 8-bit CHAR variables and output them to one or more of the parallel input/output ports on the microcontroller. The code to combine the flags and the actual output to the port should be placed in a copy of the Put_outputs() routine residing in the subdirectory reserved for development of the timing control system. It will then be a simple change to redirect the include file from the Put_outputs() routine in the main loop subdirectory, to the routine in the timing control development directory. An example of this type of Put_outputs() routine is shown below.

Code Snippet 5.8

```
Void Put_outputs()
{
    unsigned char GPIO_A, hold;
    GPIO_A  = 0;
    GPIO_A |= skptmr_display_task          *1;
    GPIO_A |= skptmr_alarmcontrol_task     *2;
    GPIO_A |= skptmr_alarmtone_task        *4;
    GPIO_A |= skptmr_button_task           *8;
    GPIO_A |= skptmr_timebase_task         *16;
    GPIO_A |= skptmr_Error_task            *32;
    Hold    = GPIO_A | 64;
    PORTA = Hold;
    PORTA = GPIO_A;
    return;
}
```

The exercise and test version of the `Put_outputs()` routine combines all of the flags from the current pass through the system into a single 8-bit byte, and then outputs the value with the 7th bit set and then cleared. This parallel output tells us the current status of all the timer flags and provides a timing marker to indicate when the output was last updated. Using this output system, we will be able to use an oscilloscope to measure both the time period of the main system loop, and the divided output of the skip timers.

Note: It is always a good idea to keep all files, currently under development, or in use for the development, in an isolated subdirectory. During the course of the development, we will be using custom replacements for some of the modules in the main loop, for the purpose of exercising and testing the tasks and function under development. By keeping the custom modules, and the modules being developed, in a separate directory, we limit the possibility of accidentally making modifications to the wrong file. And, more importantly, we eliminate the potential for accidentally replacing a completed file with a temporary exercise and test file.

Once the output function is written and tested using some simple bit set and bit clear commands inside the timer routine, we can begin the actual development of the system timer function.

The first step is to configure the hardware timer to be used for regulating the system timer tick. The actual values required to configure the operation of the timer will be specific to the microcontroller used for the project, so we can't show a generic example. However, the design of a microcontroller timer is such that it can be configured to provide a flag, and potentially an interrupt, when it rolls over from 0xFF to 00. If this feature is available on the microcontroller selected for the project, then this is the desired configuration. The preselector should also be programmed to match the specifications in the component-level design generated in the last chapter. Labels corresponding to the control registers for the timer peripheral should have already been defined in the include file supplied by the compiler, so configuration of the timer is simply a matter of adding a few assignment statements to the `Init_Timers()` function in the timer development directory.

The code required to sense the roll over can then be added to the `Timer()` routine. It should consist of a simple while statement that holds up execution of the routine until the timer roll-over flag is set. The routine can then clear the flag and return. This will fix the timing of the main loop to the roll-over period of the timer, which can then be verified by measuring the time between pulses on bit 6 of the parallel input/output port.

Code Snippet 5.9

```
While (status.tmr_ovrflo!==1);      // routine will wait until overflow is set
Status.tmr_ovrflo=0;                // clear overflo bit once detected
```

If the hardware timer in the microcontroller is not capable of generating an interrupt, or does not have an independent flag to indicate a roll-over, there are software methods for determining the 0xFF to 00 transition. The method simply monitors the most significant bit of the timer and waits for it to change from 1 to 0. We could look for a value of 00 in the timer, but if the number of instruction cycles per system tick is less than 4–10 cycles, there is the possibility that the routine may miss the 00 state of the timer. Monitoring the most significant bit is safer and almost as simple a test.

Code Snippet 5.10

```
While (timer.bit7==0);      // hold while msb of timer is 0
While (timer.bit7==1);      // hold while msb of timer is 1
```

The code operates by holding the timer routine while the msb of the timer is zero, then holding while the msb of the timer is set. This releases the hold condition on the high-to-low transition of the msb of the timer. Even if the msb is set, indicating that over half the tick has passed, this routine will hold until the msb clears once again indicating the high-to-low transition of the bit. And, the high-to-low transition only occurs when the timer rolls over from 0xFF to 00. Watching for the transition will still detect the roll-over; even if the routine is too slow to see the actual 00 value in the timer, it only has to detect the msb roll-over to register the roll-over of the counter. It does introduce a few instruction cycles of uncertainty to the detection, but no more uncertainty that watching the roll-over interrupt flag.

There was also the possibility that we would not be able to select a system clock that would allow the use of the 0xFF to 00 roll-over of the timer. As a result, we will need to also set up an interrupt function that is called on the roll-over of the timer. In this routine, the first action should be to load the timer with a value, which will force the timer to roll over prematurely. To calculate this value, use the following equation:

$$\text{Timer\_load\_value} = 256 - ((\text{Tick} / \text{Instruction\_time})/\text{prescaler})$$

Equation 5.1

The equation calculates an offset for the timer, corresponding to the difference between the normal roll-over of the timer, and the shortened roll-over needed to generate the proper system tick. The `Timer_load_value` may need to be further offset to account for the interrupt response time of the microcontroller, so testing the tick using a flag on an input/output port is recommended. The offset can then be fine-tuned to produce the exact system tick required.

Once the interrupt routine is working, a simple semaphore flag can be used to communicate the roll-over condition to the system timer routine in the main loop. The timer routine in the main loop will then use the flag as its regulating flag, in place of the normal roll-over flag.

One of the more difficult problems in building the timer system is determining whether the system tick has been overrun. Basically, an overrun condition occurs whenever the time required to execute the code in the current pass through the loop is longer than the system tick. Detecting an overrun tick is important in that it is one of the more important error conditions in the system. It is also a condition that should be detected in the design and testing of the system, so having a test for the condition is helpful in the integration-testing phase of the design.

One method for detecting an overrun condition is to test the timer overflow interrupt flag immediately following the call to the timer function. If the flag is set, then the timer has probably overrun the system tick. Loading the current value of the hardware timer should then give an indication of the amount of overrun, provided the system has not overrun the tick, twice over.

If the system has overrun the tick by a small amount, it may be possible to just restart the loop and live with the small timing offset on that particular pass through the loop. If the overrun is larger, then an error recovery system will have to evaluate all the current skip timers to determine if a task missed its chance to execute. If not, skip timers would have timed out, and then even a large overrun can be forgiven. However, if a task was scheduled to run, and it was in the middle of a timing-critical function, then the system may have to declare a hard error. Then the system error recovery task can reset all of the software functions that were dependent upon the timing of the missed task and restart the system from a known good condition.

If there is the possibility that the system could overrun the system tick, twice over, then additional code may be needed in an interrupt routine. This additional code would be responsible for keeping track of the number of times the interrupt occurs without handshaking from the main system timer routine. The overrun counter operates by incrementing a counter every time the timer rolls over. When the timer routine in the main system loop detects the roll-over condition, it queries the counter to determine if it holds the value 01. If it does, the system did not overrun the tick, and the timer function can clear the counter and restart the loop. If the counter value is greater than 01, then the system has overrun the tick multiple times, and the error recovery task for the system will probably have to reset the system and restart from a known good condition.

Once the basic timing function is complete, then the skip timer systems can be added to generate the execution flags for the various tasks in the system. The general form for a skip timer is the following:

Code Snippet 5.11

```
If (--display_task_skptmr == 0)
{
    display_task_skptmr = display_task_reloadvalue;
    display_task_goflag = true;
}
```

The skip timer is decremented and, if zero, reloaded with the skip value for the task, and a trigger flag is set to indicate to the task that it is time for it to run. The `display_tsk_goflag` will then be cleared by the task state machine, indicating to itself on the next pass that it has received the indication on the last pass and already executed a state in response.

Other variations of skip timer may also require an external event in conjunction with the skip timer timeout, or in place of the skip timer timeout. One such skip timer is the timebase task in our alarm clock example. In this case, a trigger from the external 60-Hz timebase is supposed to trigger an increment of the current time. However, if five consecutive pulses from the 60-Hz timebase are missed, then the system will switch over to an internal timebase. To implement this type of system, a more complex function is required. The following is an example of how this system could be implemented:

Code Snippet 5.12

```
if (60Hz_pulse == true)
{
    if (system_mode!=Power_fail_mode)    //normal operating modes for the system
    {                                    //use a short timeout = to 60Hz period + 1
        timebase_task_skptmr = (timebase_task_reloadvalue/60)+1;
        if (--60Hz_postscaler == 0)
        {                                //the postscaler sets the goflags every 60
            60Hz_postscaler = 60;
            timebase_task_goflag = true;
            time_increment = true;
        }
    }
    else                                 //60Hz pulses have resumed after power fail
    {
        if (--missed_60Hzpulse_counter == 0) system_mode = determine_sys_mode();
        timebase_task_skptmr = (timebase_task_reloadvalue/60)+1;
    }
}
If (--timebase_task_skptmr == 0)         //skiptimer timeout, missed pulse, powerfail
{
    if (system_mode == Power_fail_mode) //power fail, do goflags & set 1sec timeout
    {
        timebase_task_skptmr = timebase_task_reloadvalue;
        timebase_task_goflag = true;
        time_increment = true;
    }
}
else                                     //missing pulse, count & reload skiptimer
{
        timebase_task_skptmr = (timebase_task_reloadvalue/60)+1;
        if (++missed_60Hzpulse_counter > 4)
        {                                //5th missing pulse, change mode & timeout
            missed_60Hzpulse_counter = 5;
            system_mode = Power_fail_mode;
            timebase_task_skptmr = timebase_task_reloadvalue;
        }
    }
}
```

The resulting timer function operates two skip timer constructs simultaneously. The first is for the internal timebase and is driven by a conventional software skip timer `timerbase_task_skptmr`. The second construct is for the external timebase and is triggered by the 60Hz_pulse flag. Both halves of the timer operate differently based on the state of the system, specifically if the system is in power-down mode or not.

Let's start with the system in a nonpower-down mode where 60-Hz pulses are received regularly and the skip timer for the timebase task is reloaded to a period slightly longer than the period of the 60-Hz pulses. The result is that the skip timer never times out. Every 60 pulses from the 60-Hz input, the 60Hz_postscaler counter reaches zero, and the 1Hz `time_increment` flag for the display task and the `goflag` for the timebase task are set.

If a 60-Hz pulse is not received before the skip timer times out, the skip timer is reloaded with the short period time-out value, and the missing pulse is counted in the `missed_60Hzpulse_counter` variable. If five 60-Hz pulses are not received, then the `missed_60Hzpulse_counter` variable reaches a value of 5, the system mode is changed to power fail, and the skip timer is reloaded with a value which will generate a 1-Hz timeout.

While the system is in the power fail mode, the skip timer will continue to generate a `goflag` for the timebase task, generate a `time_increment` flag for the display routine, and reload the skip timer for a 1-second time-out.

When 60-Hz pulses resume, the skip timer for the timer is reloaded with the short time-out period, the missed_60Hzpulse_counter variable is decremented, and no `goflags` or `time_increment` flags are generated. If five successive 60-Hz pulses are received, then the system mode is reset to the appropriate operating state, and the 60-Hz half of the timer system takes over operation.

While the system may seem complicated, it does handles the necessary power loss detection and switch-over required for the time base of the clock as defined in the requirement document. If the description is not adequate for understanding the operation of the skip timer, refer to the flowchart in Figure 5.1 for clarification.

Figure 5.1   *Flow Chart of Power Fail Detect*

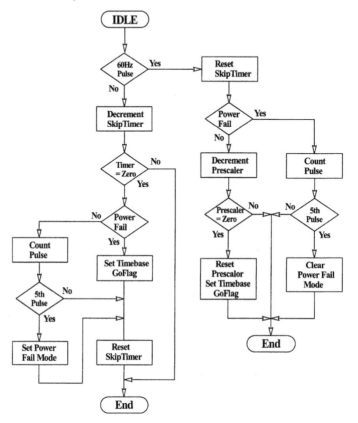

The algorithm in the previous example does have one problem with its operation—it loses the first five pulses, upon resumption of the 60-Hz input. However, this inaccuracy is reasonably small, and will not be noticeable until 12 power fail/resume conditions have passed. At that point, the current time will have lost 1 second. This translates to an error of less than 5%, which is approximately the accuracy of an internal oscillator used in a typical microcontroller. So, even with the lost pulses, the error will be less than the typical error in the microcontroller internal oscillator over the course of 1–2 seconds. Assuming that clock operates for the majority of its life using the 60-Hz time-base, this would produce only a very small error in timekeeping compared to the inaccuracy of the internal timebase. So, the potential error in timekeeping is within the tolerance of the internal timebase, and complies with the specification in the requirements document.

Once the skip timer systems have been added to the timer function and tested for accuracy, the timer function is essentially complete and can be fully commented. Remember that much of the text required for commenting the code is already written and stored in the design notes for the design. Simply copy the applicable text from the design notes file into the top of the timer source file and add the appropriate punctuation to designate it as a comment. Then the individual section of the timer source code can be commented using whatever reasonable comment style is appropriate.

Note: Having a good header comments section in the source listing is not a license to fail to comment the individual lines of code. The comments on the code should be descriptive of what the code is doing and not just an English translation of the command. All labels in the code should be descriptive and follow the naming convention developed in the last chapter. Any temporary variables should also have descriptive names and use the prefix designated for the timer system. If the way in which a routine is coded obscures the algorithm, then an additional header style comment may be called for just prior to the section of code in question. Remember that we are trying to answer any question now, rather than put up with an endless string of questioning phone calls later. Be accurate, be verbose, and supply any information that will be helpful in understanding the operation of the system later on.

Building a Testing Driver Routine

Because this design methodology produces software components, which are then combined together in the integration phase, much of the interconnectivity of the modules will not be available when the individual modules are being written and tested. So, we will need a *test driver routine* to simulate the signals from the other modules in order to adequately test the individual modules in the design.

A test driver routine is, at its simplest, a table-based arbitrary data generator. It is driven by the timer routine, and generates preprogrammed sequences of data on the task-to-task data pathways for the purpose of simulating the activity of another task in the system. To accomplish this function, it will need a skip timer in the timer to regulate its timing, and it will need access to the communications variables used to communicate with the tasks. You may remember that the reason given for using interface macros and subroutines was the ability of a test system to easily interface with the tasks without modifying their operation.

It is important to note that one of the reasons that we use a table-based test driver is that the test system is then automatic, and requires no action from the designer to operate. It is in fact perfectly reasonable to design a test driver that could repeatedly test a task over and over, with only a minor change in timing between the tests. This is a valuable tool in that it allows very thorough automated testing sequences to be generated, certainly more thorough than could be accomplished by testing the software function manually.

Also, if the test driver is designed to link the tables into the driver through an include file, multiple different tables, performing multiple different test sequences, can be generated. This collection of different test sequences is a ready-made test library that can be modified to generate new test sequences, or reused as is to look for new problems that may have cropped up during the integration phase of the design. In short, using a test driver simplifies the testing process, automates the testing process, and can more thoroughly test than testing manually.

While the test driver is typically only an output to system, it can be modified to do some data capture as part of its operation. The captured data can then either be stored in memory on board the microcontroller, or sent serially to a collection computer with more storage. Also there is no reason that the test driver could not include both a time stamp and an indicator of what drive data was used to produce the captured data. Using this system, the designer can set up a test before going home for the evening, then retrieve and review the data the next morning. This is definitely better than pulling an all-nighter on the bench-testing software, and the results are more likely to be accurate. The results could even be loaded into a spreadsheet for graphing and analysis.

How do we build a test driver? Well, as was stated previously, the driver is table driven, so it can be assumed that there will be a data table involved and the table will have constant data in it. If we borrow a concept from the port output test routine used to test the timer, we can even compress the data storage by packing multiple bits of data together to save space. Using this concept, the following initial design is a good place to start:

Code Snippet 5.13

```
(created in an included test file)
      char testdate[180] = { test data}

(modifications to the main loop file)

      #include <testdriver.inc>

      void Get_inputs()
      {
          test_driver();
          return;
      }

      void Priority_handler()
      {
          display_task();
          return;
      }

(created in a separate test driver file)

      #include <testfile.inc>
      #include <pathways.h>

      int index = 0;

      void test_driver()
      {
          static int skiptimer = 0;
          if (--skiptimer == 0)
          {
                  currenttime = testdata[index++]*65536;
                  currenttime += testdata[index++]*256;
                  currenttime += testdata[index++];
                  blank = testdata[index] & 0x01;
                  flash = testdata[index++] & 0x02;
                  skiptimer = (testdata[index++]*256)+testdate[index++]
                  if (index > 180) index=0;
          )
      return;
      )
```

The resulting routine test_driver(), is capable of driving all the input variables and functions of the display task. It accesses the display data through the currenttime variable, and controls flash and blanking through their communications variables. It even controls its own timing by reloading the skip timer from the table data.

The driver operates based on values stored in the two variables skip timer and index. Skip timer operates in the regular manner of all skip timers—it counts down each pass through the main system loop, and when it reaches zero, the driver generates new data for the task state machine. The variable "index" is the pointer into the test data and is used to retrieve the different values for driving the display task. Because skip timer is defined as static and index is defined outside the function, they will retain their data from one call of the test driver to the next. So, the system will step through the test data, placing the information into the communication pathway variables based on timing driven by the skip timer.

There are two important features of the driver that should be noted: one, this skip timer is not reloaded with a fixed value, so it can shift its timing relative to the execution of the display task; and two, the pointer "index" wraps around from the top of the data array to the bottom, so the test can be set up to run continuously. This is particularly handy when trying to debug a problem using an oscilloscope, or when performing stress tests on the electronics driving the displays. All the designer needs to do is set up the test data and let the system run. The displays will cycle through the test sequence, exercising the display, drivers, and software. In fact, this particular setup would be a good piece of test code to pass on to the support group for debugging display-related problems in units returned for repair.

One of the potential features mentioned previously is the ability to capture data and log it to some kind of in-system, or external storage. This allows the test system to not only exercise the hardware and task software, but also gather information about the performance of the system. The exact method for storage will depend on the resources available in the microcontroller, so we will discuss three different options here.

The first option is to store the information in an internal nonvolatile storage. The data can then typically be retrieved using a programmer for the microcontroller. However, due to the small size of typical on-chip storage, this method is of somewhat limited value as it can only store small amounts of data. The next option is to connect an external serial EEPROM to the microcontroller. These memories can hold upwards of 1–2 megabits of data, so the storage limitation is not as much of a problem. This system does have the drawback that a serial routine and programming commands will have to be created in the microcontroller. The third option is to serially link the microcontroller to a second system with non-volatile storage. This option has the capability for the largest storage, and the serial interface needs not be as complex as option two.

In the first option, due to the limited storage capability, the best method for storing data is to store only event information. This can be in the form of error counters, time-stamped events, or data capture triggered by specific events. The first step is to build the memory write routines for the internal storage. Typically there will be example routines in the datasheet for the microcontroller, the storage control routines need only pass an address and data, and the supplied write routine will store the value. The next step is to build a system that can trigger a write based on a specific trigger. This routine can monitor data—either system data or data in a peripheral control register—and when a match is detected, the routine passes the appropriate data to the write routine and the data is logged. The following is an example of such a routine:

➤

Code Snippet 5.14

```
(modifications to the main loop file)
      #include <testdriver.inc>
      void Put_outputs()
      {
         data_logger();
         return;
      }

(created in a separate test driver file)

      #include <pathways.h>
      int   time_stamp = 0;

      void write_ee(char data_in, address_in)
      {  // code taken from the microcontroller data sheet
         return;
      }

      void data_logger()
      {
         static   int   skiptimer = 0;
         unsigned char temp_cntr_data;
         if (--skiptimer == 0)
         {
               skiptimer = reload_value;
               If (time_error)
               {
                     temp_cntr_data = read_ee(time_error_addr) + 1;
                     write_ee(temp_cntr_data, time_error_addr);
                     write_ee((time_stamp & 255), (time_error_addr+1));
                     write_ee((time_stamp / 256), (time_error_addr+2));
               }
               If (display_error)
               {
                     temp_cntr_data = read_ee(display_error_addr) + 1;
                     write_ee(temp_cntr_data, display_error_addr);
                     write_ee((time_stamp & 255), (display_error_addr+1));
                     write_ee((time_stamp / 256), (display_error_addr+2));
               }
               time_stamp++;
         )
      return;
)
```

The data-logging routine is designed to count the total number of timer and display errors in the system, as well as logging the time stamp of the last error. Because the system is only counting errors, and not logging every occurrence, it only requires six memory locations for storage of the data. While logging the time stamp for every occurrence would be more helpful, the last time stamp does tell the designer where to look in the trace buffer memory of an emulator for the last event.

If the internal storage is insufficient, or not available, then external memory can be used to store data. Serial EEPROM memory typically uses one of two basic synchronous serial interface systems. Some microcontrollers even have an on-chip synchronous serial interface peripheral designed to generate the physical layer of the various communications formats. However, the variety of memory sizes and interface protocols is too complex to go into here, so the reader is directed to the applicable application notes for the microcontroller to be used in the design. Most, if not all, manufacturers provide application information on how to interface external EEPROM memory to their microcontrollers.

If the microcontroller has an on-chip interface peripheral, the routines for communicating with the external memory are relatively simple. If the microcontroller does not have an on-chip interface peripheral, then the interface will have to be generated in software. And, even if an interface peripheral does exist, there is an advantage to generating the interface in software—the resulting software will be far more portable. This is because all microcontrollers have parallel I/O, but not all microcontrollers have a synchronous serial interface peripheral. So, if the system can afford the additional execution time, it is generally preferable to create the interface in software.

Because an external EEPROM memory can have so much more storage capability, the method of data logging can also be modified. Now instead of just counting the error, the routine can actually log each individual error with a time stamp. The following is an example of what this version of the data-logging routine might look like:

Code Snippet 5.15 ────────►

```
(modifications to the main loop file)
    #include <testdriver.inc>
    void Put_outputs()
    {
        data_logger();
        return;
    }

(created in a separate test driver file)

    #include <pathways.h>
    int  time_stamp = 0;
    int  index = 0;

    void send_ee(char data_in)
    {   // code taken from the microcontroller data sheet
        return;
    }
    void start_ee(int addr_in)
    {   // code to start an eeprom data write
        return;
    }
    void stop_ee()
    {   // code to end the eeprom write command
        return;
    }

    void data_logger()
    {
        static   int  skiptimer = 0;
        if (--skiptimer == 0)
        {
            skiptimer = reload_value;
            If (time_error)
            {
                start_ee(index);
                send_ee(time_error_code);
                send_ee(time_stamp & 255);
                send_ee(time_stamp / 256);
                send_ee(',');
                stop_ee();
                index +=4;
            }
            If (display_error)
            {
                start_ee(index);
                send_ee(display_error_code);
                send_ee(time_stamp & 255);
                send_ee(time_stamp / 256);
                send_ee(',');
                stop_ee();
                index +=4;
            }
            time_stamp++;
        )
        return;
    )
```

In this routine, if a time or display error condition is detected, the appropriate error code is stored along with the 16-bit time stamp. A comma is also inserted as a delimiter and to pad out the data to 4 bytes. The reason for padding the data is because EEPROM memories with a serial interface typically perform their write operations within a fixed block size in memory. The blocks can be between 16 and 128 bytes in length, and the boundaries are on regular increments of a power of two. What this means for the user is if a routine tries to write a multiple byte group of data that would cross one of these boundaries, then the logic in the memory will wrap the overlapping data back to the start of the memory block. This results in data being stored out of sequence, and valuable data at the start of the block would be over written. By padding the group of bytes to be written out to an even 4 bytes, the routine is guaranteed to never overlap a boundary in the external memory.

Another feature of external serial interface memory, is the ability to load a group of bytes and then initiate the write of the entire group by ending the command. This routine takes advantage of this feature by creating three separate interface functions, one to start the write command and load the starting address, one to send a single data byte, and one to terminate the command, initiating the write process. While each byte could be written individually, it would require that the write command and address be sent prior to each byte, and the time required for the memory to complete its write function would be multiplied by 4, one interval for each byte written.

The final version of the data-logging function is one in which the data is sent to a secondary system for storage. Typically, the secondary system is a PC or other type of workstation, and the serial interface is RS-232. The data is then sent serially over the interface, and a terminal program running on the second machine simply captures the data and stores it in a file on its disk. Because modern PC and workstations have such large hard drive storage capacity, the storage space for this type of data logger is essentially infinite. In addition, the available range of software tools available for PCs and workstations means that analyzing the data will be significantly simplified.

The only problem with this type of data-logging system is the time required to transmit the data from the microcontroller to the second system. Serial interfaces on PCs and workstations are limited to 56K bits per second or slower. Even the slew rate capability of the RS-232 transmitters and receivers will limit the upper speed of transmission and the distance between the microcontroller and the second system. So, while this system does have essentially an unlimited storage capacity, it does have a limited data bandwidth.

Using this type of data logging will require a combination of the previous two systems. We will no longer be able to store every occurrence of every error. Instead, we will have to pick and choose which events are important enough to log every event, and only keep totals on error data that is not so important. We also may have to create a serial transmit function in software, if the microcontroller does not have an on-chip asynchronous serial interface peripheral. Fortunately, this type of serial interface is not difficult to generate. However, it does require specific timing to operate properly. This means that the general timing of the system could be affected.

There are two options for dealing with this problem: one, a serial interface peripheral can be connected to the microcontroller using a faster synchronous serial interface; or two, the serial interface routine can provide an external signal indicating when it is active. In the first option, an asynchronous interface peripheral with a synchronous serial control interface can be connected to the microcontroller. There are a couple of devices available commercially to perform this function, or a separate microcontroller with the capability to receive asynchronous serial communication can be programmed to provide the translation function. In fact, building up just such a test fixture for a designer's toolbox is good idea.

While this method is not an economically attractive idea for the final design, using a simple translator for testing only costs the use of two to three input/output pins for the duration of the testing. And, by off-loading the overhead of generating the slower data stream to the external peripheral, the timing for the main microcontroller should not be affected to any greater degree than interfacing to an external EEPROM memory.

The second option is probably easier to implement, but it does complicate timing measurements that need to be made as part of the software testing. Basically, a parallel input/output pin is programmed to operate as a busy indicator. When the output is high, the software serial peripheral engages in transmitting data to the second system. When the output is low, then the system is executing the normal system software. If the output is connected to the gate function of a counter time, then the total time spent in the serial interface routines can be measured and then subtracted from other measurements of the system's performance. It will double up equipment requirements for measuring timing in the system, but it does eliminate any timing offset due to the data-logging test function of the system.

As far as software to support the interfaces, the routines developed for the external serial interfaces are equally applicable to option 1. Using the routines designed for data logging to internal memory are also equally applicable to option 2, with the provision that the busy output be set at the top of the routine and cleared at the bottom.

So far, we have examined ways in which we can generate arbitrary sequences of data for driving software systems under development, and methods for logging data generated by the systems being developed. There is a third method for debugging system timing that should be examined. In previous sections of this chapter, we discussed a trouble-shooting routine for development of the system timer. In that system, the individual goflags, driven by the skiptimers, were output on a collection of the microcontroller's parallel input/output pins. This allowed us to measure the timing of the timer system directly with an oscilloscope.

We can design a similar system to aid in the debugging of a state machine. In a state machine, the state variable indicates the current state of the task by the value present in the variable. If we brought that value out and observed it in relation to other system stimuli, then we can see how the state machine is reacting to events in the system.

A simple way to do this is to just copy the appropriate bits of the state variable to any open input/output pins available on the microcontroller. In fact, the pins only need to be available for the duration of the testing, so pins that have a use later in the development can be pressed into temporary service while the test is being carried out. Below is an example of a routine that could be used for this type of testing:

Code Snippet 5.16

(created in a separate test driver file)

```
#include <display.h>

// this function is called from the Put_output() routine in the main loop
void data_logger()
{
    unsigned char data_logger_temp;
    data_logger_temp = GPIO_PORT & 0xC3;
    GPIO_port = ((display_state_variable & 0x0F) * 4) | data_logger_temp;
    Return;
}
```

The routine makes a copy of the current port data and masks off the bits that will be used to output the task state. It then copies the applicable bits from the task's state variable, masks off any extra bits, and then shifts the bits to an open group of bits in the parallel input/output port. Both results are then or-ed together and output on the parallel port. For this example, it is assumed that bits 2–6 were available, so a multiplication of 4 is required, and bits 2–6 had to be masked off of the original port data.

Now, using a logic analyzer, the state of the task state machine can be monitored and compared to other inputs to the system. Other data within the system can even be compared with the state variable, provided the additional data is output using a similar routine.

Of the different troubleshooting techniques presented, this last technique is probably the most useful in that it uses test equipment that is typically already on the developer's desk, and it can be reconfigured simply by changing the Put_output() routines. It also points out another simple technique that a designer may choose to exploit—specifically, the tendency of microcontroller manufacturers to create chips in families.

What this means for the designer is that the microcontroller chosen for the project may not be the largest chip made by the manufacturer. Other chips in the family may have larger program/data memory, and/or more pins and peripherals. Using larger chips in the family may provide additional resources during the development process. And, because both larger chips and the chip selected for the design are grouped into a family, the addresses chosen for the peripherals that are used by the system will typically not change when moving from one device to another. However, if the peripherals do move, all the designer need do is abstract the address and pin locations using #define statements and labels. The assembly/compiler will then do the translation, rendering the differences between the microcontrollers invisible to the code.

For now, this completes the section on development aids and tools. One thing that should be noted though is that all the time and effort spent on designing these tools and aids need not be lost when the module or the project is complete. In fact, the work invested in the development of these tools is a valuable resource that should be used and reused throughout the design and the designer's career. The designer is encouraged to save each version of test code created during the development of the project. The old routines can be modified into new routines for the various modules that make up the design. The old routines can even be checked into the designer's library of functions for reuse on the next project. The old routines are even valuable to the support engineers that will be tasked with writing test programs for both production and return/repair. So take the time to document any test code that is generated as part of the design process, save it in the archives along with all the test data that is collected, and reuse it when possible to shorten the design process. It also wouldn't hurt to put a small write-up on the test code in the design notes for the project, so the engineers that come along behind you know that it exists, and that it was the method for acquiring the test data included with the project files.

In the first two phases of the design, we defined the communications system for the design. The various paths that the data would move over were defined as data pathways. Further, a protocol was assigned to aid in the data transfer and to guarantee the proper transmission of the data. Our next step in the design is to generate the macros and functions needed to access and monitor the communications pathways of the design. These are the blocks that the tasks and systems within the design use to access the data in the communications pathways.

The define statements for the variables should have been completed in the last chapter, so all that is needed are the code blocks that will be used to send, receive, and test for data. We will step through the various protocols, defining the necessary access functions needed to properly send and retrieve the data.

As the simplest of the three protocols, we will start with broadcast. In a broadcast protocol, the data to be sent is posted to a globally visible variable. No handshaking is required to implement the protocol, but a data valid flag may be included in the system to notify the receiver whether or not the data currently in the variable is complete and valid. So, for the simplest implementation, without the data valid flag, no additional code is required. The receiving function can access the data directly from the global variable, as the following example shows.

```
Display_data_hours = 5;
```

Code Snippet 5.17

Or, If the data available flag is required, then a simple test function or macro is convenient to abstract the active/inactive convention of the variable.

```
Unsigned char CurrentTimeCheck()
{
    if (currentTime_data!valid = false) return 1;
    else return 0;
}
```

Code Snippet 5.18

In this function using active true logic, a data not valid flag is inverted to produce a 1 if the data is valid, and a zero if it is not. This type of function is convenient for changing the logic of a variable if the convention of the variable is different between the various tasks that use it. In fact, this type of conversion/access function is also convenient if the data format is different between the various tasks. For example, if the most convenient format for Current_time in the timebase task is a long int, and the most convenient format for the display task is multiple BCD nibbles, then a conversion is required. If the conversion is performed in the access routine, this simplifies both tasks and lets them communicate in the format that is most efficient for their operation.

——————————————————▶

Code Snippet 5.19

```
Void get_current_display_time()
{
    long cnvrt_var;
    cnvrt_var = timebase_time;

    display_data[5] = cnvrt_var / (60 * 60 * 10);    // convert 10s of hours
    cnvrt_var -= display_data[5] * 60 * 60 * 10;

    display_data[4] = cnvrt_var / (60 * 60);         // convert 1s of hours
    cnvrt_var -= display_data[4] * 60 * 60;

    display_data[3] = cnvrt_var / (60 * 10);         // convert 10s of minutes
    cnvrt_var -= display_data[3] * 60 * 10;

    display_data[2] = cnvrt_var / 60);               // convert 1s of minutes
    cnvrt_var -= display_data[2] * 60;

    display_data[1] = cnvrt_var / 10;                // convert 10s of seconds
    cnvrt_var -= display_data[1] * 10;

    display_data[0] = cnvrt_var;                     // convert 1s of seconds
    return;
}
```

Here, the data is sent by the timebase task and received by the display task, so the conversion is from long in the timebase to array of nibbles in the display. As long the native data formats for each task are specified in their respective listings, there should be no confusion concerning the transmission of the data. However, if the information in not included, then the designer can expect a phone call from support asking what is going on in the software. So, be clear and verbose in the commenting of both tasks and in the header file that defines the communication pathway variables.

There are a couple of options as to where the routines to access the pathway variables might reside. They can be appended to the include file that houses the task that they serve. This ties the operation of the routine to the task that uses it, but its connection to the pathway variables is not readily apparent. In addition, any changes to the format of the pathway variable will necessitate searching through all the include files for the system.

Alternately, the access routines could be placed in an include file tied to the main system header file that defines the system communication pathway variables. This ties it directly to the pathway variables themselves, but it leaves the connection to the task that utilized the routine somewhat hazy. Of the two options, the second is the preferred location for two very good reasons: one, if the design convention is to place access routines into the header's include file, there will be only one place to go looking for these routines during the debugging process; and two, it gives the designer the option to replace the main system header's include file with another file containing a test-driver system for automated testing of the task during development.

So, we handle the problem of identifying the task that uses the function by good commenting and use the header's include file for housing all access routines and macros.

Continuing on, the next protocol is the semaphore. As we discovered in the last chapter, there are two different implementations for this protocol: the two-way handshake and the four-way handshake. Because the possibility exists for a communications error condition to occur with both the two- and four-way handshaking, not to mention state lock error conditions, it is strongly recommended that interface functions be used for testing and accessing semaphore communications data.

In the two-way system, we have one variable that is set by the sending function and cleared by the receiving function. While this seems simple enough, it is still a good design practice to build functions for the set, clear, and test activities, as they provide the design with clear documentation of the protocol within the main system header file. Most compilers will replace the function calls with an inline copy of the function during optimization anyway, so we improve the readability of the code and it won't even cost the design any program memory space.

Code Snippet 5.20

```
char set_display_goflag()
{                                   // if flag is already set return an error
    if (display_goflag == true) return 0xFF;
    else
    {
        display_goflag = true;
        return 0;                   // if flag was clear, set and return OK
    }
}

char clear_display_goflag()
{                                   // if flag is already clear, return an error
    if (display_goflag == false) return 0xFF;
    else
    {
        display_goflag = false;
        return 0;                   // if flag is set, clear and return OK
    }
}

char test_display_goflag()
{
    return display_goflag;          // return the state of the flag
}
```

Note that the set and clear routines contain a test of the goflag, prior to the set or clear. This is included for two reasons: one, it can be used as a error test—if the bit is set and the sending routine tries to set it again, then the sending routine has overrun the receivers ability to accept data and the error code returned by the routine of problem; and two, having the test built into the set and clear routines can speed up the communications. For example, if the sending routine sets the bit and gets a zero back, then it knows the handshake has started. If it gets a 0xFF back, then it knows the bit is set and it will have to resend the event on its next pass. This saves the task the overhead of testing the bit before it attempts to set it. The same two reasons are valid for the clear function as well. So, the three routines can be reduced to just two, using the return error code system.

A four-way handshaking system operates in much the same way, with the exception that there is more error checking in the set, clear, and test routines. To recap, a four-way handshake starts with the sending task setting an alert flag. The receiver then sets its acknowledge flag to demonstrate that it has seen the alert. The receiver then processes the event and clears the acknowledge flag. This informs the sending task that the receiver has received and processed the event. The sender then clears the alert flag to end the handshaking.

In addition, there are two error conditions possible with the four-way handshake. If the sender clears the alert flag before the receiver clears the acknowledge flag, then the transfer is being aborted by the sender. And, if the receiver sets the acknowledge flag without the alert flag set, then a synchronization fault has occurred.

As with the two-way handshaking system, set, clear, and test routines will be needed to handle the interface to the flags. In fact, due to the error check built into the transfer, the routines are not considered optional, as they were with the two-way system. The possibilities for missing an error condition more than justify the minor inconvenience of accessing the flags through function calls. Also, as was noted in the two-way discussion, most compilers will replace the function call with an inline copy of the routine anyway.

Code Snippet 5.21

```
char set_display_goflag()
{                       // if flag is already set or ack is set return an error
   unsigned char errorcode;
   if ((display_goflag == true) | (display_goack == true)) errorcode = 0xFF;
   else
   {
      display_goflag = true;
      errorcode =  0;  // if flag was clear, set and return OK
   }
   return errorcode;
}

char clear_display_goflag()
{                       // assume no error
   unsigned char errorcode = 0;
                        // if flag is already clear, return an error
   if (display_goflag == false) errorcode = 0xFF;
   else
   {                    // if ack flag is still set, return an abort
      if (display_goack == true) errorcode = 0x7F;
      display_goflag = false;
```

Code Snippet 5.21
     (continued)

```
    }
    return errorcode;
}

char set_display_goack()
{                       // if ack is already set or flag is clear return an error
    unsigned char errorcode;
    if ((display_goflag == false) | (display_goack == true)) errorcode = 0xFF;
    else
    {
        display_goack = true;
        errorcode = 0;    // if ack was clear and flag was set, set and return OK
    }
    return errorcode;
}

char clear_display_goack()
{                       //assume no error
    unsigned char errorcode = 0;
                        // if goack is already clear, return an error
    if (display_goack == false) errorcode = 0xFF;
    else
    {                   // if goflag was clear, return an abort
        if (display_goflag == clear) errorcode = 0x7F;
        display_goack = false;
    }
    return errorcode;
}

char test_send_condition()
{                       // return the state of the flag(bit0) and ack (bit1)
    unsigned char test_var = 0;
    test_var = (test_display_goflag * 1) + (test_display_goack * 2);
    return test_var;
}
```

The six routines comprise the four actions and single test routines required for a four-way handshake. The set and clear display_goflag routines set and clear the display_goflag and test for error conditions. The set and clear display_goack routines perform the same service for the acknowledge bit in the handshaking system. The test_send_condition returns a value equal to the two flags, the goflag is encoded into bit 0 of the return value, and the goack flag is encoded into bit1. In addition, the two clear routines also test for and return error codes for an abort condition.

As you can see from the examples, using functions for this handshaking system is well worth the effort. Trying to code the error and abort check directly into a state machine would make the resulting code very difficult to read, let alone modify, with any degree of confidence. In addition, making the set and clear functions into macros would allow the designer to create as many copies as needed for any number of four-way handshaking semaphore data pathways.

The final protocol requiring access and test routines is the buffer protocol. From the last chapter, we know that there are four ways to configure the two pointers in a buffer protocol implementation:

1. Input pointer points to the next location to receive a value in the buffer. Output pointer points to the next location to retrieve a value from the buffer.

2. Input pointer points to the next location to receive a value in the buffer. Output pointer points at the last location a value was retrieved from the buffer.

3. Input pointer points to the last value entered into the buffer. Output pointer points to the next location to retrieve a value from the buffer.

4. Input pointer points to the last value entered into the buffer. Output pointer points at the last location a value was retrieved from the buffer.

The difference between these four combinations is the comparison required to determine if the buffer is full, empty, or it contains data but is not full. Only two of these three conditions have relevance to design—*full*, and *not empty*. So, we need a test routine that tests for full, and not empty. We need access routines to save a value into the buffer, and one to retrieve a value from the buffer. And, we need support routines to increment the pointers, with wraparound, so they can increment circularly through the buffer space.

Let's start with the pointer increment routines as they are used by all of the other routines. To make an increment routine for a circular buffer, we need to know the size of the buffer so we can wrap the pointer at the correct value. It would also be nice to have a routine that can increment any pointer. The routine should accept the current value of the pointer and the maximum size of the buffer, and return the pointer value that corresponds with the next position in the buffer. For proper operation, the maximum buffer must be greater than 0, and equal to the number of locations in the buffer. A pointer value of zero should also point to the first location in the buffer. To make the routine as portable as possible, it should work for any 8-bit pointer and any buffer size up to 255.

Given these requirements, our increment routines will look like the following:

Code Snippet 5.22

```
Unsigned char inc_buff_pntr(unsigned char pntr, maxbuff)
{
    if (++pntr >= maxbuff) pntr = 0;
    return pntr;
}
```

This increment routine will increment any pointer value passed to it, until the value is equal to the maximum buffer size, at which point the value is reset to zero. If we have an array that was defined by the statement `char buffer[Maxbuff]`, we can increment a pointer into this array using the function call `pointer=inc_buff_pntr(pointer, Maxbuff)`.

A faster, smaller variation on this increment routine relies on the buffer size being a power of two. In the variant, the increment command changes from a pre-increment command, embedded in a conditional, to a straight math function using a logical "and" to limit the value range. An example of this type of routine is shown below:

Code Snippet 5.23

```
Unsigned char inc_buff_pntr(unsigned char pntr)
{
    pntr = (++pntr & 0x0F);     // variable range limited to 0-15
    return pntr;
}
```

Using either of the increment functions, we can now create, store and retrieve functions for the buffer. Assume that our store pointer is the global variable inbuff, the retrieval pointer is the global variable outbuff, and the buffer storage is a global array called buffr[maxbuff]. Further assume that we will be incrementing the pointers after the data has been stored or retrieved (combination 1 from the previous table). Then, our routines should look like the following:

Code Snippet 5.24

```
Void store(unsigned char datain)
{
    buffr[inbuff] = datain;
    inbuff = inc_buff_pntr(inbuff,maxbuff);
    return;
}

unsigned char retrieve()
{
    unsigned char get_buff_hold;
    get_buff_hold = buffr[outbuff];
    outbuff = inc_buff_pntr(outbuff,maxbuff);
    return get_buff_hold;
}
```

The two test routines, test for buffer full and test for data in buffer, will rely on comparing the two pointers to determine the status of the buffer. From Chapter 2, we know the following about the pointers:

Table 5.1

IF (Storage   == Retrieval)   then buffer is empty
IF (Storage+1 == Retrieval)   then buffer is full
IF (Storage   <> Retrieval)   then data present

So, we need test routines which can determine if (Storage+1 == Retrieval) to detect a buffer-full condition, and (Storage <> Retrieval) to detect if data is available in the buffer. In addition, they must detect when (Storage+1 == Retrieval) is complicated by the wraparound nature of the pointers. However, we do have a pointer increment function, so the simplest test is just to increment the inbuff pointer and check for equality. The resulting test routines are shown following:

Code Snippet 5.25

```
Unsigned char test_buffr_full()
{
    if (inc_buff_pntr(inbuff,maxbuff) == outbuff) return 0xFF;
    else return 0;
}

unsigned char test_data_available()
{
    if (inbuff != outbuff) return 0xFF;
    else return 0;
}
```

To create variations of these store-and-retrieve functions for the other pointer conventions, just substitute the appropriate increment and compare functions.

A note concerning the naming of access functions: just as the variables defined in the last chapter required a naming convention, the access functions written in this chapter should also have a naming convention that is consistent with the variable names. The name should have a prefix that connects the function to the data pathway that it handles. The name of the function should be descriptive of what the function does, and, if needed, have a postfix that defines something specific about the function. For example, a routine to store data into a buffer could be named currenttime_store_postinc(), to indicate that it stores data into a buffer in the currenttime data pathway, and it uses the post increment format. The more descriptive the name for the routine, the more readable the final task state machine code will be.

Once all of the access and test functions have been created for all of the data pathways, it is a good idea to create a second include file that consists of just the prototypes for the variable access and test functions. This template file can then be used to substitute test driver and data logging functions into the data pathways of the system for the purpose of testing the tasks and software functions during development and test. Having a template file simplifies the interface for the test driver, allowing the driver to be added through a simple function call in the template. It also guarantees that the format will be the same as the final pathway variables in the final system. The templates also make a convenient conduit for capturing support variables such as pointers and constants like maxbuff, because the data is already present within the function. Also, any modifications to the values, necessary to compress the data for storage, will not affect the original variables.

One quick note on the testing of access and testing routines for buffer protocols: make sure to test the functions with the pointers pointing at all combinations of the second to last, last, first, and second positions in the buffer. This should catch any error combinations of pointer conventions. Remember, the buffer will always report it is full when there is one location still open in the buffer. This extra empty location is needed because, without it, the wraparound nature of the pointers causes a buffer-full condition to look exactly like a buffer-empty condition.

Once all the functions for all of the protocols have been written and *thoroughly* tested, they should be rigorously commented. This should include a full header comment in the include file containing:

- A list of tasks and software functions that use the function.

- Variables that are used by or accessed using the function.

- The range of values that the function is designed to handle.

- Any applicable descriptions of algorithms that the functions employ. This would include the pre-or post-increment convention for pointers used to access a buffer.

Once the access and test routines are complete and the template file has been generated, it is time to move on to the implementation of the task state machines. One of the first decisions is which task to build first. When making this decision, I always consider which task will be the most helpful in creating the other tasks in the system. Input functions are useful for entering information into the system, but we already have the test driver system. We could build the error task, or the timebase task, but then we would have to rely on our debugging system to display the results. So, the best task to start with is generally whatever variation of display task is used by the system.

If we build the display task first, then we can use it to show us the results of the timebase task. Similarly, the button task, with its commands, can use the display for debugging. About the only task that can't make use of the display task directly is the error task, and, if we format the flags of the error task as numbers, even the error task benefits from having a working display.

So, we start with the display task. From the previous chapter, we know that the display task is a data-indexed state machine. It scans the six displays with two alternate states that produce blank digits in the fifth and sixth digit position. Recalling this information from the last chapter, we have:

Notes

```
DISPLAY STATE MACHINE TYPE:      DATA INDEXED
```

STATE	DIGIT FUNCTION	Condition	If true	If false
0	Display tens of hours	always	1	
1	Display ones of hours	always	2	
2	Display tens of minutes	always	3	
3	Display ones of minutes	alarm mode	6	4
4	Display tens of seconds	always	5	
5	Display ones of seconds	blank	7	1
6	Blank display	always	7	
7	Blank display	blank	6	1

```
ALGORITHM FOR CONVERTING 24HOUR TO AMPM
  K is a temporary variable
  digit0 is the tens of hours digit
  digit1 is the ones of hours digit

  K = (digit0 * 10) + digit1          // convert digits to 0-23 value

                                      // test for time of 13:00 - 24:59
                                      // in AMPM mode, displaying hours

  If (state = 0) and (AMPM_mode = true) and (K >= 13)
  {
        digit0 = (K - 12) / 10        // subtract 12 and take tens digit
        digit1 = (K - 12) - 10        // subtract 12 and take ones digit
  }

STATE MACHINE INPUTS:
Three flags: alarm_enable, blank, AMPM_mode
  All three flags are positive true logic

Two arrays: Time_data[6]* and Alarm_data[6]*
  *Note, data is in 24:00 hour format for

  STATE MACHINE OUTPUTS:
      One state variable: Display_state

      Two I/O ports:          Segments(7) and Digit_drivers(6)

      Two LED indicators: PM and ALARM_ON
                          Indicators are positive true logic
```

From this, we know what variables the system will require, the algorithm for the AM/PM versus military timer conversion, the format of the hardware to be driven, and the individual states of the state machine.

Let's start with the state decoding. The range of states is 0–7 inclusive, so we can use an unsigned CHAR to hold the state of the state machines. Remembering our naming convention, we name the state variable Display_state. Based on the state transitions listed in the design documentation from the last chapter, we can build a basic state decoder with the appropriate state transitions. The following is one example of how this section could be written:

Code Snippet 5.26

```
switch (state)
{
    case 0, 1, 2, 4, 6:     Display_state = Display_state + 1;
    case 3:                 if (alarm_enable == true)   Display_state = 6;

                            else                        Display_state = 4;
    case 5, 7:              if (blank == true)          Display_state = 7;

                            else                        Display_state = 1;
}
```

The SWITCH statement is convenient for grouping together those states that have a common transition, such as 0–4 and 6, and 5 and 7. This section should then be placed in the function call for the display task and tested using the test driver developed earlier. The result can then be viewed using a Put_output() style of function and a logic analyzer. If the control bits are also output, then the state transitions can be compared with the triggers that cause the transition.

Once the basic state logic is working, it is time to access the data and display it on the LEDs. For now, we will skip handling the 12/24 hour switch-over, and just concentrate on getting data onto the LEDs. We will, however, put in the logic to switch between the alarm time and the current time information, as this is already built into our state decoding.

———————————➤

Code Snippet 5.27

```
Void Display_task()
{
    if (state < 6)
        {
            if (display_alarm == true)
                {
                    temp_data = Alarm_data[Display_state];
                }
            else
                {
                    temp_data = Time_data[Display_state];

                }
            segment = segment_table[temp_data];
            digit = column_table[Display_state];
            Alarm_indicator = Alarm_enable;
        }
        else
        {
            digit = all_off;
        }
    switch (state)
        {
        case 0, 1, 2, 4, 6: Display_state = Display_state + 1;
        case 3:             if (alarm_enable == true)  Display_state = 6;
                            else                       Display_state = 4;
        case 5, 7:          if (blank == true)         Display_state = 7;
                            else                       Display_state = 1;
        }
    return;
}
```

The first conditional statement separates the displaying states, 0–5, and the blank states, 6 and 7. In the blank states, the digit drivers are all turned off and the displays are blank.

If the state variable points to one of the active display states, the first test is to determine whether it is the alarm time or current time displayed. This determines which array the data is pulled from, Alarm_data or Time_data.

The digit value is then determined using a table and the state variable. The result is then output to the hardware digit driver. One final action is to output the alarm-enabled indicator by setting the port pin connected to the indicator driver equal to the alarm-enabled flag.

The final section is the state transition logic developed previously in the example.

To test this section of the display task, we again set up our test driver to load a variety of values into both arrays and to periodically change the control variables alarm_enable and blank. A logic analyzer will once again be useful to monitor the progression of the digit drives, and to verify that the time an individual display is driven does not change between time display and alarm display. It would also be a good idea to run the system for an extended period of time displaying 88:88:88 to determine the stress on the hardware digit and segment drivers.

Note: The data tables being used to direct the test driver routine should be saved following each test, along with a short write-up of the test results. Of particular interest is any anomalous behavior and the cause of the problem. This information will be very valuable when we start integrating the various task state machines into a complete whole. Quite often, a problem that appears in module testing will reappear in integration testing. Knowing what caused the problem in the module test will typically provide the required insight to find the problem in the integration test, so be clear in the description of the problem and the cause, and be verbose.

Once this section of the design has been verified, it is time to add the 12/24-hour conversion logic to the task. The difficulty with this conversion is that the most efficient way to handle this problem is "on the fly." If we handle it prior to display, we will either have to have two sets of data, or we will have to make the conversion every time the current time or alarm time are incremented. As two sets of data is redundant, and changing on the second is really no more complicated that just converting as we display, we should just make the task capable of handling both types and convert as needed for the display.

To do the conversion, we first need to determine if the digits about to be displayed need to be converted. This is easy; states 0 and 1 handle the tens and one of hours, so conversion is needed for states less than 2. The next step is to load a temporary variable with a binary value equal to the hours. We can ten offset that value by subtracting a decimal 12 if needed. We then convert the result back to BCD and display appropriately. The following shows how this is added to our existing state machine:

Code Snippet 5.28

```
Void Display_task()
{
    if (state < 6)
        {
            if (display_alarm == true)
                {
                    temp_data = Alarm_data[Display_state];
                    if (state == 0) K = (Alarm_data[0] * 10) + Alarm_data[1];
                }
            else
                {
                    temp_data = Time_data[Display_state];
                    if (state == 0) K = (Time_data[0] * 10) + Time_data[1];

                }
            if (state < 2) & (AMPM_mode == true) & (K >= 13)
                then
                {
                    AMPM_indicator = true;
                    if (state == 0)
                        {
                            segment = segment_table[(K - 12) / 10];
                        }
                    if (state == 1)
                        {
                            segment = segment_table[(K - 12) - 10];
                        }
                }
            else
                {
                    AMPM_indicator = false;
                    segment = segment_table[temp_data];
                }
            digit = column_table[Display_state];
            Alarm_indicator = Alarm_enable;
        }
    else
        {
            digit = all_off;
        }
    switch (state)
    {
        case 0, 1, 2, 4, 6:   Display_state = Display_state + 1
        case 3:               if (alarm_enable = true)   Display_state = 6
                              else                       Display_state = 4
```

→

Code Snippet 5.28
  (continued)

```
        case 5, 7:          if (blank = true)        Display_state = 7
                            else                     Display_state = 1
    }
    return;
}
```

The new temporary variable is K, and it holds the binary equivalent of the hours. We test for AMPM and if the time is after 12:59. If the conditions require it, we then subtract 12 and convert back to tens and ones of hours. The second conditional separates the result back into individual digits and outputs the segment data for the appropriate state, and 12/24-hour convention. Finally, the AMPM indicator is set if the time is after 12:59 and AMPM mode is set, otherwise it is cleared.

The only pieces left in the design are the additions for timing control, and error detection and correction. The timing control portion of the design limits execution of the task to only specific passes through the main loop based on the LED_goflag. And, we added a second flag (LED_test) to drive a test for a blank condition. The test was needed so we could blank the display within the required response time.

Regarding the error detection and correction, the only test required was to check the range on the state variable and, if it was out of range, we are to reset it to a blank state to restart the task.

Adding the timing controls as conditional statements, and adding a range check on the state variables, produces the following additional code:

→

Code Snippet 5.29

```
Void Display_task()
{
    if (Display_state > 7)        Display_state = 7;
    if (LED_test)
    {
        if (blank == true)        Display_state = 7;
        LED_test = false;
    }
    if (LED_goflag)
    {
```

Code Snippet 5.29
    (continued)

```
LED_goflag = false;
if (state < 6)
    {
        if (display_alarm == true)
            {
                temp_data = Alarm_data[Display_state];
                if (state == 0) K = (Alarm_data[0] * 10) + Alarm_data[1];
            }
        else
            {
                temp_data = Time_data[Display_state];
                if (state == 0) K = (Time_data[0] * 10) + Time_data[1];

            }
        if (state < 2) & (AMPM_mode == true) & (K >= 13)
            then
            {
                if (state == 0)
                    {
                            segment = segment_table[(K - 12) / 10];
                    }
                if (state == 1)
                    {
                            segment = segment_table[(K - 12) - 10];
                    }
            }
            else
            {
                segment = segment_table[temp_data];
            }
            digit = column_table[Display_state];

    }
    else
    {
        digit = all_off;
    }
switch (state)
{
    case 0, 1, 2, 4, 6: Display_state = Display_state + 1;
    case 3:                 if (alarm_enable == true) Display_state = 6;
                            else                      Display_state = 4;
    case 5, 7:              if (blank == true)        Display_state = 7;
                            else                      Display_state = 1;
}
return;
}
```

The first conditional statement checks the range of the state variable and resets it to a blank state if it is out of range. The next conditional statement looks for a blank flag on every other pass through the loop, and sets the state variable to a blank state if the flag is set. And, the third conditional statement only executes the state machine on every fifth pass through the loop, when the goflag is set. Note that both the second and third conditional statements include code to clear the appropriate flag. This closes the handshaking on the variables and prevents the task from repeating every pass through the loop. So, if the task is running too fast, look for this omission.

As before, test this final version of the code using the test driver software and a logic analyzer if available. Be sure to check the response timing to a blank flag, and adjust the relative timing between the display and test driver to verify the response time is always within the specification.

In this section, we have talked about testing the operation of the task using the test driver software and a logic analyzer. Now, I know that quite often, a project may not have the budget to afford a logic analyzer. There are a couple of options. One: the testing of the timing can be accomplished using a virtual microcontroller in a software simulator. There are a number of these available on the internet, and a little searching will often turn up a good simulator, for not much cash. Two: an oscilloscope can sometimes be substituted for a logic analyzer by encoding the digital information using resistor arrays. This involves using a digital-to-analog converter, or DAC, to convert multiple bits into a single voltage that can be displayed on a single channel of the oscilloscope. The DAC can also be implemented using an R2R ladder and an op-amp. The circuit is also available on the internet and in many textbooks on mixed-signal design.

Remember, not having the budget to get the perfect test equipment is not be a barrier, it is an opportunity to show off our ingenuity. After all, we *are* developing the display task first, because we want to use it as a simple logic analyzer for all the other tasks.

The next type of state machine we will tackle is an example of an execution-indexed state machine. From the previous chapter, we have the component-level design for the button task state machine. To review the requirements, the notes appear below:

Notes

```
State names for Button task
0.    Wait_4button       Idle state, waiting for a button press
1.    Wait_4bounce       Wait state, waiting for the contacts to stop bouncing
2.    Decode             The button is combined with other buttons and decoded
3.    Alarm_plus1        Command: Increment alarm time by 1 minute
4.    Alarm_plus10       Command: Increment alarm time by 10 minutes
5.    Time_plus1         Command: Increment current time by 1 minute
6.    Time_plus10        Command: Increment current time by 10 minutes
7.    Toggle_AMPM        Command: Toggle AM/PM versus military time
8.    Alarm_on           Command: Disable alarm
9.    Alarm_off          Command: Enable alarm
10.   Initiate_snooze    Command: Snooze alarm
11.   Repeat_delay       Wait state for autorepeat of increment commands
12.   Button_release     End state for button release
13.   Error              Error conditions may use this state
14.   Default            Decode this state for all other values
```

Current State	Condition	Next State if true	Next state if false
Wait_4button	Button pressed	Wait_4bounce	Wait_4button
Wait_4bounce	100msec delay	Decode	Wait_4bounce
Decode	Alarm_set & Slow_set	Alarm_plus1	
Decode	Alarm_set & Fast_set	Alarm_plus10	
Decode	Time_set & Fast_set	Time_plus1	
Decode	Time_set & Slow_set	Time_plus10	
Decode	Fast_set & Slow_set	Toggle_AMPM	
Decode	Alarm_switch_on	Alarm_on	
Decode	Alarm_switch_off	Alarm_off	
Decode	Alarm_enabled & Alarm_active	Initiate_snooze	Button_Release
Alarm_plus1	always	Repeat_delay	
Alarm_plus10	always	Repeat_delay	
Time_plus1	always	Repeat_delay	
Time_plus10	always	Repeat_delay	
Toggle_AMPM	always	Button_Release	
Alarm_on	always	Wait_4bounce	
Alarm_off	always	Wait_4bounce	
Initiate_snooze	always	Button_Release	
Repeat_delay	1 second delay & Button is held	Decode	Wait_4button
Button_Release	Button is released	Wait_4button	Button_Release
Error	Reset from Error task	Wait_4button	Error
Default	always	Error	

Notes

State	Action	Input	Output
Wait_4button	Test for button press	Button	none
Wait_4bounce	Delay and test	Button	none
Decode	decode command from button	none	none
Alarm_plus1	increment alarm time	Alarm_time	Alarm_time
Alarm_plus10	increment alarm time by 10	Alarm_time	Alarm_time
Time_plus1	increment time	Alarm_time	Alarm_time
Time_plus10	increment time by 10	Alarm_time	Alarm_time
Toggle_AMPM	Toggle AMPM_flag	AMPM_flag	AMPM_flag
Alarm_on	Set Alarm_enable flag	none	Alarm_enable
Alarm_off	Clear Alarm_enable flag	none	Alarm_enable
Initiate_snooze	Test for conditions and Set snooze flag	Alarm_enable Alarm_active	Snooze
Repeat_delay	delay 1second & test button	button	none
Button_release	test for button release	button	none
Error	Notify error task & Reset state machine	Reset	Button_error
Default	set statevariable to Error	none	none

Based on this information, we can start by defining a state variable and building a state decoder for the system. Using the naming convention, the state variable should be called Button_state. Using a SWITCH/CASE statement to implement the decoder, we get the following:

Code Snippet 5.30

```
Void Button_task()
{
    switch(Button_state)
    {
        case Wait_4button:
                                break;
        case Wait_4bounce:
                                break;
        case Decode:
                                break;
        case Alarm_plus1:
                                break;
        case Alarm_plus10:
                                break;
        case Time_plus1:
                                break;
        case Time_plus10:
                                break;
        case Toggle_AMPM:
                                break;
        case Alarm_on:
                                break;
        case Alarm_off:
                                break;
        case Initiate_snooze:
                                break;
        case Repeat_delay:
                                break;
        case Button_release:
                                break;
        case Error:
                                break;
        case Default:
    }
    return;
}
```

The basic framework is very simple, with a separate case of each state. And, because the various state names have been declared using a #define, we can use the name in place of an obscure number. If the system is to be implemented in assembly language, then the framework may not be quite this simple. Range checking will be required to decode the default state, and a jump table will be needed to decode the other states in the task. The microcontroller manufacturer's web page will typically have examples of how to build a jump table. And if they don't, check the internet for postings by other designers that have already developed a solution.

As with the data-indexed state machine, the decoder should be tested using the test driver and a variation of the Put_outputs() routine. Remember to test every possible value in the state variable; just because it catches the values just above the error state does not mean it will not mess up with higher values. As always, save your test file and results, as human memory is fallible and harddrive space is cheap. Be clear and be verbose in your write-up; it will save you phone calls from support later on.

Once the decoder is working, the next step is to build in the state transitions. These are just conditional statements that look for the trigger events defined in the component level, and make assignments to the state variable. Also review the various looping, subroutine, and goto constructs described in Chapter 2, since this is where they will be used. With the addition of the state transition, the routine should look like the following:

Code Snippet 5.31

```
Void Button_task()
{
    switch(Button_state)
    {
        case Wait_4button:  if (newbutton_press())         Button_state = Wait_4bounce;
                            break;
        case Wait_4bounce:  if (--button_dly_cntr == 0)    Button_state = Decode;
                            break;
        case Decode:        switch (decode_bttn())
                            {
                                case Alrmset_Slow:  button_state = Alarm_plus1;
                                                    break;
                                case Alrmset_Fast:  button_state = Alarm_plus10;
                                                    break;
                                case Timeset_Slow:  button_state = Time_plus1;
                                                    break;
                                case Timeset_Fast:  button_state = Time_plus10;
                                                    break;
                                case Tggle12_24:    button_state = Toggle_AMPM;
                                                    break;
                                case Alarm_On:      button_state = Alarm_on;
                                                    break;
```

```
                                     case Alarm_Off:      button_state = Alarm_off;
                                                          break;
Code Snippet 5.31                    case Snooze:         if (Alarm_enabled & Alarm_active)
   (continued)                                            {   button_state = Alarm_plus1;
                                                          }
                                                              break;
                                     Default:                 break;
                                  }
                                  break;
        case Alarm_plus1:         Button_state = Repeat_delay;
                                  break;
        case Alarm_plus10:        Button_state = Repeat_delay;
                                  break;
        case Time_plus1:          Button_state = Repeat_delay;
                                  break;
        case Time_plus10:         Button_state = Repeat_delay;
                                  break;
        case Toggle_AMPM:         Button_state = Repeat_delay;
                                  break;
        case Alarm_on:            Button_state = Wait_4bounce;
                                  break;
        case Alarm_off:           Button_state = Wait_4bounce;
                                  break;
        case Initiate_snooze:     Button_state = Button_Release;
                                  break;
        case Repeat_delay:        if ((--delay_cntr == 0) & button_held())
                                  {
                                          Button_state = Decode;
                                  }
                                  else    Button_state = Wait_4button;
                                  break;
        case Button_release:      if (button_held() == 0)    Button_state = Wait_4button;


                                  break;
        case Error:               if (Button_fault == 0)    Button_state = Wait_4button;
                                  break;
        case Default:             Button_state = Error;
   }
   return;
}
```

As you may have noticed, there are a couple of shortcuts in the code. Some of the test conditions use procedures to return a binary deciding bit, and some new counter variables were introduced. However, overall, the code follows almost directly from the component definition generated in the last chapter. The documentation was such that the state transitions almost wrote themselves. This is one of the advantages of using a top-down design methodology—all the hard choices are made long before the designer starts typing.

Once the state transitions are complete, it is back to the test driver for more testing. Remember to test both sides and all combinations of variables in each conditional statement. Record the results, as they will be helpful in debugging at the integration phase of the design.

The next step is to add in the functionality for each of the states. This will include increment routines for the time and alarm time, toggling of control bits, and writing the subroutines that were used in the last step to simplify the listing. Because of the size of the resulting code, it is becoming impractical to list the complete task code after every addition. So from this point on, the listing will be abbreviated to only include the relevant sections. In addition, sections that are substantially similar to a presented section may be passed over for brevity, and left to the reader as an exercise.

We'll start with the `newbutton_press()` routine. This function checks the current state of the command buttons and determines if any have changed state; if so, then the routine returns a 1. To perform this check, we will need a variable, which represents the previous and current state of the inputs. From our design in Chapter 3, these flags were grouped into the data pathway named Command buttons. For convenience, we will assume that they are defined within a union, occupying bits 0–6 of an unsigned CHAR named Command_buttons. port, and the individual bits use the extension Command_buttons.flags. xxxx, with the xxxx representing the individual flag names. We will also define a static variable Command_buttons_old.

---→

Code Snippet 5.32

```
Static unsigned char Command_buttons_old = 0x3F; //define with all switches open

Unsigned char Scan_buttons()
{
    if ((Command_buttons.port & 0x3F) != Command_buttons_old)
    {
        command_buttons_old = Command_buttons.port;
        return 0xFF;
    }
    return 0;
}
```

The result is a relatively simple function that compares the old state against the current state—in fact, the routine is so simple that it seems inefficient to build a procedure around so simple a function. However, it should be remembered that one of the objectives is to create a software library. By building this into a function, we accomplish two things: one, it documents the function clearly, and two, if it ever becomes necessary to change the function, the change only has to be made in one logical location. And, the compiler optimize will probably remove the function call and include the code inline anyway, so why not go for better readability and documentation?

Another function that was thrown into the design was the decode_bttn() function. Its purpose is to test the various combinations of button combinations and return an unsigned CHAR with a value corresponding to a valid command, or an out of range value that the switch statement can ignore. It will also return a value the switch statement will ignore, in the event that only one button of a two-button command has been pressed. Note, we will need the other half of the Command_buttons.flags.xxxx definition to build this function. So, we will assume the following:

Code Snippet 5.33

```
Command_buttons.flags.Fast     = Fast Set button press, active low
Command_buttons.flags.slow     = Slow Set button press, active low
Command_buttons.flags.Time     = Time Set button press, active low
Command_buttons.flags.Alarm    = Alarm Set button press, active low
Command_buttons.flags.Snooze   = Snooze button press, active low
Command_buttons.flags.Alrmon   = Alarm enable switch, enabled = active low
Unsigned char decode_bttn()
{
    unsigned char dcodbtn_tempvar;
    dcodbtn_tempvar = Command_buttons.port & 0x1F;      // remove the alarm switch
    switch(Command_buttons.port)
    {
        case    B'00011001':  return Timeset_Slow;
        case    B'00011010':  return Timeset_Fast;
        case    B'00010101':  return Alrmset_Slow;
        case    B'00010110':  return Alrmset_Fast;
        case    B'00011100':  return Tggle12_24;
        case    B'00001111':  return Snooze;
        default:              if (Command_buttons.flags.alrmon)  return Alarm_On;
                              else                               return Alarm_Off;
    }
}
```

A little explanation is required for the operation of this routine. A momentary press of a two-button combination drives all of the commands, with the exception of the alarm on and alarm off commands. So, the command cannot be executed until both buttons are pressed. However, the alarm's on and off commands have to be executed on any change. To handle both cases, the system is designed to look for the two-button combination, and if it fails to find a valid combination, it sets either the alarm on or off depending on the state of the switch. This will cause an alarm on or off command, in the event of a single button press, an illegal button combination, or an actual change in the state of the alarm on off switch. But, because the alarm on and off commands just copies the state of the switch into the alarm_enabled flags, repeatedly executing an alarm on or off command does not harm the system, and it allows the routine to be quite simple.

However, this information does need to be copied into the documentation for the function. If it is not, then the support group may spend days writing a fix for the routine, only to find out that the function was designed to work this way. Good documentation not only documents how things work, but also how they work in ways you may not suspect.

Once the various embedded functions are written and tested, the other code in each of the states can be generated and tested. For this routine, the code will mainly consist of increment by 1 and increment by 10 functions. To implement these functions, it will be necessary to create a BCD add function for the data in the alarm time and current time variables.

Now some may ask, why not just store these variables as INTs or LONGs? The math will be much simpler, and it will save space in the data memory. That is true but, remember, how often is the math needed and how often is the data displayed? By putting the math in the buttons and timebase tasks, the addition routines are only executed once a second at most. If we were to use INTs and LONGs for the data storage, that would mean that the conversion from INTs or LONGs to display data, would have to be executed every time the display task displayed the next digit. This would be a heavy drain on processing power; the more efficient use of processing time is to keep the data in the most convenient format for the task that uses it most often. That is the display task, so we keep the data in BCD digits. Besides, if the addition takes more than once cycle to complete, it is not a serious problem. We would simply design the task to take two states to perform the addition, as opposed to just one state. The display task, on the other hand, has much less time between skip timer time-outs to do its job.

Using our knowledge of how math routines work from Chapter 1, and the order in which the data is stored in the array, a BCD addition of 10 minutes to the current time would look like the following:

Code Snippet 5.34

```
unsigned char Add10_tempvar;


case Time_plus10:  Button_state = Repeat_delay;
                   Time_data[2]++;                              // +10 minutes
                   If (Time_data[2] > 9)                        // carry?
                   {
                       Time_data[2] = Time_data[2] - 10;
                       Time_data[1]++;                          // +1 hours
                       If (Time_data[1] > 9)                    // carry?
                       {
                           Time_data[1] = Time_data[1] - 10;
                           Time_data[0]++;                      // +10 hours
                           Add10_tempvar = Time_data[1] + (Time_data[0] * 10);
                           If (Add10_tempvar >= 25)             // roll over?
                           {
                               Time_data[1] = 0;
                               Time_data[0] = 1;
                           }
                       }
                   }
```

While the routine is a little cumbersome, it will only be executed once or twice a second, and it is certainly simpler than performing a binary-to-BCD conversion 360 times a second. The alarm set commands and the time-plus-1-minute blocks of code are done the same way.

Once all of the action section in each of the tasks has been added and the system is ready to test, we have two options: we can configure the test driver to exercise the task, or we can link it together with the finished display task and test it manually. In reality, we should do both, using the display task for simple initial testing and the test driver to exercise the task fully. The display task is convenient in that we can press buttons and observe the results. However, the test driver can more thoroughly exercise all combinations of buttons and timing. Designers should not let the ease of testing with the display task lure them into skipping the test with the test driver. Problems that appear in the integration-testing phase of the design have their roots in problems in the task design. A more thorough test here and now will find these problems, and do it far easier than testing at the integration phase. There are few suspects at the task level, and the whole question of timing interaction is removed. So, test now while it is easier, rather than wait and pay more later.

There is a small housekeeping step that needs to be taken care of, that is to add in the logic that drives the display_alarm flag for the display task. This bit is set whenever the Alarm set button is pressed, this causes the display task to show the alarm time whenever the alarm time is being set. It is also a good time to review the design notes for any other small details that may have been dropped in the design process.

Once the details have been taken care of and the routine is complete and tested, it is time to add in the code to handle the timer goflag, and the code for handling error detection and recovery. Just like the display task, there is a skip timer for the button task. And, just like the display task, it will gate the execution of the state machine, so we need to add the same type of conditional statement to the top of the state machine:

Code Snippet 5.35

```
Void Button_task()
{
    if (Button_goflag)
    {
        switch(Button_state)
        {
```

The error detection and recovery mechanisms designed in the previous chapter require that the button task report any recoverable or hard errors to the error task state machine. So, other than syntax errors in the user interface, the only error regularly checked in the button task, is the corruption of the state variable. The error is detected in the default state, and handled in the error state. The code necessary to handle these conditions appears below:

Code Snippet 5.36

```
        case Error:   if (Test_Buttonfault() == 0) Button_state = Wait_4button;
                      break;
        case Default: Set_Buttonfault();
                      Button_state = Error;
    }
}
```

The Button_fault variable is a semaphore flag between the button task and the error task. The Set_Buttonfault() routine sets the variable notifying the error task of the problem, and the error task allows the button task to reset by clearing the variable.

The series of states in the error task associated with a button task error, poll the Button_fault flag, and when it is set, they take the appropriate action. For our design here, these actions include:

1. Clearing the alarm_display flag.

2. Verifying that the alarm_enable flag is set correctly.

3. Verifying that the alarm_active flag is cleared if the alarm_enable flag is cleared.

4. Disabling the Alarm tone task if the alarm_enable flag is cleared.

5. And resetting the Alarm control task if it is in the wrong state.

All this is done to insure that other tasks are not left in an inappropriate state when the button task state variable is reset, although the test for the alarm_enable flag and the alarm_active flag are already handled separately by the error task, so they can be eliminated from the list if program memory becomes limited. They are included here for completeness, but they are not absolutely necessary.

With the error detection and recovery systems in place, the button task is complete, and so is the design example for an execution-indexed state machine. The last type of state machine to be covered is the hybrid type. Fortunately, the hybrid is just what the name implies: a combination of the data and execution-indexed types. So, the design format is very similar to those that have already been covered.

To begin the implementation, start with the data-indexed portion of the design, as this section is typically a sub-function to the execution-indexed section of the design. Build the data-indexed block of the hybrid state machine, in the same way as the data-indexed state machine. Define a state variable with an appropriately descriptive name and the arrays of data and constants. Next, build the state transitions section of the code. When these are complete, test them thoroughly using the test driver software.

Next, build in the algorithm for the state machine. For a sampling system, this would typically involve recovering data from the analog-to-digital converter, testing it against supplied limits and saving the results. For a software serial peripheral, it would mean shifting the data through the carry bit, and copying the carry to the output pin. Once the activity has been coded, it should then, once again, be tested.

The final steps of designing in the timing and error handling are skipped as they will be coded into the execution-indexed portion of the system that is wrapped around the hybrid. Instead, the next step is to build the state decoder for the execution-indexed section of the design. This is accomplished in the same manner as the design in the previous section. Once coded, it is thoroughly tested with the test code and the test data, as always, archived with the project.

The next step is to build in the state transitions for the execution section. Remember that the data-indexed section of the design will reside in one of the execution-indexed states, so there must be a condition that switches the design from data indexing, back to execution indexing. Typically, this is a condition based on the data-indexed state variable.

One note on state variables in hybrid state machine designs. The designer is often tempted to combine the data-indexing and execution-indexing variables into a single variable. While this is possible, and it does save one more byte of data memory, in practice it can be complicated to implement. A group of states must be decoded to the same block of code, and when using the variable as an index into an array, there must be an offset subtracted. If the number of states in the execution-indexed section of the design changes, then there is the very real possibility that the offset will have to change, for the data-indexed section to work correctly. So, while it is possible, there are other places in the design that are better sources of data memory savings. Using a combined state variable is complicated to implement, difficult to document, and the code is difficult to understand with its unexplained offsets and grouped states. The better choice is to use separate variables.

When the state decoder and state transitions have been tested, the next step is to add the actions in each state. This includes the data-indexed block that started this design. Making a header comment in front of the data-index section is a good idea, but it can also break up the flow of the execution-indexed state machine construct. A more readable alternative is to call the data-indexed block as a subroutine. The subroutine name should identify the block as the data-indexed portion of the design, and the state variable declaration will have to be external to the routine so its scope will include both the data and execution-indexed sections of the design. Using this format, a proper header comment can be placed over the data-indexed subroutine, and the flow of the execution-indexed part of the design is undisturbed. With the proper optimization setting in the compiler, the system should even delete the function call overhead and include the code inline within the execution-indexed routine.

As always, each step of the design should be thoroughly tested, with the test code archived and the test results included in the design notes for the design. And, while we are on the subject of documentation, the header comments for the various tasks should include the design notes generated in Chapters 2 and 3. Remember that part of the reason for documenting all the design details and notes was to have a source of comments for each of the system blocks. Using the notes from the design notes file automatically provides a clear description of the design. But, more than that, it also documents *why* the design was done the way it was. Understanding how something works is useful for understanding a new design when a support engineer receives it. Understanding why it was designed a specific way tells the support engineer how it can be modified for bug fixes and upgrades, without introducing new problems that the designer has already encountered and designed around.

When all of the task state machines, including the error task, are complete and tested, it is time to start on the priority-handling system. In the last chapter we examined several different systems, both to manage a complete design and for handling smaller portions of the design. In this chapter, we need to implement and test the designs.

The first impulse is usually to start building the priority handlers around the complete task state machines. While this may seem like a good short-cut in the development, it suffers from one major drawback. When an error occurs, there is always the question, is it an integration problem, or is it a bug in the priority handler code? So, it is recommended that, where possible, the design of the priority handler should be separated from the individual tasks.

For the passive system, this is done by once again routing the goflags out a parallel port. If the passive system is operating correctly, then no two bits on the ports should be set at the same time. A simple test with a logic analyzer should confirm the operation.

For a more exhaustive test, the goflags can be used to trigger a data logging function. In this logging function, 16 flags are set up, one for each combination of goflags. Each time a goflag is set, the flag corresponding to the current combination of flags is set. If the passive priority handler is working, then only the 1, 2, 4, and 8 flags should be set. If another flag is set, then the combination of goflags associated with that flag were active at the same time. To aid in troubleshooting, a 16-bit variable can be associated with each flag. When the flag is set, a time stamp is loaded into the 16-bit variable to show the most recent time the specific combination of flags was set. The following example code shows how this is accomplished.

⟶

Code Snippet 5.37

```
Union skip_flags
{
    struct
    {
        unsigned char    display_goflag:1;
        unsigned char    button_goflag:1;
        unsigned char    alrm_cntrl_goflag:1;
        unsigned char    timebase_goflag:1;
        unsigned char    unused:4;
    } flags;
    unsigned char        bytewide = 0;
}

Static unsigned char hit_flags[16] = {0,0,0,0,0,0,0,0,0,0,0,0,0,0,0,0};

Void data_logger()
{
    if (skip_flags.bytewide > 0)
    {
        hit_flags[skip_flags.bytewide] = 1;
    }
    skip_flags.bytewide = 0
    return;
}
```

The declaration for the skip timer goflags combines all of the skip timers together into a single byte. The byte is then used to determine when a new flag is set; if the normal state of all flags is zero, then a value greater than zero indicates a new flag is set. The combination of the flags is then used to index into the array, setting the location corresponding to the combination of flags. Finally, the flags are cleared for the next pass through the system loop. The result will be an array of chars which should all be zero, expect for the locations 1, 2, 4, and 8. Note, if locations 1, 2, 4, and 8 are not all set, then this is also an indication of a problem as the missing set location was never called by its skip timer. The problem should be investigated and the problem corrected before running the test again.

Tuning the passive system requires that the designer adjust the initial values of the skip timers for all the tasks using the priority handler. While the optimal system is to calculate the initial values, there will be times when the overall execution time of some tasks may shift due to modifications that are made to the system. When this happens, the optimal system is still calculation. However, if the original documentation is not available, there is still the option to adjust the timing manually. But it will require that the support engineer adjust the values, and then test to validate the timing. This back and forth adjust and test format is slow, as the testing will require time to run, but eventually a new set of initial values can be determined using the system.

In a time-remaining priority handler, the basis of the system is knowing how much time is left in the system tick. To do this, it is necessary to access the hardware timer that drives the system timing. The value is then compared to a database of execution times, indexed by task and state. Reading the timer simply involves reading a 16-bit value from the hardware and accessing the database table; performing the comparison is simple. The challenge is compiling the information for the execution time database. The following shows how the code for the priority handler works:

Code Snippet 5.38

```
Static unsigned int database[4][16];    // array [task][state]

Void Time_remaining()
{
    unsigned int time_diff;
    if (timebase_goflag)
    {
        time_diff = 0xFFFF - sys_timer;
        if database[3][timebase_statevar] < time_diff) timebase_task();
    }
    if (button_goflag)
    {
        time_diff = 0xFFFF - sys_timer;
        if database[1][button_statevar] < time_diff) button_task();
    }
    if (display_goflag)
    {
        time_diff = 0xFFFF - sys_timer;
        if database[0][display_statevar] < time_diff) display_task();
    }
    if (alarmcntrl_goflag)
    {
        time_diff = 0xFFFF - sys_timer;
        if database[2][alarmcntrl_statevar] < time_diff) alarmcntrl_task();
    }
}
```

The four sections of the routine are identical, but they act upon different tasks, based on a different index into the database and different state variables. In fact, this routine could be rewritten using a FOR/NEXT loop and a SWITCH statement, but the current implementation will not be significantly larger. Plus, it is easier to modify the order of the tasks in the current implementation, and the order places higher priority on the first task in the list, and a lower priority on the later tasks in the list.

To build the database, it is necessary to build a special data-logging system. This data-logger captures the start and return time each time a task is called. The start time is subtracted from the return time and the resulting value is the execution time for that task executing that state. The results are stored in a large data memory array that is indexed by task number and state number for the task. However, rather than just store the data, it is first compared to the data already in the array and only stored if it is greater than the original value. This builds up an array of worst-case execution times for the various tasks and states. The following is an example of how this can be done:

Code Snippet 5.39

```
Static unsigned int database[4][16];  // array [task][state]
Static unsigned int start_time;        // this value supplied by timer
Static unsigned char task_nmbr;        // this value supplied by timer

Void time_logger()
{
   unsigned int     stop_time;
   unsigned char    gen_state;
   unsigned int     time_diff;

   stop_time = sys_timer - K;           // K is number of cycles between call & now
   switch (task_nmbr & 0x03)
   {
        case 0:    gen_state = display_statevar;
                   break;
        case 1:    gen_state = button_statevar;
                   break;
        case 2:    gen_state = alarmcntrl_statevar;
                   break;
        case 3:    gen_state = timebase_statevar;
                   break;
   }
   time_diff = stop_time - start_time; // assumes an incrementing system counter
   if (time_diff > database[task_nmbr][gen_state])
   {                                    // if new time is larger replace old time
        database[task_nmbr][gen_state] = start_time - stop_time;
   }
    return;
}
```

The timer function of the main loop is modified to supply two values, a number indicating the task that is running on this pass through the loop and the value of the timer just prior to the task state machine being called. The task number is used to access the correct state variable and to index into the timing database. If the new time is longer than the old time in the database, the new value replaces the old value.

The tasks are then set up in the system using the same offset skip timer system as the passive priority system. While the passive system will not get the optimal usage of execution time that a time-remaining system will, it does exercise the task sufficiently to perform the execution timing test.

Once the passive priority system is running with the tasks, data-logger, and the test driver, the system is left to run through the test routine. Note that the various tasks should not be linked together, but should be completely driven by the test driver to minimize the potential for interaction problems. The test routine should also exercise all modes and combinations of task inputs, both the expected and unexpected. Remember that the purpose is to determine the worst-case timing, so try all combinations of inputs, even if the combination is not normal to the system.

The alternative time-remaining system is just a variation on the original. The only difference is that it calls an initial set of tasks using another system, such as the passive system, and then calls housekeeping functions if time permits. This system uses the same routines as the previous implementation. The designer still needs to measure the execution timing of the housekeeping function so the system can know if there is sufficient time remaining for their execution. So, the only real difference in implementation is the initial group of tasks called before the priority handler.

The variable-order system is designed to call a different list of tasks, based on the system mode. This involves two design needs, a list of the tasks required in each mode, and a method for determining the system mode. For our clock example, we have the list of tasks by mode, and a common mode variable that multiple sources within the design update as changes are needed. The only thing left is to build the SWITCH statement for the implementation. From the previous chapter, we have the following design notes on the system priorities:

Code Snippet 5.40

```
Void variable_order(unsigned char mode)
{
    switch (mode)
    {
        case Timekeeping:                       TimeBase_task();
                                                Display_task();
                                                Button_task();
                                                Error_Task();
                                                break;
        case TimeSet:                           Button_task();
                                                Display_task();
                                                TimeBase_task();
                                                Error_Task();
                                                Break;
        case AlarmPending, SnoozeMode:          TimeBase_task();
                                                AlarmControl_task();
                                                Display_task();
                                                Button_task();
                                                Error_Task();
                                                Break;
        case AlarmSet:                          Button_task();
                                                TimeBase_task();
                                                Display_task();
                                                Error_Task();
                                                Break;
        case AlarmActive:                       TimeBase_task();
                                                AlarmTone_task();
                                                AlarmControl_task();
                                                Display_task();
                                                Button_task();
                                                Error_Task();
                                                Break;
        case PowerFail:                         TimeBase_task();
                                                Display_task();
                                                Error_Task();
                                                Break;
        case ErrorMode:                         Error_Task();
                                                Display_task();
                                                Button_task();
                                                Break;
        Default:                                mode = ErrorMode;
    }
}
```

The system is quite simple to implement, as it just needs the various lists of tasks for each system mode. It is even simple to combine this priority handler with some of the other priority-handling systems previously discussed. For example, using passive with this system just requires the designer to add the initial presets to the system, and add a simple mode change routine to re-offset the skip timers of tasks that have been disabled during the previous mode. This type of system is a good idea anyway, as a disabled task has probably timed out while it was disabled and re-enabling the task will mean the task will run on the first pass after a mode change.

Another system that can be combined with the variable-order system is the time-remaining system. Using this combination, the state machine of the variable order is modified with the basic block of the time-remaining system. Specifically, each call to a task in the variable-order system is replaced with the similar block from the time-remaining routine. The following demonstrates the required change:

Code Snippet 5.41

```
case PowerFail:  TimeBase_task();
                 Display_task();
                 Error_Task();
                 Break;
```

is replaced with:

Code Snippet 5.42

```
Case PowerFail:
    if (timebase_goflag)
    {
        time_diff = 0xFFFF - sys_timer;
        if database[3][timebase_statevar] < time_diff) timebase_task();
    }
    if (display_goflag)
    {
        time_diff = 0xFFFF - sys_timer;
        if database[0][display_statevar] < time_diff) display_task();
    }
    if (error_goflag)
    {
        time_diff = 0xFFFF - sys_timer;
        if database[5][error_statevar] < time_diff) error_task();
    }
    break;
```

The result is a system that changes the list and priority of the tasks that are called, based on the system mode. Further, if a task has a low priority and the majority of the task has already been used, then the task will be deferred to the next pass through the loop. This system optimizes the processor throughput and adjusts the task priorities based on the requirements of the system. To minimize the program memory impact, the basic building block of the time-remaining system could be boiled down into a single function, with the necessary information pass in. For example:

Code Snippet 5.43

```
Unsigned char time_test(char goflag, task_nmbr, state_var)
{
    if (goflag)
    {
        time_diff = 0xFFFF - sys_timer;
        if database[task_nmbr][state_var] < time_diff) return 0xFF;
    }
    return 0;
}
```

The main priority handler can now use this routine to determine whether to call a task or not, as the following code example shows.

Code Snippet 5.44

```
Case PowerFail:
    if (time_test(timebase_goflag, 3, timebase_statevar)) timebase_task();
    if (time_test(display_goflag, 0, display_statevar)) display_task();
    if (time_test(error_goflag, 5, error_statevar)) error_task();
    break;
```

The result is smaller and much more readable in the final version of the routine.

The excuse-me, excuse-you system involves one task deferring its execution or state change based on the status of another task in the system. The difference between the two systems is whether the task making the decision to defer is the task that will defer, or is the task that forces another task to defer.

Let's start with the excuse-me version of the system. When a task is ready to change from a low-priority state to a high-priority state, the excuse-me system gates that decision with the status of a related task in the system. As an example, consider the alarm control and alarm tone tasks in our design. The alarm tone task operates much faster than the alarm control, so it has a high probability of executing on the same tick as the alarm control task. If the total execution time of the two tasks is sufficiently long to interfere with other tasks in the system, then some method is needed to prevent the two from stacking up and overrunning the system tick.

We use the excuse-me system to handle this. When the alarm control task determines that the alarm tone task should be run, it will defer any transition that will move the task into a high priority, specifically a high priority that will require longer execution times. It does this by monitoring the alarm tone task, to determine when the alarm tone task is busy generating a tone and when it is idle as part of the quiet section of the modulated alarm tone.

By limiting its execution of high-priority, long execution states to only those times when the alarm tone is idle, it interleaves the execution of the two tasks so that both tasks never execute long states in the same tick. If the alarm tone task is not running, then the excuse-me system is idle and the alarm control task makes any transition required for its operation.

The implementation is fairly simple. The alarm control task includes a set of conditional statements at the top of its state machine that will only allow a transition if the alarm tone is not active, and, if the alarm tone task is not in a long execution state, or if the alarm control state transition is to a state with a short execution time. The following demonstrates how this is coded.

Code Snippet 5.45

```
Void alarm_control_task()
{
        if  ((alarm_tone_active==0)|
            (alarm_tone_statevar!=tonegen)|
            (executiontime[alarmcntrl_statevar] < tone_time))
        {
            switch (alarmcntrl_statevar);
        {
            case
```

The code gates the change in state by delaying the execution of the next state until such time that the alarm tone task is not active, not in its tone generation state, or the next alarm control state is short enough to not interfere. While this is fairly simple, it does assume that there is only one long execution state in the alarm tone task. In more complex systems, the conditional may have to rely on a second execution time database that holds the execution times of several states.

Of course, the test routines generated in the Time Remaining priority handler would work equally well here to build both execution time databases.

The excuse-you priority handler is a little more complex, in that it touches several tasks. The controlling task contains code to determine when one of its state changes will shift the priority of the task. When it detects such a transition, the task then broadcasts a flag indicating that all low-priority tasks must defer execution until such time as the controlling task transitions out of its high-priority mode. This means additional code for both the controlling tasks and the low-priority tasks that must defer their execution.

For example, when the error task in our alarm clock example determines that a server-error condition has occurred, the error task will then transition to a series of states that will reset the appropriate task state machines. Because the display and alarm tone tasks are not affected by this task reset, they are considered low priority and are deferred until the error task has completed its reset. The following shows how this would be coded.

Code Snippet 5.46

```
{additions to the display task}
Void Display_task()
{
    if (defer_task != true)
    {
        if (state < 6)
            then
            {
                if (display_alarm == true)
                    then
```

```
{additions to the alarm tone task}
void alarmtone_task()
{
    if (defer_task != true)
    {
```

```
{additions to the error task}
    case poll_timebase:    if (timebase_error == true)
                           {
                                error_statevar = master_reset;
                                defer_task = true;
                           }
                           break;

    case end_masterst:     error_statevar = poll_alarm_cntrl;
                           defer_task = false;
```

The additions to the error task set and clear the defer flag used by the display and alarm tone flags. If the flags are set, the display and alarm tone tasks are essentially disabled until the error task completes its reset of the other system task state machines. While this is fairly drastic for the system, the error task will need to complete the reset quickly or else it may affect the accuracy of the time base. Less drastic systems could be employed, which only prevent a state transition to a higher priority state in the lower-priority tasks. In either case, the function of the priority handler is to free up execution time in the system tick for higher-priority tasks.

The last priority handler to examine is the parent/child system. In this priority handler, a parent controls the execution of a child. It is accomplished by including a conditional statement in the child state machine that only allows the child to decode its current state if the enabling flag is set. The parent then allows the child to operate by setting the enabling flag. Once the child has completed its task, it can then clear the enabling flag, putting itself back to sleep until it is needed once more. The parent may also force the child task to sleep, if it determines that the function performed by the task is no longer needed.

This form of priority handler is especially useful for arbitrating control between two parent tasks, over the control of a common child task. Whichever parent task takes control of the child task first, need only enabled to the task. The secondary parent is then prevented from taking control until the first parent releases the child by clearing its enabling bit, or until the child completes its task and clears the bit itself.

A good example of a task pair that would benefit from a parent/child priority handler is the alarm control and alarm tone task. The alarm tone is only used when the alarm control task determines that the alarm time is equal to the current time, and the alarm function is enabled. So, the alarm control task is already in control of the alarm tone's operation. Using the parent/child system just simplifies the control of the alarm tone task. The following is an example of how this control would be coded.

⟶

Code Snippet 5.47

```
{additions to the alarm tone task}
void alarmtone_task()
{
    if (child_alarmtone_enable == true)
    {


{additions to the alarm control task}
    case check_time:        if (alarm_time_check() == 1)
                            {
                                alarmcontrol_statevar = generate_alarm;
                                child_alarmtone_enable = true
                            }
                            break;



    case generate_alarm:    if (alarm_enabled != true)
                            {
                                alarmcntrl_statevar = inactive;
                                child_alarmtone_enable = false;
                            }
```

The variable child_alarmtone_enable is the gating flag that the parent, alarm control, uses to control the execution of the child, alarm tone. When the variable is set, the child executes, and when it is cleared, the child does not. As before, getting the entire execution of the child is pretty drastic; however, the variable can also be used as part of a condition statement, which handles a state change as well. The only advantage to gating the execution of the entire task is that the child task is saved the overhead of implementing an IDLE state in which to wait for the next enable flag. This is an important point to note should a designer need to save a few program memory words here and there in the design.

The final block to implement is the error detection and recovery system. Fortunately, most, if not all, of the system has already been implemented in our creation of the system task. The only pieces left in the design are the initialization and configuration of any hard fault hardware-based supervisory system, and the error task itself.

The initialization and configuration of the hardware supervisory systems will be specific to the microcontroller hardware used, so discussing them here is not possible. The only recommendations that should be made are:

1. Label the individual control and configuration bits so they have descriptive names.

2. Clearly note in the design notes how the systems are configured and any algorithms specific to their use.

3. Build the functions into descriptively named routines.

4. Add all new communications pathways to the communications plan and documentation.

The error task state machine should also be completed at this time. It will typically be an execution-indexed state machine, although a hybrid may also have advantages. The specifics of its design will be unique to each design. The system for our example alarm clock design is designed using the requirements that have been accumulated during the course of the design and implementation exercise. Those requirements are documented here for reference, although the actual design of the state machine is left up to the reader, as an execution-indexed state machine design has already been presented.

List 5.1

```
State names for Error task
0.  Initial           power up state for the state machine
1.  Poll_alarm         check alarm control task for statevariable corruption
2.  Poll_timebase      check timebase task for statevariable corruption
3.  Poll_buttons       check button task for statevariable corruption
4.  Sanity             state to check alarm enabled, alarm active, and snooze
5.  Restore_Sanity     state to reset alarm enabled, alarm active, and snooze
6.  Master_reset       reset controlling task in the event of sv corruption
7.  End_masterst       release system from reset
8.  Error              error condition in error task
9.  Default            all undefined states decode here
```

→
List 5.1
(continued)

Current State	Condition	Next State if true	Next state if false
Initial	Timeset command	Poll_alarm	Initial
Poll_alarm	alarm task error	Master_reset	Poll_timebase
Poll_timebase	timebase task error	Master_reset	Poll_buttons
Poll_buttons	button task error	Master_reset	Sanity
Sanity	Missmatched variables	Restore Sanity	Poll_alarm
Restore_Sanity	always	Poll_alarm	
Master_reset	always	End_masterst	
End_masterst	ack of all resets	Poll_alarm	
Error	always	Master_reset	
Default	always	Error	

State	Action	Input	Output
Initial	Flash display & force 12:00 time	Timeset	Current_time Flash Mode
Poll_alarm	Check alarm error flag & set mode	Alarm_error	Mode
Poll_timebase	Check timebase error flag	Timebase_error	none
Poll_buttons	Check buttons error flag	Buttons_error	none
Sanity	Check alarm variables	Alarm_enabled Alarm_active Snooze	none
Restore_Sanity	Reset alarm variables	Alarm_on	Alarm_enabled Alarm_active Snooze
Master_reset	Clear control task	none	Reset_alarm Reset_timebase Reset_buttons
End_masterst	Wait for acknowledge	Reset_alarm Reset_timebase Reset_buttons	none
Error	Reset state machine	none	none
Default	set statevariable to Error	none	none

Note that the error state machine should be built just like any other state machine in the system. Start with the state decoder, then the state transitions, the state actions, then the timing, and error detection/recovery. The state machine should also have the same level of documentation, if not better documentation due to its interaction with all of the other tasks in the system. As with all the other tasks, after a section is written, it should be tested thoroughly using the test driver and whatever datalogging routines are deemed necessary. Once each step of the testing is complete, then the test code should be archived and the results noted in the design notes for the system.

Once all of the tasks, timers, communications pathways, priority handling, and error detection/ recovery systems have been built and tested, it is time to start integration and testing of the complete system. While this may seem like a simple enough task, it is typically one of the most frustrating to accomplish. Why should this be? All of the components are complete and working, so it should just be a simple matter of stringing all the components together to create a whole. Well, yes, the individual components are complete and tested, but they have not been tested with one another. It is less a matter of whether the components work, and more a matter of whether they work and play well with others.

The process of integration is also littered with numerous land mines waiting to catch the unwary designer. One of the worst is impatience. If a designer gets impatient and just throws the tasks together and hopes for the best, then the designer, with *very* rare exceptions, can expect to be severely disappointed. In all my designs, I have never had a group of tasks just drop together and work. There have always been at least two or more problems to be sorted out and the individual component testing did not find the problem.

So, how can the components be combined with the least trouble? We start by picking two tasks that have interleaved functions—for example, the button task and the display task. Or, alternatively, we could have chosen the time base and display tasks. The idea is to choose two tasks that interact with each other regularly. Personally, I would choose the display and button tasks, because they can be initially tested manually, without writing a test driver routine.

The next step is to link the two tasks with a common skip timer value and an offset that puts one task in the tick immediately following the first. This allows putting one breakpoint at the start of the first task, and stepping all the way through the end of the second task. Once the tasks are linked, step through their execution one tick at a time, watching the communications variables between the tasks. If the operation of both tasks is correct, then offset the two tasks by one state and step through again. Repeat this process until each state in the first task has been executed with every other state in the second task. This process should identify most, if not all, of the interaction problems between the two tasks.

Once the tasks are working well together, add the normal skip timer reload values to the timer and allow the system to operate at its normal rate. To supply data from other related tasks that are not currently included in the system, it may be necessary to add the test driver to the system. A test routine can then be used to generate the missing control and data that will normally be supplied by the missing tasks.

The test driver can also act as an exerciser for the system by overriding selected input variables to simulate input from the user. This will allow the designer to automate much of the integration testing for the system, performing a much more thorough test than could be accomplished manually.

The two main interactions that cannot be tested at the component level are inadvertent variable corruption and timing issues. Let's start with variable corruption, as that is the simpler problem to tackle.

Even if a task tested out perfectly, and showed no outward signs of problems, there still exists the possibility that the task may inadvertently corrupt adjacent variable storage. There are a number of ways this can happen:

1. A pointer may not have been initialized the first time it was used to store a value.

2. A pointer may have been incremented beyond the last data value and then used for a read or write.

3. An index variable into an array may have been set beyond the last location in array and then used for a read or write.

4. If a pointer is used in a loop, the last pass through the loop may have left it in an undefined location. Then the next time the loop is used, the pointer points to an invalid location.

5. A hand-coded math routine may be used on the wrong data type.

Whatever the reason, a memory location was read or written to that does not belong to the routine doing the work. When the task was stand-alone, the problem would not have appeared, but now that other routines have their data storage around the problem task's data, it is becoming corrupted.

There are a couple of different ways to identify the problem and the likely suspect. The first is to limit the number of suspects by only adding one task to the design at a time. If a new task is added to the system and a problem appears, remove the task and see if the problem disappears. This one simple rule of thumb can save designers hours of debugging time, so go slow, add one at a time, and test thoroughly. Too many designers have pulled their hair out searching for a needle-sized problem in a proverbial haystack of suspects.

The second way to identify the problem is to review the test data from the component-level implementation. Remember that we tested both the normal and abnormal conditions through each step of the component implementation. This is why, if we know the symptom, by reviewing the test results we should be able to identify the suspect variable by searching for a similar symptom in the test results. It is then just a simple matter of reviewing the data memory map to find out which tasks have variables in close proximity, and now we have a list of suspects to examine.

The third method involves using an emulator for the microcontroller. Most emulator systems have an option to specify a group of variables for surveillance. When the emulator reaches a breakpoint, the values in these variables are then retrieved from the emulator and displayed. The user interface will also typically identify any variables that have changed from the last time the emulator was halted.

By placing a breakpoint at the start of the timer routine, and placing the variables used by a suspect task in the surveillance window, a designer will know in which system tick the corruption is occurring. It is then simply a matter of running the design from breakpoint to breakpoint, until one of the variables is changed, even though the task using the variable was not called. A quick check of the skip timers should then pinpoint the suspect task.

Once the suspect task has been identified, the state variable can be used to narrow down the search to a specific state. Note that the value of the state variable is the next state to be executed, so it may take a little detective work to backtrack to the guilty section. If the problem is still elusive, put the breakpoint at the top of the suspect task and then repeatedly run the task until the variable is corrupted. This should narrow the search down to a specific command. Remember, the task works, it just has an unforeseen consequence to its operation. Designers should take their time and step through the problem logically.

The second group of suspects in problems that develop at integration are timing related. Often, the coding of a task state machine is designed around the mistaken assumption that the only place data will change is at the state in which the data is tested. This means that a change in the value of a variable partway through a sequence of states may have consequences that the designer did not consider.

Another common pitfall is using actual input port registers as a source of data in a state. If the timing of the port bit change is asynchronous to the system-timing tick, then it is certainly possible that the state of a port may change during the execution of a task state, and can also change between states when the system is performing other tasks.

Both problems have a simple solution: if a variable is used over the course of several states, or the variable is an external port, then the value should be captured and stored in a shadow variable. The capture can occur either at the start of the sequence of states, or at the start of the current system tick. And the shadow copy of the data should be the variable used during the course of the task's work. Because the designer controls when the data is copied from the source into the shadow variable, the designer also establishes the variable's lifetime.

While this solves the problem, it does not identify the suspect. To find the variable causing the problem, take the task back to the automated testing system using the test driver. Adjust the timing of the test driver so that the data present in the suspect group of variables is modified at a specific time relative to the operation of the task. Then repeat the test, slowly incrementing the timing offset between the test driver and the task, until the problem appears.

Once the timing is known, move one variable at a time, back to the original timing, leaving the others with the timing of the failure. Retest between each variable timing change; when the error disappears, the last variable moved will be the suspect.

A shadow variable can then be defined for the suspect variable, and the system can be retested with all of the variables changing at the time that exhibited the problem. If the problem does not reappear, then the problem has probably been corrected. To assure the problem is gone, repeat the time shift and test routine through all of the combinations of states and variables. If no new problems appear, the designer can be reasonably sure the problem is corrected.

Note that the code to change the variables on a sliding time scale is valuable and should be archived both in the design and in the designer's personal library of valuable functions. This may have been the first time that the function was needed, but it won't be the last.

Integration should then continue, adding functions one at a time, with thorough testing between each addition. Note that the error task should be saved for last, as its purpose will be to correct errors in the system. This means that, in order to test the task, it will be necessary to introduce errors to test this module. Adding the error task last prevents the error task from responding to errors that are in the process of being debugged, and it is probably best to only introduce new bugs once all of the design bugs have been removed.

To test the error task, the test driver should be included in the system, with a test program that can override specific variables in the system. These variables should include all the state variables for the various tasks, including the error task, and system status variables that the error task is charged with monitoring, such as alarm_enabled, alarm_active, and snooze. The test driver should also force the system into all of the different system modes, so the mechanisms for switching between modes can be thoroughly tested. This also allows the designer to test the system's response to various system modes.

Once all of the tasks have been added and the complete system thoroughly tested, the design work for the system is complete. However, that is not to say that the designer's job is done. There is still the task of harvesting useful routines for the designer's library, and additional documentation that should be added to complete the system.

Let's start with the documentation for the system, as it will be the more tedious task. First of all, the design notes should be reviewed for any additions or edits that may be needed. The file should have been kept current during the design process, but even I don't always keep up with the edits like I should. So, now, before we forget, the design notes files should be cleaned up.

Once the notes file is current, the next step is to review and update the requirements document. During the course of the design, numerous changes will have been made, and the requirements document should reflect the final product. Any notes concerning features that did or did not work should be added in the appendix, so future documents can avoid problems that have already been identified. When reviewing and updating the requirements document, remember that the product will be marketed based on what this document says, not on what the product actually does, so it is critically important that the document accurately represent the features, functions and capabilities of the final system.

Next, any updates or additions to the main system file, its header file, and any main system include files should be made. This is also the point at which the files should have a revision history added to the header comments. This history will live with the design from this point forward, and the first version of code that is submitted to product testing should be labeled A0 or the equivalent for reference. Any changes from now on can be tracked, as well as the appropriate updates and changes made to the support documentation—specifically, the requirements document and the design notes.

Any updates and edits required for the individual task include files and header files should also be made at this point. Depending on the size of the project, individual revision histories may also be added at this point. Note that any change in the task files revision history should also be reflected in the main system revision history.

An archive of all the test data, test procedures, and test functions should be compiled with a directory indicating the capabilities of each piece of test code, and the various test procedures that can be implemented using the test code. Task, function being tested, and revision (if any) should categorize the test data. This will help the support staff understand how the test code can be used and how they can modify it for test and diagnostic functions, both in repair and for test code on the assembly line.

Finally, a short report with any information that the designer thinks may be relevant to the design should be compiled. This report need not have a specific format; it can even be a list of things to note about the design. The purpose is just to capture any and all information relevant to the design, before new design challenges and time purge the information.

At this point, the design work on the project is complete and all of the information can be archived. If the archive software has the ability to include file structure, placing the entire work environment into the archive is also a good idea. If there is ever a problem and the designer has to recreate the development system, this archive will be valuable in that it can recreate the look and feel of the environment, and that will make getting back into the design easier.

While the design is complete, there is still some work for the designer to accomplish. When we started out on this design methodology, one of the stated purposes was code reuse. Code reuse shortens design cycles by providing the designer with prefabricated building blocks to start the system. So, our last task as designers on this project is to mine the design for usable blocks for our library.

First of all, I strongly recommend that the files from which we mine the routines must be in a completely unrelated directory structure. There is nothing more annoying than completing a design and then inadvertently damaging one or more files while trying to carve out useful functions. So, make a different set of directories and copy the system design documentation off to a back-up before starting the mining process.

A good place to start mining for library routines is the timing function for the main loop. The configuration and initialization constants for the hardware timer will be useful for any future design with this particular microcontroller. Also, most microcontroller families share one or more of the system peripherals, so there is a chance that the information may be applicable to more than one microcontroller.

To extract the function, simply copy the block of code into a text editor. If the block is a complete function, then retain the function definition and the header comment. Next, go to the test code archive and copy out any test functions used to verify the timer's operation. Include it in the same file, but separate the code with comments and a description of what the test code verified. Also, go to the design document and gather together any specific information concerning the design decisions and calculations that went into the generation of the configuration and initialization constants and routines, or its test code. This information should be included in the text file above the header comment for the function.

Once the file is complete, give it a descriptive name and save it into the directory structure that holds the library. Add a couple of notes on the organization of the library, for convenience. Build a structure with folders for each different type of routine, timers, priority handlers, data functions, error detection/recovery, and state machines. This makes it easier to find a block because they are subdivided by type, and it reduces the number of candidates to review.

The skip timer section of the system timer is also a good source of library material. Even though the functions are relatively simple, a standard working template is always useful as both an example and a starting point for more complex functions. And, in our design example, the skip timer system for both the display and the time-base tasks were not all that simple.

The documentation generated for the skip timer and system timing design should also be copied and pasted out of the design notes. Any notes on decisions made concerning the operation of a timer interrupt and the main system clock should also be included. Configuration and initialization of the interrupt structure and the interrupt service routine are also valuable.

Once all the code has been pulled together, any test routines and data should be appended to the file as well, before it is archived in the library.

Another good area to mine is the main system header file. We went to a considerable effort to create the various access and test functions for all the communications pathways, so it would be inconvenient if we couldn't reuse that code. Copy all the related functions into a common file, include the variable definitions from the main system header file, and add all applicable header comments from both the functions and the definitions. Include any test functions and data from the test archive, as we did with the timer system. Separate the code with comments and, as always, your comments should be clear, complete, and verbose. Finally, go to the design notes and copy in all the design information for the individual pathway, include timing calculations, size estimates, and any design decisions that affected the design of the pathway protocol, functions, and variable definitions.

The system tasks are some of the most valuable code for a library, but it can also be the most difficult to extract due to the combination of several software functions into a common task. So, extracting the code, start by copying over the complete task state machine, without modifications. That way, if there is ever any question about the design, we will know how the original was designed. Extract the test driver and test routines from the test archive and include them in the file as well. Be sure to separate the two blocks of code with comments, and add in all entries from the design notes that concern the operation of the block.

Only after the complete task has been copied in should modifications be made to try and strip out the unwanted sections of the design. Do this by copying the source into another file and then strip down the function. When the extraneous pieces have been removed, the task should be tested using the original test driver, with modified test functions that account for the stripped down nature of the state machine. After the new, stripped state machine has been tested and debugged, it can then be copied into the original library source file for archiving. As with other pieces that we have mined from the design, the new test functions and test data should be included in the file with the state machine.

One final piece of information concerning the task should be included—the section of the requirements document that drove the original development. The reason to include this is for documenting future design requirements documents. During the course of this design, the requirements document was updated to reflect changes in the design goals. Putting a copy of the final version of the requirement in the library saves time in the next design by retaining well-worded descriptions of the task, which can be pasted into the next design's requirements document as part of its upgrade during the design.

Another good source for the library are the system priority handlers. These blocks controlled the order in which the functions within the design are called. As they are relatively simple, there will not be a great deal of code to copy. In fact, the scattered nature of the implementation will make some snippets obscure without the inclusion of some of the surrounding code. So, cut generously when you carve out the priority functions; the fat can always be trimmed in the next design. Also, the time and effort spent on the system and component level of the design is valuable in that it can save design time in the next system. Be sure to copy anything related to the priority information, and include all test functions and code as well.

The final section to mine is the error detection and recovery systems. This includes both the error task state machine and any embedded functions within the individual task state machines. As with the priority handlers, cut generously when the embedded functions are carved out of the state machines. Include all the design notes information related to the error functions, and include the appropriate sections from the requirements document as well.

Once all the various blocks have been removed, copy the new library files into their respective folders. It would also be helpful to include a text file in each folder that lists the name of the library files, and a short description of the functions that they contain. Some designers may want to go so far as to distill the various files down further, into a standard library of basic functions. Whatever the level of effort expended, keep the file current and, with each new design, weed out older blocks that can be replaced by newer, more efficient examples.

Also keep a separate back-up of the library folders in the event of a system crash. Over time, most designers become somewhat dependent upon their libraries, and often looe time and energy recreating functions that have been lost in a disk crash.

This completes the design methodology for creating multitasking code with state machines. I hope that you have found something in the process that will help you in your future designs. I have taught this system for several years now, and I am always amazed at the number of engineers that use this system or something very much like it.

On several occasions, I have talked with engineers after the presentations that have stated, "I do almost exactly what you talked about except...." Initially, I apologized for what I thought was a waste of their time, but almost all have stated that it was not a waste because they felt validation that someone else was using a similar system to what they had developed.

So, I leave it to you as designers, to take from this system what works for you and incorporate it into your personal coding style. You should not feel obligated to take everything I have presented—just use what works for you and discard the rest. As I have stated several times in this book, design is influenced by the talents and outlook of the designer, so it should come as no surprise that we all create systems that are slightly different in the details, even if they agree in the main points.

The next chapter will examine whether or not this book has met its objectives. It is not a required part of the methodology, but it does clearly outline what the methodology should achieve. Read it or not as you see fit, and thank you for reading my words on a subject that I have come to feel strongly about.

6

Does It Do the Job?

In Chapter 1, we established that it was in a designer's own best interest to design code that could accomplish several important goals. The code should be quick to write, efficiently use development time, and be simple to debug. It should help minimize material cost, generate clean documentation, and be modular in design. Further, it should be extensible and be able to multitask. The question is, does the design methodology presented here meet these lofty goals?

Let's start with quick development and efficient use of development time. With many designs, rewrites and modifications can significantly lengthen the development time, so any system that clarifies what the customer wants at the beginning should both shorten the development, which by definition makes a more efficient use of development time.

The design methodology presented here started out with a dissection of the designs requirements document. This dissection carved up the document, looking for every possible nuance of the design, from timing information to the functions and features of the design. When information was found to be missing, the design was held until the questions and ambiguities were resolved. Only when a completely clear picture of the design was generated, did the methodology more on to even the highest level of the design.

So, yes, I would judge that the methodology did make an efficient use of the development time in that it reduced the rework associated with missed communications between the group that defined the system and the designers that actually generated it.

Further, the top-down nature of the design methodology supported the efficient use of design time, because it forces designers to consider every aspect of the final product before they generate a single line of code.

The next point was the requirement that the system create code that is simple to debug. While the methodology does not prevent designers from making syntax errors, it does prevent unintended interactions by its modular nature, and the use of state machines to implement the individual tasks. Typically problems are generated, not by the specific code, but by how different blocks of code interact in real time. Because this methodology forces the various blocks to execute at specific times, and with some degree of synchronization, the possibility of problems through interaction is reduced. Further, the build-and-test, build-and-test, sequence of the design limits the development of large bugs by eliminating the small bugs early, before they can evolve into the larger ones.

The top-down system design also forces the designer to consider how the various blocks in the system will interact, before the actual blocks are generated. In this way, the interactions are planned and accounted for in the design of the blocks, before they have a chance to create unintended interactions.

Concerning material cost, the free nature of the design methodology provides an initial reduction in the system cost by not introducing a usage fee. Further, the modular system nature of the design lends itself to the use of software-based peripherals in place of more expensive hardware. And that same modular nature facilitates the later introduction of hardware replacement, when components of the system suffer end of life.

Concerning other production costs, the modular nature of the design methodology also lends itself to the creation of test and evaluation software that uses many of the regular components of the software design. This shortens the test and qualification process for components, and reduces the support overhead required to maintain and upgrade the system over its product life. Its self-documenting nature also decreases the time required for support engineers or new designers to become fluent in the system's operation.

We mentioned documentation, and that is one of the key requirements for the design methodology. That is, generating clear and accurate documentation, so that support and collateral information can be generated quickly and accurately with only minimal support from the design team. This methodology generates design notes as part of the requirements document dissection, the system-level design, the component-level design, and the implementation/testing phase of the design. In short, the methodology generates documentation at every step of the design, noting not only how the system works, but also why the system works the way it does. "How" is important to the support engineers because it allows them to understand the system's operation. The "why" is what allows them to go beyond support, to upgrade and modifications for bug fixes and product life extension.

Two related requirements are modularity and extensibility. Modularity requires that each function or task within the system be its own standalone block, and that it be testable as a unit, and reusable with only a minimal understanding of its interface to the system. Extensibility takes the requirements of modularity and extends them to the full system. The interface between the modules, and the modules interface to the system, should be clearly defined so new modules can be added using the existing module interfaces as a prototype.

The modular nature of the task state machines, the system of communications pathways, the timing system, and the priority handlers all combine to define a simple yet flexible system interface that will allow the addition of future modules with a predictable effect on the system. Further, due to the top-down nature of the design, the effect on the system can be predicted before the design of the new module is started. It need only have a system and component level of definition to be evaluated for its compatibility with the existing design. So, by our definition of modularity and extensibility, the design methodology complies with these requirements as well.

The last two design requirements are reuse and multitasking. The modular nature of the various tasks and systems in the design make the reuse of software blocks within the system both simple and easy. This is because the top down design approach clearly defines the interface to every major code block in the design. With a knowledge of how the block works and how it is designed to connect to external systems, reuse is just a matter of mining the blocks from the final design and building a series of folders to hold the blocks.

Multitasking is a requirement that is central to the design methodology. In fact, we spent a considerable amount of time in Chapter 2 evaluating multitasking operating systems to determine what the specific needs are for multitasking. What we determined was that multitasking required, one, a method for switching between multiple tasks without losing context information; two, that a method for communication was needed to handle the transfer of information and event timing between the various tasks; three, that a system of regulating the execution timing of the individual tasks was necessary for real-time control and monitoring; and four, that a method for shifting priorities in the system was needed to respond to changes in the system mode.

The design methodology presented creates systems to handle each of these requirements. State machines provide a means of breaking up tasks and provide a means whereby individual blocks of the task can be executed, in order, with only the state variable to maintain the current status of the task. A communications system composed of variables and access/test functions provides for the communications needs of the system. Specific protocols handle different communications needs, including different rates of transmission and reception, and the transfer of event timing. The timing system and the definition of a system tick provide for the regular timing of the system. Further, the flexible nature of the timing system provides a means for each task to change its timing as needed for changing requirements. Finally, simple priority-handling systems allow the system, and even small subsets of the tasks, to ship execution time from low priority tasks to higher priority tasks based on the needs of the system or the task.

So, overall, the methodology meets its requirements as set out in Chapter 1. It is modular, extensible, real-time, multitasking, self-documenting, simpler to design, and promotes the reuse of software blocks. The result is a simple, low-cost method for designing better multitasking software systems without the use of packed software operating systems or specialized hardware. The final design is scalable, simple to support, and easy to modify with a predictable outcome.

Index

ELSEVIER SCIENCE CD-ROM LICENSE AGREEMENT

PLEASE READ THE FOLLOWING AGREEMENT CAREFULLY BEFORE USING THIS CD-ROM PRODUCT. THIS CD-ROM PRODUCT IS LICENSED UNDER THE TERMS CONTAINED IN THIS CD-ROM LICENSE AGREEMENT ("Agreement"). BY USING THIS CD-ROM PRODUCT, YOU, AN INDIVIDUAL OR ENTITY INCLUDING EMPLOYEES, AGENTS AND REPRESENTATIVES ("You" or "Your"), ACKNOWLEDGE THAT YOU HAVE READ THIS AGREEMENT, THAT YOU UNDERSTAND IT, AND THAT YOU AGREE TO BE BOUND BY THE TERMS AND CONDITIONS OF THIS AGREEMENT. ELSEVIER SCIENCE INC. ("Elsevier Science") EXPRESSLY DOES NOT AGREE TO LICENSE THIS CD-ROM PRODUCT TO YOU UNLESS YOU ASSENT TO THIS AGREEMENT. IF YOU DO NOT AGREE WITH ANY OF THE FOLLOWING TERMS, YOU MAY, WITHIN THIRTY (30) DAYS AFTER YOUR RECEIPT OF THIS CD-ROM PRODUCT RETURN THE UNUSED CD-ROM PRODUCT AND ALL ACCOMPANYING DOCUMENTATION TO ELSEVIER SCIENCE FOR A FULL REFUND.

DEFINITIONS

As used in this Agreement, these terms shall have the following meanings:

"Proprietary Material" means the valuable and proprietary information content of this CD-ROM Product including all indexes and graphic materials and software used to access, index, search and retrieve the information content from this CD-ROM Product developed or licensed by Elsevier Science and/or its affiliates, suppliers and licensors.

"CD-ROM Product" means the copy of the Proprietary Material and any other material delivered on CD-ROM and any other human-readable or machine-readable materials enclosed with this Agreement, including without limitation documentation relating to the same.

OWNERSHIP

This CD-ROM Product has been supplied by and is proprietary to Elsevier Science and/or its affiliates, suppliers and licensors. The copyright in the CD-ROM Product belongs to Elsevier Science and/or its affiliates, suppliers and licensors and is protected by the national and state copyright, trademark, trade secret and other intellectual property laws of the United States and international treaty provisions, including without limitation the Universal Copyright Convention and the Berne Copyright Convention. You have no ownership rights in this CD-ROM Product. Except as expressly set forth herein, no part of this CD-ROM Product, including without limitation the Proprietary Material, may be modified, copied or distributed in hardcopy or machine-readable form without prior written consent from Elsevier Science. All rights not expressly granted to You herein are expressly reserved. Any other use of this CD-ROM Product by any person or entity is strictly prohibited and a violation of this Agreement.

SCOPE OF RIGHTS LICENSED (PERMITTED USES)

Elsevier Science is granting to You a limited, non-exclusive, non-transferable license to use this CD-ROM Product in accordance with the terms of this Agreement. You may use or provide access to this CD-ROM Product on a single computer or terminal physically located at Your premises and in a secure network or move this CD-ROM Product to and use it on another single computer or terminal at the same location for personal use only, but under no circumstances may You use or provide access to any part or parts of this CD-ROM Product on more than one computer or terminal simultaneously.

You shall not (a) copy, download, or otherwise reproduce the CD-ROM Product in any medium, including, without limitation, online transmissions, local area networks, wide area networks, intranets, extranets and the Internet, or in any way, in whole or in part, except that You may print or download limited portions of the Proprietary Material that are the results of discrete searches; (b) alter, modify, or adapt the CD-ROM Product, including but not limited to decompiling, disassembling, reverse engineering, or creating derivative works, without the prior written approval of Elsevier Science; (c) sell, license or otherwise distribute to third parties the CD-ROM Product or any part or parts thereof; or (d) alter, remove, obscure or obstruct the display of any copyright, trademark or other proprietary notice on or in the CD-ROM Product or on any printout or download of portions of the Proprietary Materials.

RESTRICTIONS ON TRANSFER

This License is personal to You, and neither Your rights hereunder nor the tangible embodiments of this CD-ROM Product, including without limitation the Proprietary Material, may be sold, assigned, transferred or sub-licensed to any other person, including without limitation by operation of law, without the prior written consent of Elsevier Science. Any purported sale, assignment, transfer or sublicense without the prior written consent of Elsevier Science will be void and will automatically terminate the License granted hereunder.

TERM

This Agreement will remain in effect until terminated pursuant to the terms of this Agreement. You may terminate this Agreement at any time by removing from Your system and destroying the CD-ROM Product. Unauthorized copying of the CD-ROM Product, including without limitation, the Proprietary Material and documentation, or otherwise failing to comply with the terms and conditions of this Agreement shall result in automatic termination of this license and will make available to Elsevier Science legal remedies. Upon termination of this Agreement, the license granted herein will terminate and You must immediately destroy the CD-ROM Product and accompanying documentation. All provisions relating to proprietary rights shall survive termination of this Agreement.

LIMITED WARRANTY AND LIMITATION OF LIABILITY

NEITHER ELSEVIER SCIENCE NOR ITS LICENSORS REPRESENT OR WARRANT THAT THE INFORMATION CON-TAINED IN THE PROPRIETARY MATERIALS IS COMPLETE OR FREE FROM ERROR, AND NEITHER ASSUMES, AND BOTH EXPRESSLY DISCLAIM, ANY LIABILITY TO ANY PERSON FOR ANY LOSS OR DAMAGE CAUSED BY ERRORS OR OMISSIONS IN THE PROPRIETARY MATERIAL, WHETHER SUCH ERRORS OR OMISSIONS RESULT FROM NEG-LIGENCE, ACCIDENT, OR ANY OTHER CAUSE. IN ADDITION, NEITHER ELSEVIER SCIENCE NOR ITS LICENSORS MAKE ANY REPRESENTATIONS OR WARRANTIES, EITHER EXPRESS OR IMPLIED, REGARDING THE PERFORMANCE OF YOUR NETWORK OR COMPUTER SYSTEM WHEN USED IN CONJUNCTION WITH THE CD-ROM PRODUCT.

If this CD-ROM Product is defective, Elsevier Science will replace it at no charge if the defective CD-ROM Product is returned to Elsevier Science within sixty (60) days (or the greatest period allowable by applicable law) from the date of shipment.

Elsevier Science warrants that the software embodied in this CD-ROM Product will perform in substantial compliance with the documentation supplied in this CD-ROM Product. If You report significant defect in performance in writing to Elsevier Science, and Elsevier Science is not able to correct same within sixty (60) days after its receipt of Your notification, You may return this CD-ROM Product, including all copies and documentation, to Elsevier Science and Elsevier Science will refund Your money.

YOU UNDERSTAND THAT, EXCEPT FOR THE 60-DAY LIMITED WARRANTY RECITED ABOVE, ELSEVIER SCIENCE, ITS AFFILIATES, LICENSORS, SUPPLIERS AND AGENTS, MAKE NO WARRANTIES, EXPRESSED OR IMPLIED, WITH RESPECT TO THE CD-ROM PRODUCT, INCLUDING, WITHOUT LIMITATION THE PROPRIETARY MATERIAL, AN SPECIFICALLY DISCLAIM ANY WARRANTY OF MERCHANTABILITY OR FITNESS FOR A PARTICULAR PURPOSE.

If the information provided on this CD-ROM contains medical or health sciences information, it is intended for professional use within the medical field. Information about medical treatment or drug dosages is intended strictly for professional use, and because of rapid advances in the medical sciences, independent verification of diagnosis and drug dosages should be made.

IN NO EVENT WILL ELSEVIER SCIENCE, ITS AFFILIATES, LICENSORS, SUPPLIERS OR AGENTS, BE LIABLE TO YOU FOR ANY DAMAGES, INCLUDING, WITHOUT LIMITATION, ANY LOST PROFITS, LOST SAVINGS OR OTHER INCIDENTAL OR CONSEQUENTIAL DAMAGES, ARISING OUT OF YOUR USE OR INABILITY TO USE THE CD-ROM PRODUCT REGARDLESS OF WHETHER SUCH DAMAGES ARE FORESEEABLE OR WHETHER SUCH DAMAGES ARE DEEMED TO RESULT FROM THE FAILURE OR INADEQUACY OF ANY EXCLUSIVE OR OTHER REMEDY.

U.S. GOVERNMENT RESTRICTED RIGHTS

The CD-ROM Product and documentation are provided with restricted rights. Use, duplication or disclosure by the U.S. Govern-ment is subject to restrictions as set forth in subparagraphs (a) through (d) of the Commercial Computer Restricted Rights clause at FAR 52.22719 or in subparagraph (c)(1)(ii) of the Rights in Technical Data and Computer Software clause at DFARS 252.2277013, or at 252.2117015, as applicable. Contractor/Manufacturer is Elsevier Science Inc., 655 Avenue of the Americas, New York, NY 10010-5107 USA.

GOVERNING LAW

This Agreement shall be governed by the laws of the State of New York, USA. In any dispute arising out of this Agreement, you and Elsevier Science each consent to the exclusive personal jurisdiction and venue in the state and federal courts within New York County, New York, USA.

Printed and bound by CPI Group (UK) Ltd, Croydon, CR0 4YY

03/10/2024

01040334-0006